The Tanks Are Coming Through Now

The Brigade Battles at Gazala, 27 May-18 June 1942

Neal Dando

Helion & Company Limited
Unit 8 Amherst Business Centre
Budbrooke Road
Warwick
CV34 5WE
England
Tel. 01926 499 619
Email: info@helion.co.uk
Website: www.helion.co.uk
Twitter: @helionbooks
Visit our blog at blog.helion.co.uk

Published by Helion & Company 2023
Designed and typeset by Mach 3 Solutions (www.mach3solutions.co.uk)
Cover designed by Paul Hewitt, Battlefield Design (www.battlefield-design.co.uk)

Text © Neal Dando 2023
Maps drawn by George Anderson © Helion & Company Ltd 2023
Front cover: Valentine tanks training in the Western Desert, 27 March 1942.
(Crown Copyright 1957)

Every reasonable effort has been made to trace copyright holders and to obtain their permission for the use of copyright material. The author and publisher apologize for any errors or omissions in this work and would be grateful if notified of any corrections that should be incorporated in future reprints or editions of this book.

ISBN 9-781804512-32-6

British Library Cataloguing-in-Publication Data.
A catalogue record for this book is available from the British Library.

All rights reserved. No part of this publication may be reproduced, stored in a retrieval system, or transmitted, in any form, or by any means, electronic, mechanical, photocopying, recording or otherwise, without the express written consent of Helion & Company Limited.

For details of other military history titles published by Helion & Company Limited contact the above address or visit our website: http://www.helion.co.uk.

We always welcome receipt of book proposals from prospective authors.

Contents

List of Maps	iv
Acknowledgements	v
Abbreviations	vi
Introduction	viii
1 Planning	13
2 Terrain	35
3 Training	46
4 Opening Battles South, 26–31 May	64
5 Cauldron	83
6 Armoured Battles, 29 May–13 June	110
7 Infantry Battles	129
8 Bir Hacheim, Breakout and Final Battles	144
Conclusion	164
Note on Sources	169
Bibliography	173
Index	181

List of Maps

1	The Gazala Position, 27 May 1942.	i
2	Minefields as per South African Map, spring 1942.	ii
3	Detail from 15th Panzer Division Sketch Map, May 1942.	iii
4	Detail of 4th Armoured Brigade Battle Position Ack. 4th Armoured Brigade positions: 60th = 1st KRRC, 5th RTR, red, green yellow = company positions.	iv
5	4th Armoured Battle Positions South, 27 May 1942.	v
6	The 2nd Highland Light Infantry (2nd HLI) Attack, Operation Aberdeen, 5 June 1942.	vi
7	4th/10th Baluch Regiment Position on 5–6 June, 1942.	vii
8	The 2/Scots Guards locality, Rigel Ridge.	viii

Acknowledgements

I would like to thanks the staffs at the National Archives, Kew, Bovington Tank Museum Archives and the Imperial War Museum for their kindness and help in making my visits worthwhile in collating details from the archives. I would also very much like to thank key players at Helion & Company, proprietor Duncan Rogers, Stephen Ede-Borrett for his patient final editing of the manuscript, along with Dr Michael LoCicero and the rest of the team for all of their support, especially for turning the original draft into a book. I would also like to thank my mother Hazel and brother Stuart for their constant support, along with old friends, Graham Godfrey, Geoff Martin and Robin Folkes, and old school pal Marcus Hayes MBE for all of their support and 'keep it going' attitude which is what all writers need. Any errors or omissions in the text are purely my own.

Neal Dando
12 September 2023

Abbreviations

AA guns	Anti-aircraft guns, mostly 40mm Bofors in the field
Ariete	Italian Armoured Division attached to DAK
AT guns	Anti-tank guns, British were mainly 2pdr with increasing numbers of 6pdr guns (aka Roberts guns) arriving just before and during the battle
Battalion	Infantry unit of up to four companies, plus an HQ company, 400–800 men
Battery	Eight guns, with three batteries making up a typical regiment. Sometimes a regiment also had a fourth AT battery of 2pdr/6pdr anti-tank guns
CIGS	Chief of the Imperial General Staff, General Sir Alan Brooke in 1942
C-in-C	Commander-in-Chief
COS	Chief of Staff (also COS Committee)
Dafadar	Indian Cavalry Sergeant
Deir	Crater like depression, sometimes more than a mile across, with raised slopes providing potential defensive positions, once occupied
DAK	Deutsches Afrika Korps, the armoured Corps which led most of the fighting for Panzerarmee, (15th Panzer, 21st Panzer and 90th Light Divisions)
Jock Columns	Small mixed groups of artillery, AA, A/T guns and supporting infantry companies, sent into forward areas to harass enemy positions and to reconnoitre
MET	Mechanised enemy transport, trucks, half-tracks, tow tractors, et cetera
PAA	Panzerarmee Afrika, the main Axis force in Libya
PAK	German anti-tank guns
Mk III	Panzer Mark III, German main battle tank with 50mm gun
Mk IV	Panzer Mark IV, German heavy tank with short 75mm gun
MMG	Medium machine gun
RASC	Royal Army Service Corps
RE	Royal Engineers

Recce	reconnaissance – a small patrol or a few vehicles sent out to report on the enemy.
RHA	Royal Horse Artillery
RTR	Royal Tank Regiment, an armoured unit of 3 Squadrons, approximately 51 tanks
TEWT	Tactical Exercise Without Troops (a map Kriegspiel/wargame).
Trieste	Italian Motor Division attached to DAK
Trigh	A desert track, used by both sides, which could be relatively large. The Trigh Capuzzo was said to be up to 100 yards wide in places. The surface was often ground into fine dust by the hundreds of vehicles using them, which clogged everything. They were generally marked by numbered barrels to aid navigation
Troop	A small group of 3 to 5 tanks or guns, there could be between 2 and 5 troops per squadron
VCIGS	Vice Chief Imperial General Staff, Lieutenant General Sir Archibald E. Nye
WDAF	Western Desert Air Force

Introduction

I did not see Lannes at Ratisbon
Nor MacLennan at Auldearn
Nor Gillies MacBain at Culloden,
But I saw an Englishman in Egypt.

A poor little chap with chubby cheeks
And knees grinding each other,
Pimply unattractive face –
Garment of the bravest spirit …

His hour came with the shells,
With the notched iron splinters,
In the smoke and the flame,
In the shaking and terror of the battlefield.

Word came to him in the bullet shower
That he should be a hero briskly,
And he was that while he lasted…

He kept his guns to the tanks,
Bucking with tearing crashing screech,
Until he himself got, about the stomach,
That biff that put him to the ground,
Mouth down in sand and gravel,
Without a chirp from his ugly high-pitched voice

'Heroes'
Sorley Maclean [1]

---

1   Victor Selwyn (ed.), *Poems of the Second World War: The Oasis Selection* (London: Everyman, 1987), p.101.

The Battle of Gazala was fought over 26 days during the hot and dusty early summer of May–June 1942. Despite the countless examples of courage and self-sacrifice by Eighth Army troops, it proved to be a heavy defeat which led to the collapse of the defensive line, the rapid loss of Tobruk, and a long, ragged retreat back to the Alamein position in Egypt, where the next major battles were fought. This battle showed the dogged spirit of the men on all sides, to keep going no matter what. During those blistering, gritty days General Ritchie's Eighth Army engaged Rommel's Panzerarmee. They fought hard yet suffered numerous daily defeats and overruns along with high casualties; they also gained some occasional minor victories in some actions. Yet they were still able to regroup and fight again in defence of the ill-fated Tobruk. Later during the long retreat into Egypt, they attempted to hold the Axis at Mersa Matruh before finally halting at Alamein, where the fighting began again in early July.

From an Allied perspective, the battle represented both the very best of the heroic fighting spirit from British, Empire and Free French Troops, as well as arguably the nadir of leadership, especially from the higher echelons of division, corps and army command. Harold Pyman, the G1 with 7th Armoured Division HQ, said in his later memoirs, that while the soldiers fought well, they were badly led, and that, 'it was the only occasion…that I heard British divisional and brigade commanders tearing each other asunder over the wireless in the heat of battle.'[2] It also showed the Axis commander, General Rommel was at the height of his powers of leadership, always active at or near the front line headquarters, responding quickly to new threats from the Eighth Army. In these daily battles he pushed his experienced Divisions of the Afrika Korps to the brink of exhaustion to gain the prize of Tobruk, which had eluded him in 1941.

Following success in the Crusader battles of late 1941, Eighth Army had advanced west and occupied much of Cyrenaica, but in the process it had over-extended itself again, with too few units in the forward areas due to the difficulties of maintaining supply. The new year brought continued bad weather, which slowed the over-long supply routes and turned forward landing grounds into a mire. As in 1941, Rommel quickly took advantage of renewed deliveries of fresh panzers, to drive the British front line eastwards, back towards their main supply port at Tobruk. Eighth Army had been defeated and forced to retreat for a second time back across Cyrenaica, leaving behind the valuable ports of Benghazi, and the airfields around Derna and Martuba, which provided vital air cover for the convoys to Malta. With the island suffering a renewed blitz throughout the spring of 1942, the pressure from the Prime Minister and COS in London was soon on again for GHQ Middle East and Eighth Army, to begin a new offensive to push Panzerarmee back and recapture this vital sector of eastern Cyrenaica.

The retreat had largely halted by 3 February on the coast at Ain el-Gazala, west of Tobruk. The front had to be held to protect Tobruk, so the tired formations of

2   Harold Pyman, *Call to Arms* (London: Leo Cooper, 1971), p.41.

Eighth Army began forming a new line south from here for approximately 45 miles into the Libyan desert, to prevent Panzerarmee making another outflanking move inland. General Claude Auchinleck, at GHQ Cairo telegrammed General Ritchie, at Eighth Army HQ on 16 February, 'Consider it most important that development position GAZALA HACHEIM TOBRUK as conceived by you…should continue apace to give secure base for future offensive. Frontier positions should be developed concurrently.'[3] Pressure from the Prime Minister in London became more intense in this low period of the British war effort, where any success was needed to prove Britain was a viable ally. Churchill had sent Auchinleck a goodwill message on 12 February and was obviously preoccupied with events in the Far East, but by the end of the month he was asking the C-in-C Middle East what his plans were, in view of the renewed threat to Malta.[4]

For Ritchie, the forthcoming battle was envisaged as an initial defensive battle on the Gazala line, followed by a counter-offensive by the army.[5] Panzerarmee's spring offensive was to be weakened by continuous attacks on Eighth Army's defensive 'boxes' situated behind the 45 miles of minefields. Then the armoured brigades would counterattack the weakened Panzer divisions and defeat them, before forcing back the rest of Panzerarmee towards Benghazi and hopefully out of Cyrenaica. Unfortunately for Eighth Army, what actually happened was a long battle of attrition, which would leave it battered, defeated and retreating back towards Alamein by late June.

After the battle in July, General Ritchie made his report which focused on the importance of the defensive line at Gazala and how it would enable the lesser trained and formations, new to the desert theatre to defeat Panzerarmee.[6] As fresh brigades and regiments moved into the forward area, they reconnoitred numerous potential battle sites over which they could engage the enemy, especially the armoured regiments who were key to the British counterattack. Pip Roberts, then C.O. of 3rd RTR, discussed this preparation.[7] The battle for the Gazala line became a long, hard slog for all sides. By 18 June, Eighth Army had too few units which could hold the equally battered Panzerarmee south of Tobruk. There was also a good deal of command confusion, as to whether the Army was to fight on in Tobruk or retreat to the frontier and fight there. These poor command decisions placed worn-out units in exposed positions with little or no support, making the fall of Tobruk almost a foregone conclusion.

3   TNA WO 201/401: Operations: telegrams & reports, January-March 1942, Personal to General Ritchie from C-in-C 66997, 16 Feb 42.
4   TNA CAB 101/248/2: Telegrams. T.294/2. Prime Minister to General Auchinleck, 26 February 1942.
5   TNA WO 201/379: Operations in North Africa: General Ritchie's report, May–June 1942, Object of the Gazala Position.
6   TNA WO 201/379: Operations in North Africa: General Ritchie's report, May–June 1942.
7   Bovington Archive: 3rd RTR, Papers of G. P. R. Roberts, RTR\ROBERTS3. 'Experiences of an Armoured Regimental Commander in the Middle East, 1943; and the early chapters of many other papers and memoirs.

This work is partly based on a paper given in 2017 about the infantry experience; however I wanted to expand the piece to cover the whole battle. It does not try to prove or disprove any particular theories about British morale, doctrines or a 'British way' of fighting, as others have covered this aspect.[8] It is entrenched around the narrative, but also to highlight those accounts which have often been left out of other histories, to add further depth to the story of the battle. In this period of eightieth anniversaries of the Second World War I believe these actions also remind us of the sacrifice of the thousands of young men in 1942. So Gazala represents some of the typical examples of courage and duty from across all arms; men who remained frustrated by the more effective battle doctrines of Panzerarmee Afrika.

Gazala was an intense battle at times for Eighth Army but the flow of battle waxed and waned over the long summer days. The head-to-head clashes of armour altered after the first days of massed panzer columns meeting British armoured regiments in the open. Elsewhere infantry brigades with their supporting artillery often found themselves isolated and overrun. There were other days of a more cautious warfare, of reconnaissance or patrol and watchful pauses along low ridgelines made by weakened armoured regiments. Both sides continuously attempted to force the other out of key positions, through heavy and accurate shelling, followed by attacks to knock out tanks and artillery. Armoured regiments were often outflanked and forced to give up their vital ridgelines, which then undermined the remaining infantry positions, making them untenable. Eighth Army was also undermined by a higher command which was attempting to regain the initiative, by ordering too many localised attacks against Panzerarmee. Operation Aberdeen was conceived between Ritchie and his corps commanders, who then abdicated responsibility down to the two divisional commanders for the planning and execution of the attack, but the pressure had come from Auchinleck at GHQ. At the same time British command became less effective, through their constant delays, arguments, queries and changes of orders, which left the troops trying to cope with Rommel's incessant drive for Tobruk.

The chapters cover the planning, ground and training background for Eighth Army, before dividing into broadly armour and infantry battles, with the first day and last few days covered as events, rather than a straightforward linear account. Chapter 1 gives a summary of the plans and intelligence in the spring build-up, while Chapter 2 details the terrain and deployment. The problems with training and equipment are considered next. I have divided up the actions by area and type, the opening battles South covers the first two key days mainly for the motor brigades and armoured response south of Knightsbridge. Chapter 5 covers the battles in the cauldron including the actions around the destruction of 150th Brigade and Operation Aberdeen. The later

---

8   Jonathan Fennell, *Combat and Morale in the North African Campaign: The Eighth Army and the Path to El Alamein* (Cambridge: Cambridge University Press, 2011), and James Colvin, *Eighth Army Versus Rommel. Tactics, Training and Operations in North Africa 1940–1942* (Warwick: Helion, 2020), pp.128–172.

phases of the battle are divided into armoured and infantry battles because they were mostly separated, which occurred mostly across the centre, such as the 2nd Scots Guards at Rigel Ridge and other defended localities. The final chapter covers all of the fighting at Bir Hacheim, the breakout by 50th Division and the final armoured engagement which covered the retreat of units back to Tobruk or the frontier. This is to provide a fresh view for those participants whose stories reside within the archival reports and older unit histories. The documents for 1st South African Division in the north and the immortal battle made by 1st Free French Brigade at Bir Hacheim, are more limited so I have used what files I could find for their battles.

From this distance, one cannot easily imagine the endless days of combat, of being 'dog-tired' and hungry, with the constant fear of being wounded by shelling, or being under intense fire from inside a tank or crouching in a dusty shell-scrape. The title quotation is taken from a report by the A company C.O. of 4/10th Baluchs, who calmly described the overrunning of his position to his battalion HQ, by 15th Panzer Division at 0920 hours, 6 June 1942.[9] This study focuses on the experiences of the soldiers within Eighth Army and their battle to hold the line before Tobruk. After the battle, with Eighth Army in retreat, events moved rapidly eastwards, to Tobruk and then Egypt, little was done in the aftermath to clear up the bodies and debris. When 4th Indian Division returned to Gazala six months later, they counted over 60 knocked out tanks near Pt.171. Lieutenant General Tuker rightly called it a, 'great feat of arms.'[10] The Rigel Ridge was also visited by Captain N. B. Hanmer, who described the site of the Scots Guards battle:

> … none of our men had been buried … the sand appeared to have some sort of preserving quality … A position which impressed me greatly was the 6-pdr anti-tank gun positions manned by the Scots Guards. They must have fired their guns until the German tanks were right on top of them. Almost every gun had the body of a Scots Guardsman … slumped over the breach.[11]

As we pass the 80th anniversary of the battle, I felt that it was important to convey their story again.

---

9 TNA WO 169/7770: 4/10th Baluch Regiment War Diary, report of 6 June 1942.
10 Miles Smeeton, *A Change of Jungles* (London: Rupert Hart Davies, 1962), p.48.
11 David Erskine, *The Scots Guards 1919–1955* (Uckfield: Naval & Military Press, 2001), pp.107–108.

1

Planning

They call me Venal Vera,
I'm a lovely from Gezira,
The Führer pays me well for what I do,
The order of battle,
I obtain from last night's rattle ... with the Brigadier from 'Q'.

'Ode to a Gezira Lovely'
Anonymous[1]

The first months of 1942 would bring numerous defeats and problems for the Allied war effort in general and for the British in North Africa. In Cairo, security checks found a local waste paper dealer, making bags from over 800 secret maps, while officers in bars were often overheard discussing military plans.[2] All of these problems added to intelligence and planning headaches for Eighth Army, just as Panzerarmee made a sudden advance in late January. This forced Eighth Army into a precipitate retreat across Cyrenaica, which halted at Ain el-Gazala 40 miles west of the main supply base at Tobruk. Rommel had been able to outflank and defeat the few brigades south of Benghazi backwards in the 'Gazala gallop'.[3] Very quickly Panzerarmee also had its own problems. Staff officer F. W. von Mellenthin at Panzerarmee HQ, said the final thrust towards Mechili, south of the Jebel Akhdar hills, was stopped by the continuing lack of fuel.[4] With Axis columns halted, Eighth Army began to form a series of defensive boxes, from the coastal road down into the Libyan desert. Auchinleck was

---

1   Victor Selwyn (ed.), *Poems of the Second World War. The Oasis Selection* (London: Everyman, 1987), p.135. Gezira was the Sports Club in Cairo where many GHQ staff officers spent their free time.
2   TNA WO 169/4053: 1st Armoured Division War Diary, Intelligence Summary 23, 7 May 1942.
3   Many of the desert retreats were given ironic horse racing names, e.g. Matruh Stakes.
4   F. W. von Mellethin, *Panzer Battles* (Stroud: Spellmount, 2017), p.76.

quick to inform London that a forward line at Mechili-Tengeder would be outflanked and that an alternative position was being formed further back at Gazala which, 'does not suffer from this disadvantage.' He also added an optimistic comment that in the rear, the frontier line Sollum-Giarabub was being strengthened and a future offensive plan was being considered.[5]

Eighth Army had to prevent Panzerarmee from reaching the main supply base at Tobruk. Fresh brigades were rushed forward to strengthen the new line. From 50th Division, the 150th Brigade; arrived to hold at first pushed forward to Tengeder, it was ordered east across a flat sea of soft sand with few landmarks. They arrived back at Bir Hacheim from 2 February and began to create a defensive box. They would soon be relieved by the newly arrived 1st Free French Brigade.[6] The infantry surrounded each of the battalion positions with wire and minefields and then added larger dugouts for HQs and vehicles until everything was below ground level. Soon a defensive line over 40 miles long was developed from the coast down to Bir Hacheim, connected by a series of minefields. It would be strengthened and developed more intensively as more wire and mines became available. Each brigade set up defensive 'boxes' and new sites were added to as their defensive value was realised. The line would be outflanked by Axis offensive in late May and the battle would be largely fought across Eighth Army's forward area, behind the mine belt which had taken so much effort by Eighth Army's engineers and infantry.

Despite the success of the advance, the Italian commanders had been against the move away from Tripolitania from the beginning, and were keen to halt this thrust towards Tobruk.[7] The renewed pause in operations was caused by petrol shortages, but also by a need for more reinforcements, along with a period of reorganisation before they could attack again. In mid-February Rommel reported to the Fuhrer that supply was now secure but operations were limited.[8] However fuel supply issues continued into March, when DAK Quartermasters noted that the fuel situation was still a 'bottleneck' along with munitions supply.[9] Within 15th Panzer Division, H. W. Schmidt also noted [10] Rommel was still grumbling by the end of March that, 'supply difficulties, particularly getting the stuff up overland, are still a great headache.'[11] Axis plans for new attacks wavered between Malta and Libya through the spring months and were not fully decided until the dictators' conference in Austria in April.[12]

5 TNA WO 201/397: Cipher telegrams: General Auchinleck and Prime Minister, May 1941–June 1942, 1718 cipher 2/2 dated 3/2/42.
6 E. W. Clay, *The Path of the 50th* (Uckfield: Naval & Military Press reprint, 2020), p.50.
7 B. H. Liddell-Hart, *The Rommel Papers* (Boston: Da Capo, 1982), p.186. Letter to Frau Rommel 23 January.
8 Bundesarchiv: PzAOK War Diary, Folder 2: Notes for Fuhrer/Duce, 14.2.42.
9 Bundesarchiv: RH24-200/107: DAK supply War Diary, 1 March to 15 August 1942, 1 and 7 March.
10 H. W. Schmidt, *With Rommel in the Desert* (London: Constable, 1997), p.127.
11 Liddell-Hart, *The Rommel Papers*, p.186. letter to Frau Rommel 26 March.
12 J. R. M. Butler, *Grand Strategy, Vol..III, Part II* (London: HMSO, 1964), p.444.

In Libya Rommel continued to plan for a renewed attempt to defeat Eighth Army, capture Tobruk, and use it as his own forward supply port. Such a prize would give his army a firm base from which to strike into Egypt, as well as gaining hold of the various supply dumps, which included thousands of tons of petrol, ammunition et cetera, built up by the British since the Crusader battles that winter.

British plans evolved around their renewed offensive in Libya, codename 'ACROBAT', to capture Tripolitania and push the Axis west. However worsening events in the Far East, even before this sudden advance by Panzerarmee, had forced London Chiefs to discuss the factors which would affect the Eighth Army offensive. Churchill returned from Washington in mid-January and quickly updated Auchinleck on future joint plans with US forces, now that America had joined the war. Just before Rommel's counterstroke, he telegrammed that, 'The President is very much set on GYMNAST…with American participation… [He]…is therefore deeply interested in ACROBAT and there is no need to delay it in any way.'[13] The planners in London and Washington agreed to, 'close the ring round Germany and gain possession of the whole North African coast.'[14] Auchinleck was now under pressure to return Eighth Army to the offensive. In early January, General Brooke, the CIGS, had doubts about the success of a new offensive towards Tripoli and he wanted it combined with the takeover of Vichy controlled Tunisia.[15]

The COS Committee met on 13 January, and despite the desire to launch Acrobat, they also had many uncertainties which affected an offensive while still retaining Cyrenaica. They cited problems including only having one spare armoured brigade ready before late May. They wanted three full armoured divisions ready by 1 June. The Royal Navy were concerned that if Eighth Army advanced again, they would struggle to control the Eastern Mediterranean as well as the sea-routes to Benghazi, where more air reconnaissance units would be needed.[16] These issues delayed any final decision and Rommel took advantage of the British lull in operations, to make his sudden advance on 22 January. This put paid to the discussions about Acrobat until Eighth Army re-established itself at Gazala in early February.

---

13 TNA WO 201/397: Cipher telegrams: General Auchinleck and Prime Minister, May 1941 May–June 1942, SUSAN 18/1, War Office to C.-in-C Middle East, 18 January 1942.
14 Butler, *Grand Strategy, Vol. III, Part II*, p.564.
15 Alex Danchev & Dan Todman (eds), *Alanbrooke War Diaries 1939–1945: Field Marshal Lord Alanbrooke* (London: Phoenix Press, 2002), p.219.
16 TNA CAB 79/56/3: COS Committee Meeting, 13 January 1942, Minutes, Discussion of Operation ACROBAT.

Changing Plans in Cyrenaica

With Eighth Army back at Gazala, the situation in Cyrenaica and with the Allied war effort, were all affected by the events and problems which had unfolded from December 1941. Firstly, the new war with Japan now drastically overstretched the British effort, there was a lack of shipping capacity for fresh divisions being sent to North Africa, and those ships that were available were desperately needed to send reinforcements to the Far East. This forced the Chiefs of Staff to revise their opinions about operations Acrobat and Gymnast, for the time being.[17] London planners were also under pressure to resolve the issue of opening a second front in Europe in 1942, with Stalin in Moscow calling for the British and American forces to take the pressure off the eastern front by the summer of 1942.[18] Planning reviews in London were then exacerbated by the final fall of Singapore in mid-February, and naval defeats as the German pocket battleships *Scharnhorst*, *Gneisenau* and heavy cruiser *Prinz Eugen* successfully made their Channel dash to Germany. Convoys to Malta had also been heavily bombed with two valuable ships lost, so that all of these setbacks added pressure on Eighth Army to regain some momentum in the campaign.[19]

There was also the additional irritation of confused communications between London and Cairo with numerous vital telegrams often crossing over with each other, delaying final decisions. The COS and CIGS also had different views on the likely advance to be made by Eighth Army for a time, which gave Auchinleck leeway to delay his own plans. Finally, Auchinleck responded at times through the Middle East Defence Committee, which angered Churchill as it had no official remit, when Auchinleck should have replied directly as C-in-C. Middle East.[20] He did respond on 17 January, putting the emphasis on four brigade groups in Anatolia (on the northern front) supported by 24 RAF squadrons. In Libya he 'hoped' to maintain one armoured brigade and one infantry division west of Sirte, threatening Tripoli port, if reinforcements from home and fresh trucks arrived soon.[21] Auchinleck was therefore already shifting his thinking from a limited offensive in Libya to building up stronger forces re-deployed to the northern front in Persia-Iraq, to counter an expected German thrust from southern Russia. There was doubt in Cairo as to whether the Russians could hold on during 1942, but the northern front remained a central part of Auchinleck's thinking.[22]

---

17 The operations designed to clear Axis forces from Tunisia and the rest of the North African shore.
18 Butler, *Grand Strategy, Vol. III, Part II*, pp.565 and 594.
19 TNA CAB 80/34/4: COS Committee Weekly Résumé no.129, 19 February 1942.
20 Butler, *Grand Strategy, Vol. III, Part II*, pp.446–449.
21 TNA WO201/397: Cipher telegrams: General Auchinleck and Prime Minister, May 1941-June 1942, Cipher 1702, 17 January 1942.
22 Bennett, *Ultra and Mediterranean Strategy*, pp.110–111.

The loss of Cyrenaica was a blow to the campaign, as Benghazi again came under Axis control, leaving Tobruk as the next port and forward supply base. Eighth Army could still recover and strike back, if the armoured formations and logistics were brought forward. At first, London appeared to react slowly to what was happening in Libya, as Eighth Army retreated from 22 January. Despite various telegrams updating them from Auchinleck, General Brooke only mentioned it, due to the loss of Benghazi on 30 January, 'This Benghazi business is bad and nothing less than bad-generalship on the part of Auchinleck.'[23] As a new defensive line developed from Ain el-Gazala, Ritchie was strongly advised by Auchinleck not to retreat any further and through February he became more confident that everything would stabilise and that a renewed offensive would begin quite soon.[24] The plans would be delayed as most regiments needed to be reequipped and receive fresh training. They still hoped the army would advance again before Rommel was able to begin his own attack towards Tobruk.

At GHQ, the focus became more about an attack on the north or centre of the Gazala line which heavily influenced plans and deployments made by Ritchie. Eighth Army concentrated more formations there with a direct supply line from the Tobruk-Belhamed depots. Politically it placed Eighth Army and GHQ Cairo under much greater pressure, to make good the initial loss of Cyrenaica and to begin an offensive more quickly than Auchinleck would have liked. By early March, Auchinleck sent an exasperated reply to London, that the Middle East Committee was fully aware of the situation regarding Malta, '…we are trying…to present to you the situation as it appears to us, not as you would like it to be.'[25] As defeats increased in other theatres, Eighth Army appeared to be the only British force capable of striking a fresh blow in the British and Allied war effort. So that just as occurred before Crusader, greater pressure from Churchill and the COS on Auchinleck at GHQ and Eighth Army increased through the spring.

Defeats elsewhere added more pressure onto British strategy for some sort of success. As well as the reverse in Libya, the Prime Minister and COS were dealing with the worsening news arriving from the Far East. Here the successful Japanese advances effectively changed the plans for North Africa. General Brooke had appreciated the problems, 'My hopes of carrying on with the conquest of North Africa are beginning to look more and more impossible every day. From now on the Far East will make ever increasing inroads into our resources.' He noted how all of this bad news drove Churchill to be at his most critical and left even Brooke wondering why the, '…troops are not fighting better. If the army cannot fight better than it is doing at present

---

23 Danchev & Todman, *Alanbrooke War Diaries*, 30 January 1942, p.225.
24 TNA WO 201/401: Telegrams January-March 1942. Review of Situation in Libya, 26 February 1942.
25 TNA WO 201/397: Telegrams: General Auchinleck and Prime Minister, May 1941-June 1942. 4 March 42.

we shall deserve to lose our Empire!'[26] The recent military defeats and Churchill's 20 months in office, meant that he needed a political victory as well as a military one to stay in office.[27]

In Cairo, the C-in-C Middle East made the decision that despite Tobruk remaining as the primary forward supply base for Eighth Army just behind the front line, they would not attempt to defend the port for a second siege, as they had done in 1941.[28] General Ritchie was to organise the Gazala defences, and create a strike force to recapture the airfields to the west at Derna-Mechili-Martuba, with up to three armoured divisions, three brigade groups and three infantry divisions. He was concerned about the numbers of enemy medium tanks in the Derna-Martuba area, but envisaged that by 1 April and certainly by 1 May Eighth Army would be 'ready for battle' with 500 medium tanks and 150 Valentines.[29]

Increased shortages in shipping also added heavily to the problems for the war effort, and urgently affected both reinforcements to the Middle East and flexibility of future operations. The Chiefs of Staff wanted 5 armoured and 17 Infantry divisions for the Middle East, to guarantee a victory in North Africa and the defence of the northern front. With the Far East now needing more troops, the Middle East would be left with just 3 armoured and 10 infantry divisions. India had been dangerously denuded of any wholly British formation, which was viewed as a security threat to its defence. Britain did not have enough troop ships and American ship capacity was only one-third of British levels and would not improve until 1943.[30] These shortages meant that reinforcements could not be sent out and it was troopships which were most needed.[31]

The shipping crisis occupied a good deal of time by the COS Committee and in turn Auchinleck needed to win a major success as soon as possible. Brooke discussed the situation with his deputy General Archie Nye in early February and said it was a problem which, 'the PM will not face, and yet it…will affect our whole strategy during the coming year.' He later commented that the 'opening up' of the Mediterranean would release a million tons of shipping.[32] This would release the much-needed capacity for further operations elsewhere. There were similar problems in trying to send out RAF reinforcements to the Far East as the Japanese advanced rapidly across the Pacific. The COS response to the urgent requests made by the New Zealand

---

26   Danchev & Todman, *Alanbrooke War Diaries*, 18 February 1942, p.231.
27   Andrew Roberts, *Churchill Walking with Destiny* (London: Allen Lane, 2018), p.712.
28   I. S. O. Playfair *The Mediterranean & Middle East Vol. III* (Uckfield: Naval & Military Press, 2007), p.197.
29   TNA WO 201/401: Telegrams January-March 1942. Review of Situation in Libya, 26 February 1942, p.4.
30   TNA CAB 80/61/3: COS Committee Memorandum, Shipping Situation 9 February 1942.
31   Butler, *Grand Strategy, Vol. III, Part II*, pp.547–548.
32   Danchev & Todman, *Alanbrooke War Diaries*, p.225. 30 January 1942, p.227.

Prime Minister Fraser, was to side-step RAF planes and promise American Fighters which had been first allocated to the British.[33]

By mid-February Eighth Army's offensive was threatened with further delays. It was clear that formations would be sent from the Middle East to shore up the rapid collapse in Malaya. The CIGS informed Auchinleck that two divisions had to go, (as Singapore had surrendered on 15 February). He wrote, 'I realise that your plans for regaining Cyrenaica may have to be abandoned in favour of the defence of the Egyptian frontier (Sollum-Maddalena),'[34] while the northern front would only have an internal security defence. General Brooke appreciated the effect of the loss of two veteran divisions, but Auchinleck doggedly responded, 'your news entirely nullifies all previous planning...therefore the whole situation of Middle East must be reviewed accordingly.' He said the Middle East Defence Committee would make a fresh review.[35]

They responded about the transfer of divisions with a lengthy and bleak summary, which angered the Prime Minister, partly because it came from the Committee, rather than directly from Auchinleck. They argued that to defend Libya and the northern front properly they wanted at least 12 infantry divisions and ideally 17, with five brigade groups for internal security, apart from the armoured formations. With units gone to the Far East, 'we will have eight divisions and five brigade groups... It is evident that with this force we cannot maintain our position in the Middle East in the face of an attack from the North.'[36] Secondly, the Committee said that the political effect of these large-scale withdrawals on Turkey, which might drive her towards becoming a Germany ally, this would directly threaten Russia and endanger bases in the Delta and the Iraqi oilfields.[37] From London's point of view, this assessment seemed very negative and offered few ideas to aid Malta or make any defence of the northern front. They seemed to be requesting more shipping and four extra divisions for the Middle East.

These pressures on both the Prime Minister and Auchinleck developed a strain in their previous warmer relationship and one which never recovered during the summer battles. The debates continued and Auchinleck sent a lengthy report on 27 February, which outlined his reasons for delaying an offensive until 1 June. He wanted a steady build-up in the numbers of new tanks in the armoured brigades, to counter the danger that Panzerarmee might attack from the desert flank, if Eighth Army advanced towards Mechili. Equally the coastal route also had to be secured again to

---

33 TNA CAB 80/61/3: COS Committee Memorandum, Air Assistance 9 February 1942.
34 Playfair, *Mediterranean & Middle East Vol. III*, p.199.
35 TNA WO 201/398: Cipher telegrams: General Auchinleck & PM, December 1941-June 1942, 1721 Private for CIGS from General Auchinleck, 19 Feb 1942.
36 TNA WO 201/398: Cipher telegrams: General Auchinleck & PM, December 1941-June 1942, Mideast CS/747. 20 February 1942.
37 TNA WO 201/398: Cipher telegrams: General Auchinleck & PM, December 1941-June 1942, Mideast CS/747. 20 February 1942.

recapture the vital airfields which protected the convoys to Malta. He added that the supply situation was improving as the railway advanced towards El Adem, and that army planners had also highlighted problems of logistical support to any advance into Western Cyrenaica.[38] He did not mention the reality that many regiments were still training and being reequipped in the Delta, or rear areas, well into April. Churchill was extremely unhappy with Auchinleck's appreciation, and requested that he return to London to discuss matters further, which Auchinleck declined.[39] Churchill also promised more reinforcements in more detail to Auchinleck's points. He was still worried about the danger to Malta, and the strategic need to be doing something with the 635,000 men currently in the Middle East, especially with a renewed German offensive expected in Russia by May.

General Brooke reduced the PM's criticism towards Auchinleck, to a more measured response from the COS. Malta was placed under Middle East Command, because its defence was so tied in with any successful advance in Cyrenaica. Brooke believed that GHQ also needed an expert on armoured warfare so he appointed Major General Dick McCreery to join Auchinleck in Cairo. He informed McCreery that it would be an awkward appointment, but was never told that Auchinleck later basically ignored McCreery and any advice he gave.[40] McCreery effectively became an inspector of armoured regiments. It is clear that the months of February and March were not a harmonious time for the COS, trying to keep the Prime Minister in check from making rash decisions based on gut reactions to a steady stream of bad news.

Problems continued through March with more difficult exchanges. The Defence Committee was dismayed by Auchinleck's summary and called again for action. They also disagreed over the comparisons about respective tank numbers in Libya. Auchinleck detailed these totals to General Brooke, giving totals of 591 tanks with regiments and another 523 under repair. His main point was that 'other factors besides MERE issue of tanks…govern readiness of formations…such as General Grants with more powerful weapons necessitating change in tactical procedure. We must have (time to) think how to get the full value out of our material.'[41] Churchill queried the GHQ totals in the desert and argued again for even just a limited offensive towards Derna, to give more air cover for Malta bound convoys. He also promised a forthcoming visit by Sir Stafford Cripps and the Deputy Chief of Staff, General Nye, to Cairo. Churchill hoped that these two men would be able to ascertain the reality of problems, tank numbers, and general readiness for Eighth Army to take the offensive as soon as possible.

38 TNA CAB 80/61/3: COS Committee. Situation in Libya, 1 March 1942.
39 TNA CAB 101/248/3: Telegrams Prime Minister to General Auchinleck, T.343/2. 8 March 1942.
40 Danchev & Todman, *Alanbrooke War Diaries*, 2–3 March 1942, p.235.
41 TNA WO 201/397: Cipher telegrams: General Auchinleck & Prime Minister, May 1941-June 1942, 1724 cipher CS/789, 4/3/42.

General Nye's later detailed report confirmed that both Eighth Army and RAF groups were not ready for an offensive before mid-May. He added further detail, responding to all of London's queries saying that Axis tank strength was about 320 in the forward area whereas Eighth Army would only have 2nd and 4th Armoured Brigades by then. It continued pessimistically that enemy reinforcements would outweigh British even until August, but Eighth Army would have enough by May only if the Axis did not receive any further supplies of new tanks.[42]

The political outcome of this visit to Cairo largely backfired against Churchill's plan to challenge GHQ's arguments, as both Nye and Cripps, having looked at the detailed situation, agreed with Auchinleck that the army would not be ready for an offensive in March or April. Many regiments were still being reequipped and in the midst of fresh training. The Prime Minister sent a petulant comment to Auchinleck on 16 March, 'it is decided that if you must stand on the defensive until July, it will be necessary to consider the movement of at least 15 air squadrons from Libya to sustain the Russian left wing in the Caucasus.'[43] London planners had already shown that the Middle East needed 85 squadrons but only had 60 that spring. Churchill was still angry with Nye's report on 22 March, 'I do not wonder everything was so pleasant considering you seem to have accepted everything they said, and…we have to accept is the probable loss of Malta and the army standing idle while the Russians are resisting the German counterstroke desperately, and while the enemy is reinforcing himself in Libya faster than we are.'[44] Churchill remained frustrated, yet if Eighth Army began major operations it would be quickly undermined. De Guingand believed that Auchinleck suffered unfair pressure at this time, and that he was only trying to give the army a reasonable chance to be ready for the coming battle.[45]

Auchinleck maintained his stance and again replied through the Middle East Committee to press his serious doubts about the success of even a limited offensive, arguing that, the ensuing battle was likely to be fought on ground of the enemy's choosing, in the area Derna-Mechili, and this could result in Eighth Army giving up the Gazala line and Tobruk and falling back to the frontier posts at Sollum-Maddalena, 'the destruction of the British Tank Force would force the loss of these defensive positions.'[46] He added, 'We are not (repeat not) in a position at this moment to mass a superior force of tanks against the enemy.' He thought that if by the end of the month they could have two armoured brigades, then the Army might be ready for

---

42 TNA WO 201/397: Cipher telegrams: General Auchinleck & Prime Minister, May 1941-June 1942, 22/3/42.
43 TNA CAB 101/248/3: Telegrams Prime Minister to General Auchinleck, T.393/2. 16 March 1942.
44 TNA CAB 101/248/3: Telegrams Prime Minister to General Nye (Cairo), T.446/2. 22 March 1942.
45 Francis de Guingand, *Operation Victory*, (London: Hodder & Stoughton,1947), p.108.
46 TNA CAB 66/24/26: Telegram from Middle East Defence Committee, No. CC/42, dated 9th May, 1942Extract from Tel. CS849 22 March,

the end of May. XIII Corps HQ and 2nd New Zealand Division both agreed in their lessons from Crusader, that more combined training was needed across most units in Eighth Army.[47] The C-in-C Middle East felt he could hold to a later start date and so the Defence Committee reluctantly accepted mid-May as the date for a new offensive, the aim being to have a three to two ratio of armour to allow for the poorer British tank performance.[48]

Renewed Axis threats continued to build pressure for London and Cairo during April, both in the Mediterranean and the Far East. In the Mediterranean, Malta recorded the heaviest weekly air raids on Valetta and the airfields, while in the Indian Ocean, a large Japanese Carrier naval force was sited 380 miles south-east of and heading for Ceylon. This force posed a direct threat to Ceylon and India, especially after the Royal Navy force based on the Carrier Hermes was sunk on 9 April.[49] Major-General Kennedy reviewed the situation in early April, and concluded that a Libyan offensive was vital, but defences in India and Ceylon might not be strong enough and more US activity was needed in the Pacific.[50]

A new strategic review was released by the COS which threatened dire consequences to the Allied war effort and the defence of Australia, if Axis forces were allowed to dominate both the Indian Ocean and threaten oil supplies in Persia.[51] It was an unsettling review for Auchinleck and Ritchie, as they would be committing units forward into Cyrenaica which might be suddenly recalled elsewhere. On 9 April, Auchinleck reappraised the entire Middle East strategy in favour of the defence of India, because of the rapidly worsening situation in the Indian Ocean. On the same day the COS informed GHQ Middle East of the urgent need to transfer aircraft, which of course weakened air support in the Mediterranean. They also confirmed the greater threat to India and the supply route to the Middle East from Japanese naval forces. Auchinleck replied that a new offensive into Cyrenaica would be a 'tremendous risk.' All efforts should be to strengthen the defences, the Gazala line, and to send all spare resources for the defence of India. The COS disagreed in the strategic review of 10 April and considered the implications of the Japanese threats to Ceylon and Calcutta, along with the German threats to Malta and the northern front. They concluded that while forces had to be built up in Ceylon and India, the offensive in Libya should still go ahead soon to save Malta, and that continued Russian defences would cover threats to Northern Iran.[52]

47 TNA 201/522 13 Corps: Operations, November 1941-January 1942. Notes on Lessons from Recent Operations.
48 Playfair, *Mediterranean & Middle East*, Vol. III, p.202.
49 TNA CAB 80/36/1: War Cabinet Weekly Résumé 136, to 9th April 1942, situation,
50 John Kennedy, *The Business of War* (London: Hutchinson, 1957), p.220.
51 TNA CAB 80/36/1: Memorandum. COS Committee Relation of Strategy in Middle East and India, 10 April 1942.
52 TNA CAB 80/36/1: Memorandum. COS Committee Relation of Strategy In Middle East and India, 10 April 1942.

Malta suffered badly with increased bombing during February and Kesselring ordered it to be intensified throughout March. In response London increased calls on Auchinleck to recapture Cyrenaica to provide air protection for Malta bound convoys. In late February the COS telegrammed Middle East, that, 'Malta was of such importance…that the most drastic steps were needed to sustain it… We are unable to supply MALTA from the west. Your chances of doing so from the east depend on an advance in CYRENAICA.'[53] Axis pressure on Malta and the threats to its supply line from Alexandria was becoming more deadly, with both the February and March convoys being almost destroyed by enemy action. So the April convoy was now vital if a crisis was to be averted on the island.[54] The intensity of air raids increased again during April, with the airfields and the dockyard areas being pounded to rubble, leaving just six fighters for air defence. They flew over 200 sorties each day, forcing the last RN ships and submarines to leave. Malta had lost its strike force for now.[55] The island had been neutralised as a base against Axis shipping, though the Italians were still nervous of its ability to be rejuvenated.

Kesselring returned from Germany with Hitler's approval for the invasion of Malta only in late April, but Italian commanders were still worried that its coastal batteries were intact and a parachute assault would suffer heavy casualties.[56] Air defences were bolstered by the arrival of a second delivery of 61 Spitfires from the carriers *Wasp* and *Eagle*, combined with the Luftwaffe transferring Fliegerkorps II back to Russia, changing the dynamic of the constant air raids and enabling the island to slowly rebuild its defensive strength, though supply shortages would remain an issue for much of 1942.[57] By May, Malta's air defences were slowly improving with the reduction in air raids but the situation remained dangerous. The pressure also eased in the Far East, so that the Prime Minister's telegram to Auchinleck on 5 May conveyed a friendlier tone. He still requested that Middle East Command would aid the war effort the most if they would, 'engage and defeat the enemy on your western front,' rather than denude the theatre by sending troops to defend India.[58] The arrival of more Spitfires and a fast supply ship to Valetta ensured the island could continue until early June at least.[59] By mid-May the numbers of Spitfires increased with more

---

53 Timothy Bowman, *The Military Papers of Field Marshal Sir Claude Auchinleck, Vol. I: 1940–42* (Woodbridge, Boydell Press, 2021), p 322, Cipher from COS to Auchinleck, 27 February 1942.
54 Playfair, *Mediterranean & Middle East Vol. III*, p.200.
55 Denis Richards & H. St George Saunders, *Royal Air Force 1939–1945, Vol. II, The Fight Avails* (London: HMSO, 1954), pp.192–193.
56 Count Ciano, *Diary 1937–1943* (London: Phoenix Press, 2002), p.513.
57 Ernle Bradford, *Siege: Malta 1940–1943* (Harmondsworth: Penguin, 1987), pp.171–177.
58 TNA CAB 101/248/5: Telegram Prime Minister to General Auchinleck, T.691/2. 5 May 1942.
59 Kennedy, *Business of War*, p.231.

arriving from carriers.[60] This eased the critical air situation over Malta and enabled the RAF to gain local air superiority, especially with Fliegerkorps II strengths declining throughout May as it was transferred.[61]

The COS continued to assess the threat to the northern front. While they made it clear to Auchinleck that the enemy had to be driven out of Cyrenaica in order to save Malta, they also argued that if Eighth Army was pinned down in Libya, the northern front would be under greater threat.[62] Plans were made to ensure oil denial in the Middle East, as a worst-case scenario. If the Axis broke through the Caucasus, the danger to Persia and India would be very real, and if Eighth Army was heavily involved in Cyrenaica, it would be unable to respond. The COS had expressed their fears of wider threats to the Allied war effort. That any new strategy should also take into account the, 'heavy threat to shipping routes of the allied nations and of preventing the junction of Japanese and German forces by way of the Caucasus.'[63]

By mid-April, Enigma intercepts showed Luftwaffe reinforcements heading to southern Russia.[64] Auchinleck increased his arguments about the dangers to the northern front, by requesting that Middle East Command take control of liaising with neutral Turkey, in view of the Axis pressure to sway Turkey across to their side. He felt Cairo was better placed to make immediate operational decisions and would also speed up defence plans for Syria. Here Commonwealth divisions were being sent to the Syrian border to watch Turkish labourers improve their roads to the border. Brigadier Kippenberger and 5th NZ Brigade took over the Syrian-Turkish frontier in March and noted that their role was to, 'cover the heavy bomber airfield at Aleppo and to impose as much delay as possible on any invasion by the Germans through Turkey.'[65] Despite all of these concerns at GHQ, Joint Planners in London reiterated their earlier report that Axis troops in Libya were being reinforced in case their position could be exploited and that possible attacks on Syria, Iraq or Persia, through the Caucasus or Turkey, were unlikely until Russia had been defeated.[66]

Eighth Army planning discussions also contributed their views on the likely success of the next phase of operations. General Ritchie's style included regular conferences, mimicking similar events at GHQ. This contributed to the idea that Auchinleck's

60   TNA CAB 66/24/45: War Cabinet Weekly Résumé 142 to 21st May 1942, Mediterranean situation.
61   Playfair, *Mediterranean & Middle East Vol. III*, p.188.
62   Playfair, *Mediterranean & Middle East Vol. III*, p.201.
63   TNA CAB 79/19/12: Minutes of the COS Committee, Friday 13 March 1942, 13. Combined British and American Strategy.
64   TNA HW 1/513: Southern Russian Front: GAF bomber and fighter reinforcements, 19 April. 21 April 1942.
65   Howard Kippenberger, *Infantry Brigadier* (London: Oxford University Press, 1949), p.117.
66   TNA CAB 79/20/10: COS Committee Minutes, 6 April 1942, Conclusions JISC Report Enemy Intentions.

decision to keep Ritchie as Army commander, was not the right one. Michael Carver saw both men in this period, and argued that Ritchie was an honest, straightforward commander, who was too loyal to Auchinleck, and not ruthless enough to request the C-in-C to step away and leave him to command Eighth Army in his own style.[67] Long conferences at Gambut or a Corps HQ would continue throughout the battle.

Auchinleck's conference agendas were still influenced by his continued worries for the northern front and the defence of India. In mid-March, the main discussion was about plans for a three-day exercise on northern front defences, and options if German forces advanced through Turkey. While the northern front scenario was an important strategic issue, it was still distracting for Eighth Army. What is perhaps somewhat curious are the agenda topics at the higher-level GHQ conferences, which also discussed more minor issues included army publicity, use of formation signs and the duties of liaison officers. Why a major planning conference was discussing these mundane administrative issues is surprising and these could surely have been resolved at lower levels of the vast headquarters complex.[68] It was also somewhat ironic that the US Colonel Bonner Fellers attended the 17 May conference, where an early agenda topic was the poor quality of security standards inside GHQ. Again, even with an Axis offensive now fully expected in Libya, the 'Wargame – Persia' was still a major discussion.[69] These agendas give the impression of GHQ maintaining a different focus to Eighth Army HQ about Libya. Yet General Ritchie and other leaders from Eighth Army attended them.

Logistical Plans, Spring 1942

If there were doubts about whether Eighth Army had enough new tanks and fully trained units to defeat Panzerarmee, both GHQ and Army planners also had wider logistical problems for the Army to make an effective advance across Cyrenaica. Some of these doubts must have fed through to the final decisions made by Auchinleck and Ritchie. In early March GHQ Quartermasters (Q Branch) provided an important analysis about the logistical support for an advance, with some caveats. They noted there was still an, 'absence of a firm directive as to time and without a clear direction of advance.'[70] To maintain a force at 200 miles radius was 'only just possible,' Tobruk would need to operate at 1,200 tons per day and the railhead had to be extended to El

---

67 Michael Carver, *Dilemmas of the Desert War. The Libyan Campaign 1940–1942* (Staplehurst: Spellmount, 2002). pp.145–146.
68 TNA WO 201/532: Eighth Army: Commanders Conferences, December 1941-May 1942, 16 March 1942.
69 TNA WO 201/532: Eighth Army: Commanders Conferences, December 1941-May 1942, 17 May 1942.
70 TNA WO 201/419: Cyrenaica campaign: planning, March–October 1942. 12 March 1942.

Adem. GHQ also took a good deal of March to produce further plans, with the final report reaching Army HQ on 24 March.[71] They envisaged Eighth Army advancing across Cyrenaica, possibly beyond Benghazi, based on four separate force options, ranging from two divisions down to a single division. They could be supplied at 130 miles from Tobruk/El Adem or just possibly at 200 miles range. Supply echelon columns could reach the former with a four day turnaround and the latter within six and a half days. They offered detailed examples: Force A (consisting of two armoured divisions and one motor division, plus an RAF echelon – but not the whole RAF Group), would need approximately 1,600 tons per day. While lesser Forces B, C and D, each basically one infantry division, would need 1,500 tons per day as a group. If Eighth Army advanced with these forces it left a deficit in supplies at Tobruk and El Adem, of 1,900 tons per day.

Another issue was the shortage of motor transport companies, who would be needed to operate west of Tobruk, and then between Tobruk and the railhead at Capuzzo. Any advance would suffer more problems in finding new water supplies across Western Cyrenaica, to ease the burden of trying to transport it using water trucks over such distances.[72] They calculated that to advance beyond the 200 mile range, major new FMCs (large supply dumps), would be needed at the 130 mile marker, and this would require a pause in operations. It was *hoped* that if, 'an adequate water source were found during the advance, AND 'BENGHASI be opened up' the logistical position would be much more in the army's favour.[73] This was being fairly optimistic in view of the previous attempts to capture and open up Benghazi as a port, while Axis bombers could attack the sea approaches from Tripolitania. The planners proved that to advance any sizeable force, would require massive logistical support, overstretching existing supply resources of trucks and personnel.

Army planners and Brigadier C. H. Miller in Cairo, also poured a fair amount of cold water on the possibilities of Tobruk supplying army formations on operations up to 130 miles beyond Tobruk. He said that the port was unlikely to receive 1,700 TPD, and more realistic was 445 TPD possibly up to 800 TPD at best. Secondly, unless Eighth Army knew differently, there were currently only 28 supply companies, and not the 42 needed to advance. Additionally, the size of supply dump required for 60 days of petrol would be 'colossal' and that if not used quickly the petrol would go 'gummy' in the summer heat. Equally, such a supply chain would require large numbers of personnel in the forward areas, which would also increase the water, fuel and food needs. Finally, in terms of RAF support, the Air Commander (AOC)

71   TNA WO 201/421: Cyrenaica campaign: planning, March–October 1942. Estimates, 24 March 1942.
72   TNA WO 201/421: Cyrenaica campaign: planning, March–October 1942. Estimates, 24 March 1942.
73   TNA WO 201/421: Cyrenaica campaign: planning, March–October 1942. Estimates, para.7, 24 March 1942.

preferred, '...to operate with the bulk of his fighters well forward,' and would not want to split his force into two parts.⁷⁴

From GHQ, Lieutenant-Colonel Bastyan countered in detail to show that supplying operations was possible beyond Tobruk, and Brigadier Miller's second response to him was somewhat sharper, 'You will appreciate how extra-ordinarily dangerous it would be to plan...[to] maintain a force at over 2,000 TPD west of TOBRUK if in actual fact 1,700 TPD is the real figure.'⁷⁵

Both HQs were also still uncertain about the start date for an advance. The logisticians were adding to Ritchie's doubts by defining some of the supply problems even without an enemy response. As planning for a spring offensive continued, the differences between the realistic assessment from Eighth Army, against the ideas from staff officers in Cairo, were becoming more noticeable.

RAF Support

The RAF, under the title of WDAF, provided valuable air-ground support at various stages throughout Gazala and air historians have written cogent studies of this. The official history, along with the more recent work by Christopher Shores et al, have provided a comprehensive account of the daily air battles for this period,⁷⁶ while B. W. Gladman has detailed how the WDAF became more effective in the tactical battle. A new HQ provided improved air to ground support with more signals personnel and wireless trucks, all being directed by Army Air Support Control No.2 unit, (AASC).⁷⁷ RAF liaison officers were spread across both Corps and Divisional HQs and provided over 900 reports in one year.⁷⁸ Yet at 1st Armoured HQ, liaison officers were being exchanged only from late May, which did not give them much opportunity to 'promote mutual understanding' as intended.⁷⁹

The WDAF intensified day and night-time raids on Axis airfields, while aircraft would strafe and bomb any viable ground target. In early May 90th Light Division reported the effect, 'English low flying aircraft have repeatedly inflicted grave losses... the opportunity for destroying enemy aircraft has been largely neglected...by the

---

74   TNA WO 201/421: Cyrenaica campaign: planning, March–October 1942, letter to Lieutenant Colonel Bastyan 27 March 1942.
75   TNA WO 201/421: Cyrenaica campaign: planning, March–October 1942, letter to Lieutenant Colonel Bastyan 30 March 1942.
76   Richards & St George Saunders, *Royal Air Force 1939–1945, Vol. II, The Fight Avails*, and Christopher Shores et al, *A History of the Mediterranean Air War 1940–1945. Vol. Two: North African Desert February 1942-March 1943* (London: Grub Street, 2021).
77   Brad William Gladman, *Intelligence and Anglo-American Air Support in World War Two. The Western Desert and Tunisia* (Basingstoke: Palgrave Macmillan, 2009), pp.77–81.
78   TNA WO 201/500: General Auchinleck's despatch on operation 'Crusader', 1941 December–1943 November.
79   TNA WO 169/4053: 1st Armoured Division War Diary, 20 May 1942.

failure to reply with any sort of fire...'[80] They also continued with their wider operational role with attacks targeting Axis supply ships at Benghazi, any landing grounds and supply columns heading to the front along the Via Balbia. In London, the COS Air believed that the best use for WDAF bombers was in attacking Axis shipping to Tripoli, or mining the approaches and in March he was prepared to send six Lancasters to assist this task.[81] The Luftwaffe also had similar roles, by neutralising Malta and sinking Allied shipping into Tobruk, combined with daily sweeps across Eighth Army areas to catch any unfortunate supply columns and targets.

Ultra confirmed that Rommel was about to launch his offensive (Operation *Venezia*) and this gave Ritchie the excuse to halt his plans for an offensive and await the Axis attack. He intended to let the Panzer divisions be crippled on the defensive boxes and then strike with his own armoured brigades in a counterpunch. 'Should the enemy resume the offensive...it must be our endeavour to bring his armour to battle on ground of our own choosing, reconnoitred and prepared by us...where his administration would be extended to the greatest possible extent.'[82]

Meanwhile in Cyrenaica, Panzerarmee made a forward move in early April, and strong columns of 100 tanks and MT moved eastwards to close on the Gazala line, which made Eighth Army units react to be ready.[83] The Green Howards and other units along the front went to one hour's notice to move, when Tac-Rs (RAF reconnaissance aircraft) reported four enemy columns moving south near Bir Temred.[84] Both Auchinleck and Ritchie thought Panzerarmee might begin its own offensive very soon, before Eighth Army was ready to advance, thus a strong defence was needed.

The C-in-C[85] Middle East replied to London with further doubts about a successful Libyan offensive after meeting on 9 May, and responded to the Prime Minister's telegram with further analysis. More concerns were expressed about the likely success of such a limited offensive. In their view, the loss of Malta would be deplorable but not fatal to ensuring the security of Egypt, but they agreed that control of Cyrenaica would help protect convoys to Malta, although it would not guarantee that offensive power on Malta could be restored. Also, simply capturing Cyrenaican landing grounds would still mean the RAF would need time to set up new operations and a decisive victory in the expected armoured battle was not guaranteed. Finally, they argued that defeating the forthcoming Axis offensive first and only then advancing

---

80   TNA WO 169/4053: 1st Armoured Division War Diary, Intelligence Summary 23, 7 May 1942.
81   TNA CAB 79/19/24: COS Committee Meeting, 24 March 1942, Mediterranean,
82   TNA WO 201/379: Operations in North Africa: General Ritchie's report, May–June 1942, Object of the Gazala Position.
83   TNA CAB 80/36/1: War Cabinet Weekly Résumé 136, to 9 April 1942, military situation,
84   TNA WO 169/5023: 7th Green Howards War Diary, 6 April 42.
85   Auchinleck appears to have seen the Cairo Chiefs as a 'mini-committee'. It is possible that he sometimes preferred to make the issue less clear on purpose, knowing Churchill's likely reaction to delays and negative responses from GHQ Cairo.

into Cyrenaica, 'might very well be the best thing that could happen.'[86] They could not ignore continued doubts of success in battle combined with the clear logistical problems of supplying numerous divisions and RAF squadrons in Western Cyrenaica, especially while Axis forces were still capable of striking back. Somehow Panzerarmee had to be defeated without the Pyrrhic losses for the armoured brigades of another Operation Crusader.[87]

The supply situation improved for the Axis. Rommel noted that in March they had received only 18,000 tons of supplies, but thereafter the situation improved, and allowed him to develop his plans for an offensive. Secondly, he appreciated that Eighth Army would be reinforced faster than Panzerarmee by the end of May, so he had to move fast.[88] Supply documents show that Panzerarmee received another 20,000 tons of operating fuel, and 5,676 tons of ammunition, along with another 5,000 tons of other supplies in April, strengthening their position.[89] On 11 May 90th Light Division received updated orders, which confirmed the attack would be via Bir Hacheim – Acroma – Gazala – Tobruk, they would move on 'X Tag', this date was confirmed later.[90] Cavallero outlined the plans to the Italian Comando Supremo only on 12 May, confirming that Rommel intended to attack in Libya and capture Tobruk if possible and 'go as far as the old boundaries.' Then all forces would be concentrated for an assault on Malta.[91]

Eighth Army Plans – May 1942

Intelligence reports largely confirmed, that up to 13 May, there were 'no definite' signs of an immediate offensive by Panzerarmee, but it was maintaining good supplies. Which added to the pressure for Eighth Army to get on with its own attack. However, three days later, they confirmed that Panzerarmee was, 'now in a position to attack in the immediate future…and is likely to attempt passage of our minefield under cover of a dust storm or by night.'[92] As far as Ritchie was concerned, they would attack through the minefield and additional defences were needed for the middle and northern sectors, albeit behind the front line. This defence would blunt the Panzer divisions, and then be followed by an armoured counterpunch. Corps and divisions

---

86 TNA CAB 66/24/26. Telegram from Middle East Defence Committee, No. CC/42, dated 9 May, 1942,
87 Plutarch *Life of Pyrrhus*, 'Pyrrhus replied to one that gave him joy of his victory that one other such victory would utterly undo him.' Crusader had relieved Tobruk but had cost Eighth Army nearly 18,000 casualties.
88 Liddell-Hart, *Rommel Papers*, p.192.
89 Bundesarchiv: KTB225: summary of shipping deliveries for April, 3 May 1942.
90 Bundesarchiv: 90th Light Div, Armeebefehl für den Angriff, 11 May 1942.
91 Ciano, *Diary*, p.519.
92 TNA WO 169/4053: 1st Armoured Division War Diary, Operation Order No.13, 16 May 1942.

made their defensive battle plans and selected sites from which to fight during April and May. Even if units were to advance, there were still problems for some formations. The 150th Brigade HQ made it clear that any advance would affect the B echelon units moving forward to supply the brigade. If an advance was attempted, the shortage of vehicles would force 50th Division to 'milk' two brigades of their vehicles to enable one brigade to advance. In their view, the army was not in a state of readiness.[93] These were some of the basic issues which perhaps GHQ did not fully appreciate.

Intelligence came from a variety of sources, Ultra decrypts were still limited in operational detail to the Army commander. Professor Ralph Bennett worked on the Bletchley decrypts for the Middle East and confirmed that GHQ and Ritchie received clear confirmation that Rommel would attack in late May or early June, so that delays in starting the British offensive would mean Eighth Army fighting defensively at first. Secondly, Ultra provided regular updates about tank strengths for Panzerarmee, so that GHQ could see the comparison with Eighth Army totals, the latest update was sent on 7 May. Bennett argued that Ultra was not being utilised to the best advantage for planning.[94]

Other key intelligence came from RAF tactical photo reconnaissance flights (Tac-R) updating on enemy formations, their reports arrived within four hours of the photos being developed.[95] The main problem was the interpretation analysis and further patrols were needed by armoured car or jock columns to see what more detail could be gained. These reconnaissance patrols were the main ground source for intelligence. They were supported by, and possibly later frustrated by, the numerous jock columns who added details about enemy vehicles, troops and aircraft spotted. These patrols also delivered unlucky POWs back to the main HQs for processing. David Hunt, the Intelligence Officer at XIII Corps believed the POWs and signals listening gave a good indication of the coming offensive by Panzerarmee, so that the intended desert flank move was obvious.[96] Photos and other papers were also taken from prisoners, as they often photographed their journey, which inadvertently gave away vital

---

93 W. E. Bush, (ed.), *150th Infantry Brigade (50th Northumbrian Division) in the Middle East, June 1941-June 1942* (London: Green Howards Regimental Journal, 1944), p.18. Lieutenant Colonel Bush and fellow officers wrote the first account of the Brigade's actions in a POW camp in Italy, but this was found by the Italian guards. They wrote a second version when they escaped after September 1943, but they had to leave it behind in a farmhouse. The third version was written as a group comprising most of the original officers from the Brigade, gathered again in Switzerland by 1944, and this third version is that which was published by the Regimental Association of the Green Howards after they returned to the UK later that year.
94 Bennett, *Ultra and Mediterranean Strategy*, p.112.
95 TNA WO 201/500: General Auchinleck's despatch on operation 'Crusader', 1941 December–1943 November.
96 David Hunt, *A Don at War* (London: Frank Cass, 1990), p.100. though he accepted the NCO may have been planted with false information.

information about shipping and the dock situation at Naples or Tripoli.[97] The final movements made by DAK, kept Corps and Army HQs guessing that the main attack would still be made against the centre or north of the line.

Corps Level Plans

With most of the infantry/motor brigades in static roles or operating jock columns, the main forces for a counterattack lay with the two armoured divisions. Operational orders given to 1st Armoured Division show some corps and divisional training schemes about this task. The division moved to the rear at Bir el Gubi specifically for practising operational problems using one day wargames. At XXX Corps, General Norrie held a wargame to consider four 'problems-appreciations' with just the armoured division and brigade commanders, working in two teams around a model of the terrain.[98] There is no indication of who won.

Four sets of orders were issued by XXX Corps, between 16 and 23 May, which clearly show changes in emphasis to their defence plans. Intelligence given on 20 May, about Panzerarmee's attack being imminent, clearly affected changes. First AT Brigade ordered units to be prepared for an armoured battle in the rear area.[99] Operations Order No.12 (confusingly issued on 13 May) emphasised the importance of defending the left flank. They were to prevent enemy penetration south around Bir Hacheim and to counterattack west, rather than plan to counter any Axis attack on the northern sector of the line. Only 22nd Armoured would deploy against attacks in the north-west, though the two brigades were being sent in different directions. The south would be protected by 7th Armoured, to defend the various southern boxes and to destroy enemy forces moving south of Bir Hacheim.[100] Three days later new orders were received which focused on the attack in the north, with 2nd Armoured supporting 22nd Armoured to the north-west. The support for 7th Armoured Division in the south was downgraded.[101] The orders to 4th Armoured Brigade for 22 May said that attacking our weaker forces in the centre, 'tend to make this course more likely.'[102] This was a change of emphasis to the earlier orders. The intelligence confirming this had been the two Tac-R flights on 18 and 23 May, and German moves made by 15th

---

97   TNA WO 169/4053: 1st Armoured Division War Diary, Intelligence Summary 23, 7 May 1942.
98   TNA WO 169/4053: 1st Armoured Division War Diary, XXX Corps exercise No.3, Wargame, 15 May 1942.
99   TNA WO 169/4199: 1st Army Tank Brigade War Diary, Adm Order No.10, 21 May 1942.
100 TNA WO 169/4053: 1st Armoured Division War Diary, Operation Order No.12, 13 May 1942.
101 TNA WO 169/4053: 1st Armoured Division War Diary, Operation Order No.13, 16 May 1942.
102 TNA WO 169/5032: 1st KRRC War Diary, Operational Order No.6, 22 May 1942.

Panzer and 90th Light Divisions – the former to the Cherima, in the centre, and the 90th Light to Segnali, more to the south. The bulk of the armour remained in the north. Therefore, the assumption was that the attack would arrive in the north or possibly the centre, with 90th Light clearing the way for 15th Panzer.[103]

In May there was a good deal of new movement behind Panzerarmee's forward line. Axis armour neared the front line which meant that the DAK was moving forward and being made ready.[104] On 13 May, 1st AT Brigade and others halted plans because of enemy activity.[105] Appreciations showed Panzerarmee was forward in strength and protected by an increasing number of minefields, which would cripple any British counterattack. Later orders for 22 May determined that, 'the general indications are that the maximum weight of enemy attack is likely to be via the northern sector of XIII Corps, and that it will be coupled with seaborne landings.'[106] Jock columns and others noticed that the Axis lines were mostly quiet from 20 May, which added to the ruse that Panzerarmee had settled in for an attack in the north, or at best the centre, of the line.

Eighth Army therefore increased its defensive efforts in the north with new minefields being laid north of Acroma keep, to block the west side of Tobruk, and two more infantry brigade groups arrived, along with 4th and 7th RTR. The 2nd Armoured Brigade would move to 'battle positions' east of Knightsbridge, and either side of the Trigh Capuzzo. They were ready for an attack in the centre or against the northern sector. The Guards Brigade began to lay a minefield south from Acroma but left suitable gaps for traffic. In effect, a second line of minefields was being laid either side of Acroma box to give a new defensive line.[107]

DAK offered an alteration to Panzerarmee, about the approach march on 14 May. They suggested that rather than pause 3km south of Bir Hacheim, they wheel slightly further south and attack Bir Hacheim from the south after the rest period, but Panzerarmee HQ disagreed. On 18 May, Nehring and his staff conducted a TEWT to test the plans.[108] Rommel finalised his plans by 20 May by his five key divisions as the main approach to Eighth Army around Bir Hacheim. The Panzer divisions also received their instructions and the army commanders held a conference to confirm all plans.[109] The rest of the Italian infantry divisions would hold the front line and pin the Eighth Army brigades opposite them in the north. These troops also carried out

---

103 TNA WO 201/539: Eighth Army: intelligence matters, November 1941–August 1942.
104 TNA CAB 66/24/45: War Cabinet Weekly résumé 142 to 21st May 1942, Libya situation.
105 TNA WO 169/4199: 1st Army Tank Brigade War Diary, 9 May 1942.
106 TNA WO 169/4053: 1st Armoured Div. War Diary, Operational Order No.16, 22 May 1942.
107 TNA WO 169/4053: 1st Armoured Div. War Diary, Operational Order No.16, 22 May 1942.
108 IWM: DAK War Diary, 14–18 May 1942.
109 IWM: DAK War Diary, 20–21 May 1942.

diversionary attacks and movements on 26–27 May, to keep up the idea of a threat along the coast road. Meanwhile DAK and the two attached Italian divisions, Ariete and Trieste, would move south overnight and refuel south of Pt.171 in the early morning of 27 May.

Axis intelligence was mostly correct in defining Eighth Army deployment. Panzerarmee sketch maps for 20 May show the recce units to the west of the minefield; they noted three South African Armoured Car Regiments, the Kings Dragoon Guards and 9th KRRC jock columns further south with the South African brigades holding the northern boxes with 50th Division next to them, though they listed 151st Brigade in the middle at Sidi Muftah, with the RTR regiments behind them. The Free French are noted at Bir Hacheim and behind them 4th Armoured Brigade. 2nd Armoured Brigade is behind the centre. The Knightsbridge box and armoured attacks on the first day were a surprise to them, as they had 22nd Armoured and 200th Guards Brigade (by then 201st) as being well in reserve to the west of Bardia, with 5th Indian east of Sollum.[110]

As the battle opened on 27 May, 1st Armoured Division made final plans for cooperation with 4th Armoured Brigade. If the latter took up defensive position 'MAJORITY' – 1st Armoured was not expected to 'cooperate intimately'. However, if 4th Armoured took up position 'LARWOOD', 2nd Armoured Brigade would go south and take a defensive position between the Retma Box and Bir el Gubi while 22nd Armoured remained in reserve south of Knightsbridge. Effectively, 2nd Armoured Brigade would be advancing south-west, heading for Bir Hacheim, approaching the rear of 4th Armoured and coming in on the left of 22nd Brigade. The Guards Brigade was to cooperate with 2nd Armoured to form a pivot, and this could involve the partial or full evacuation of Knightsbridge. This did not happen but was a late change in the defensive role for using boxes. The orders also reiterated that 2nd Armoured Brigade would act alone but provide recce information on suitable positions for supporting infantry and gun batteries.[111] There seems to have been a lack of cooperation with 4th Armoured Brigade and even between the different brigades of 1st Armoured Division. As the first day progressed British armour engaged the Panzer divisions moving north towards Knightsbridge, but in a succession of separate engagements.

As the battle intensified by early June, London and GHQ Cairo still issued directives which became more out of touch with what Eighth Army might achieve. There was either a lack of up-to-date information or of a general understanding. On 2 June the Air Ministry insisted GHQ understood the importance of having air cover, and particularly Beaufighters, to cover the next convoy to Malta. They assumed that Martuba airfield would be captured and in use, but Martuba was approximately 40

---

110 Bundesarchiv: RH19/VIII/13: PzAOK War Diary, 7 February–25 May, Enemy deployments map, 20 May 1942.
111 TNA WO169/4053: 1st Armoured Division War Diary, Operational Order No.13, 27 May 1942.

miles west of the front line.[112] There were similar problems between GHQ departments and the embattled Eighth Army HQ. By 10 June Cairo was still planning for a British advance, despite the armoured battles around Knightsbridge reaching their climax, and within two days their defeat would lead to a gradual retreat. Q Dept was still planning for the transport needs of the expected advance towards Agheila, 'It is assumed that EIGHTH ARMY will not establish itself on the AGEILA Line before the middle of July. Thereafter a period of approx. one month…will be required to re-open BENGAHASI…'[113] They assumed Eighth Army would successfully advance and be halted at Agheila, until Benghazi had been opened up again. Both Cairo and London were clearly 'behind the curve' in understanding what was happening in the battle. Eighth Army had been constantly pressed by the need to support convoys to Malta, and to defeat Panzerarmee.

Churchill added his own pressures onto GHQ Middle East to gain any victory, especially after the defeats elsewhere in early 1942. Strategically, he hoped to gain the shorter route to India for future convoys by winning the North African campaign. This would also open up the southern flank of Europe and overstretch Axis forces required to defend the coast from Southern France to Greece. Eighth Army preparations had been a race against time. Army HQ planners calculated that an offensive across Cyrenaica was flawed by serious logistical issues in keeping enough fighting units in the front line. The Axis faced similar supply problems, to break through and capture Tobruk, as a prelude to the next phase of the campaign. Eighth Army feared that even if pushed back, Panzerarmee would be in a fighting condition, able to counterattack and sweep back again towards Tobruk. They had already forced Eighth Army to retreat twice and created a reluctance by British commanders to push forward once more without the certainty of a decisive victory over Panzerarmee, or even to make another advance across Cyrenaica without full logistical support, thus the new defensive line developed at Gazala.

112 TNA WO 201/398: Cipher telegrams: General Auchinleck and PM, December 1941-June 1942, Air Ministry to Mideast 2 June 1942.
113 TNA WO 201/420: Cyrenaica campaign: planning, June 1942, Appreciation 10 June 42

2

Terrain

This land was made for war. As glass
Resists the bite of vitriol, so this hard
And calcined earth rejects
The battle's hot, corrosive impact ...

'Landscape near Tobruk'
Joscelyn Brooke[1]

The terrain across which Gazala would be fought was vital to Eighth Army's defensive plan and subsequent counterattack. The desert west and south of Tobruk was a series of limestone plateaus bordered by escarpments and steep edges, mainly running east–west. In the southern sector there were some wide depressions bordered by low rimmed slopes. There were also large areas of open ground, much of it good going as it had top cover of stone or sand which overlaid the hard crust of limestone. These areas were good for traversing columns of armour and supply trucks, but more difficult for infantry and guns to dig in, to create an effective defensive position. More than one participant said that places on maps were often a figment of the mapmaker's imagination, as there was often little to define the place. Some heights on many ridges were not always discernible; they were still often vital crest lines, which could decide how effective a defensive position might be. The battles in 1941 confirmed that German units, 'always make for the high ground and once there it is very difficult to push them off. They dig in and deploy large numbers of anti-tank weapons.'[2] Eighth Army's plan was to manoeuvre in support of their Infantry 'boxes' and pivot around them to engage and destroy enemy armour. They would also move through the mine-marsh, in the centre and south of the line.

---

1   Selwyn, *Poems of the Second World War*, p.59.
2   TNA WO 201/450: Lessons from Operations, Cyrenaica No.1, 5 November 1941.

Increasingly warmer spring weather and more frequent dust storms also impacted on daily operations. The main problem of the *khamseens*, or dust storms, was that they hampered movement and training. The 1st RHA noted a bad *khamseen* throughout 17–18 April with the temperature reaching 105 degrees.[3] Back in March, Brigadier Kippenberger had attempted to visit General Koenig at Bir Hacheim during such a storm. He, 'penetrated the perimeter unseen…failed to find him and went out again undetected.'[4] Roy Farran also remembered two 'phenomenal sandstorms' which blew through the front during the spring.[5] Alan Moorehead talked about the heat, and that fighting in these conditions could not be tolerated. Yet when he visited the forward area, he found that, 'both British and Germans were standing up to the heat without any great difficulty. As summer advanced men became leaner and harder and browner, they ate and slept just as well and moved and thought just as quickly.'[6] The long hot days sapped the strength of many soldiers, who were living on minimal food and sleep, and being on duty or fighting for long hours from their tanks, vehicles or slit trenches.

Most commanders understood the experiences of desert operations and the problems of operations in Libya. Supply remained the main issue for the British either holding the Gazala line or attempting to move west beyond Tobruk. Lieutenant General Gott, an experienced desert hand, wrote to Harold Pyman after Crusader, with some of lessons from the winter battle, fought largely just east of Gazala. He said that high ground was vital and the enemy tactics had some weaknesses, but the importance of logistics – the 'Centre Line' in desert warfare was paramount. He argued that operations should have, 'a definite centre line for communications and supplies should be at right angles and never parallel to the hostile forces… In order to threaten this line, the enemy must make long detours which, in themselves, exhaust him and expose his own communications. The desert must be used against the enemy.'[7] Once Panzerarmee came around Bir Hacheim, Eighth Army's centre line of supply ran parallel to the enemy.

At Gazala the centre line of supply (and most communications) was the Trigh Capuzzo, track, in the centre of the forward area, traversing from the west through the Gazala minefields and heading east past Knightsbridge. This was the main supply route for most brigades in the centre and southern sector. The hundreds of vehicles using the trigh and valley either side of it had created a foot deep crust of sand by May, which was later strewn with battle debris and knocked out-tanks from the early stages of the battle. This track was a major struggle to drive along for most trucks

---

3   TNA WO 169/4555: 1st Royal Horse Artillery War Diary, January-December 1942, 17–18 April.
4   Kippenberger, *Infantry Brigadier*, p.115.
5   Roy Farran, *Winged Dagger. Adventures on Special Service* (London: Cassell, 1998), p.138.
6   Alan Moorehead, *African Trilogy* (London: Hamish Hamilton, 1946), p.309.
7   Pyman, *Call to Arms*, pp.39–40.

and vehicles.[8] The state of the track worsened with more battle debris as fighting progressed along the trigh. Along the coast ran the Via Balbia coast road which passed through Tobruk and then east to the frontier. The tarmacked Axis bypass road skirted south around Tobruk almost joining the Trigh Capuzzo just to its south. The coast road was another main supply route for the brigades deployed in the northern sector. In the build-up all supply columns remained vulnerable to sudden air attack, so daytime movement was never an easy option.

Early Development of the Line

Despite the upheavals of the January battles, and after a confused fighting retreat, the battered units settled around Gazala and south of it in early February. Defence positions and minefields developed organically, as units settled in from their retreat or arrived later to strengthen weaker sectors. Before his resignation, Lieutenant General Godwen-Austen reported that:

> Withdrawal proceeded to plan, except that the Polish Bde was halted on the GAZALA position to occupy a central sector, as the troops were too thin on the ground. The French Mobile column was withdrawn from MECHILI… 4 Independent Div developed a position echeloned in rear of GAZALA to prevent penetration between there and BIR HACHEIM. 1 Armd Div was positioned further west than planned…protected by minefields, it could operate on the left flank. By 4 Feb all formations were speedily improving their positions and morale was high. The enemy were in contact with our forward elements on the right.[9]

In the south the newly arrived 150th Brigade held Bir Hacheim and began digging a box which would be the southern end of the line. The new front line stretched south from Ain el-Gazala on the coast, some 40 miles to Bir Hacheim. The 1st Support Group (1st Armoured Division), which had fought its way back, noted that all enemy pressure was against the coast road, so it was felt this was the sector which needed the strongest defences.[10]

Eighth Army swiftly retaliated by deploying jock columns to the west, in the area up to Martuba-Tengeder. The newly arrived 50th Division nicknamed this area, 'the bloodiness' because much of it was a featureless area of difficult going. Panzerarmee did not close up to the British line until early April and moved closer again in May,

8   Moorehead, *African Trilogy*, p.327.
9   TNA WO 201/500: General Auchinleck's despatch on operation 'Crusader', December 1941–November 1943. Brief survey of Operations between 21 January and 5 February 1942 by Lieutenant General Godwin Austen, p.3.
10 TNA WO 169/4065: 1st Armoured Brigade Support Group War Diary 1942, 3–5 February 1942.

creating a no man's land for reconnaissance. By 5 February jock columns from the Guards, 150th Brigade, the Polish and Free French Brigades along with 1st South African Division were heading west, all patrolling sections of the front line. They manoeuvred in support of the reconnaissance patrols of the armoured cars from the Royal Dragoons, Kings Dragoon Guards and the S.A. Regiments. All of this patrol activity provided continuous intelligence and gave early warning of renewed threats from Panzerarmee.[11]

Eighth Army manuals described two types of minefields. First a close density field had two mines per yard, while open spaced fields had only one mine per yard. It had to be concealed to avoid detection, along with at least two dummy fields created by scratching the surface of the ground to imitate possible digging.[12] To speed up the development and to strengthen the line, companies of 60 men each were sent to assist the engineers in minelaying, along with early warning patrols going six miles forward. In the rear, brigades continued their reorganisation while other units went back to the Delta.

These first deployments hastily prevented a further advance by Panzerarmee. After returning to Gazala, 1st Support Group remained near the front. First South African Division were astride the coast road, just west of Gazala, then the Free French Brigade initially positioned just to the south at Alem Hamza. Here the line turned east, and then south again across the Trigh Capuzzo and the Trigh el Abd. This central sector was covered by 2nd Armoured Brigade and 200th Guards Brigade at Got el Ualeb until mid-April. Behind the line, 4th Indian Division held two sites west of Acroma, with the 150th Brigade, in the south at Bir Hacheim. They would soon exchange this desolate spot with the Free French. Engineers of 1st Armoured quickly laid a mine belt. The armoured brigades were in support and later carried out training exercises in the rear near Capuzzo, before returning to the front again as the situation developed.[13]

Northern Sector

The defensive boxes in the northern sector were sited close together to enable better artillery fire support. They were sited forward of the rest of the line to protect the coastal inlet at Ain el-Gazala. Their key importance was to protect one of the main trighs which traversed north out of the desert, and down the escarpment at the Serpentine pass to the coast road. This had to be held or the whole of the line would have been outflanked from the north. The South African brigades developed their MG and artillery positions, along with a strong front of wire and mines, to make

---

11 TNA WO 169/4065: 1st Armoured Brigade Support Group War Diary 1942, 3–5 February 1942.
12 HMSO, *Middle East Training Pamphlets* (Buxton: MLRS, 2011), METP No.6. Anti-Tank Mines, 1941, pp.4–5.
13 TNA WO 169/4065: 1st Armoured Brigade Support Group War Diary 1942.

any attack a hazardous prospect. The link between 1st and 2nd Brigades overlooked a depression west of the minefield, so the enemy would be attacking upslope from a bowl-like piece of ground, surrounded on three sides by South African guns. The Italians would make just such an attack early in the battle and suffer terrible casualties. The coast road continued eastwards, below the escarpment, and through Tobruk. Midway along this escarpment was another small defensive site, Commonwealth Keep at Pt.209.[14] It was held by a weak combined British/South African battalion. There was a good view south, towards the low rise at Eluet et Tamar, which became one of the key defensive sites to hold off Axis advances northwards. Units developed this site as part of a line facing south to link with the rear of 50th Division boxes.

Central Sector, Knightsbridge and Cauldron

The position of the new Knightsbridge box was seen as vital to support the line, as it blocked any potential breakthrough of the mine belt in the centre or north. It was started quite late on from 18 May and was situated on a plateau. The garrison consisted of 3rd Coldstream Guards, 2nd RHA and a company of Scots Guards. They decided to dig the defences around the RHA regiment in the centre and added 36 anti-tank guns near No.2 Company, and another battery outside the box. As elsewhere, vehicles and guns were all dug in below ground.[15] The Coldstream Guards provided the main infantry defence. They described the box area as featureless and flat around them, with the terrain rising to the low Maabus and Rigel Ridge, two miles to the north. To the west and south there were few features and the horizons degenerated into a shimmering heat haze as the summer heat began to build.

They occupied an area roughly two miles square, with the Trigh Capuzzo passing through the box east–west with one or two exits placed in the wire, with two more on the northern side. One battery of anti-tank guns from the Northumberland Hussars was deployed across the southern and western sides of the perimeter, supported by medium MG positions. The 25pdrs of 2nd RHA H and L Batteries were sited in the centre and northern sectors. All gun pits, slit trenches and vehicles were dug in with no visible parapet. Digging in would continue until 26 May, with various support units and four days of supplies dumped within the box. The shortage of ammunition was another problem, with only limited amounts arriving, along with sixteen 6pdr anti-tank guns, delivered by the Northumberland Hussars. The guardsmen greeted these improved weapons with enthusiasm.[16] All of this frenetic activity was completed just before the first attack by Panzerarmee. The perimeter wire was completed on the

14   J. A. I. Agar-Hamilton & L. C. F. Turner, *Crisis in the Desert May–July 1942* (Cape Town: OUP, 1952), p.8.
15   TNA WO 169/4982: 3rd Coldstream Guards War Diary, 18–20 May 1942.
16   TNA WO 169/4556: 2nd Royal Horse Artillery War Diary, January-December 1942. 18 May 1942.

evening of 26 May and the Guards watched the Luftwaffe bombing over most of the front.[17] Knightsbridge became the hub for Eighth Army's supply line, and had been put in place only just in time.[18] The Guards and their supporting arms would successfully defend two major attacks on the box, as well as enduring 17 days of constant shelling, until it was decided that the position was untenable.[19] This was possibly one of the only positions where Ritchie's defensive box strategy worked more effectively until the armour became too weak to pivot on either flank.

In comparison, work on the nearby Rigel Ridge defended locality was only started after the battle had begun and was never properly completed for an effective defence. The north-west flank of Knightsbridge had to be protected and so 2nd Scots Guards moved out over three days from 30 May, to occupy the position. They were also sent there to prevent Axis movement north towards Acroma and Eluet et Tamar, and to protect the 25pdrs from I Battery 2nd RHA, which engaged enemy artillery firing on Knightsbridge.

Rigel had a steep edge on both sides, up to 150 feet high, and the southern side was cut by wadis, as at El Adem. The main weakness was that it was overlooked by higher ground further east along the ridge, and at the 'toe-end' to the west, which gave artillery observation over the Guards position and the guns at Rigel. The southern slopes were convex forcing the Guards to dig their anti-tank pits and slit trenches on the forward slopes, making them vulnerable to enemy fire. Finally, most of the gun pits and rifle pits had to be drilled or blasted out of the rock. The Indian engineers only had one pneumatic drill and refused to work under shellfire, so the 6pdrs were never properly dug in. The battalion clearly understood they would need an armoured counterattack to help see off direct assault, as this position did not have the strength or depth of the main Knightsbridge box.[20]

Cauldron Sector

The central section of the minefield became a 'mine-marsh'. This was a series of separated minefields three to four miles in depth, but with various gaps for the armoured and motor brigades to pass through. The section from the Trigh Capuzzo down to the Trigh el Abd was known as Hackney marshes and below that was Stepney marshes, among them were both normal and 'secret' gaps to pass through.[21] Here 150th Brigade

---

17 TNA WO 169/4982: 3rd Coldstream Guards War Diary, 26 May 1942.
18 Richard Doherty, *Ubique: The Royal Artillery in the Second World War* (Stroud: History Press, 2008), p.119.
19 Michael Howard & John Sparrow, *The Coldstream Guards 1939–1946* (Oxford: Oxford University Press, 1951), pp.91–92.
20 Erskine, *Scots Guards 1919–1955*, pp.99–100.
21 TNA WO 201/392: 1st South Africa Division: Gazala defensive battle, operational reports, 19–26 June 1942, map overlay. Only this folder, in the report by Bush and

took over the Guards old Got el Ualeb position, which covered the Trigh el Abd. They ended up with an over-large perimeter, designed to overlook both the Trigh Capuzzo along Tamar Ridge to four miles south, the Trigh el Abd, heading south-east. The gaps were to be covered by artillery fire, or medium machine guns up to 1,000 yards. Another 10 miles south again was the Free French Brigade at Bir Hacheim. Behind this sector, 4th Armoured Brigade was deployed to protect the southern or left flank of the army.

The northern edge of the cauldron was the Bir et Tamar Ridge, considered one of the highest ridges in the area. Along it were the 'pimples', the uneven lumps and bumps of the high points 202, 203 and 204. General Lumsden said this ridge was the most important one in the whole battlefield, as it looked south over the whole cauldron down to Got el Ualeb.[22] The eastern side of the cauldron was bordered by the Aslagh ridge, which became a wide plateau in places but also split into a saddle feature, with the B.180 height on the north side and the B.100 height in the south. In between was almost a narrow valley leading into the Cauldron. This was to be the sector for much of the fighting. West of Aslagh, the depression was six miles wide; an expanse of low ground, criss-crossed by a few small ridges and heights in the middle, to the mine-marsh in the west and roughly the same from Sidi Muftah in the north-west down Ualeb in the south-west corner. With both trighs leading west to Axis supply bases, the whole area increased in importance for them. The Trigh el Abd passed through Got el Ualeb, and headed south-east towards Bir el Gubi, so provided another useful route to flank Eighth Army.

Below the cauldron the mine-marsh continued south and around Bir Hacheim before returning north again. This created a second line of minefields behind the front line, running north like a fish-hook as far as Bir Harmat on the Hacheim track. These two minefields in the south were joined in the middle by a third minefield traversing east–west near the Rotunda Ualeb. Units attempting to breakthrough into this space between would find themselves surrounded by a double band of minefields. Early on in the battle, 90th Light Division was delayed in making gaps to rejoin Panzerarmee across this sector. Once they had opened up these extra gaps they proved useful to Rommel when he outflanked 5th Indian Division caught up in the cauldron.[23]

The central-southern part of the battlefield behind Bir Hacheim was a rough sector of low ground which stretched 15 miles to the east. There were numerous low ridges which provided potential hull down positions for armour against a thrust from the south. It was here that 4th Armoured Brigade encountered DAK on the first day, as it headed north towards Knightsbridge. To the east the escarpment was broken by numerous wadis which led up to a high and wide plateau, bounded along its northern

Lieutenant Cowtan mentions the marsh names.
22 TNA WO 201/537: 1 Armoured Division: report on operations in Western Desert, May–July 1942, p.18.
23 IWM: E127: 90th Light Division War Diary, 15 May–5 July 1942.

edge by the steep El Adem escarpment, and in the south by the 7th Motor Brigade's Retma Box position. In the centre of the plateau, 7th Armoured Division sited its HQ at Bir Bueid. The series of gullies and defiles on the western side included the Giof el Baar area, and provided the leaguer position for 8th Hussars, which had space enough for recreation and training grounds. The plateau above also became a useful safe area for numerous B echelon supply units for the brigades in this sector. These small columns of supply vehicles were constantly dodging enemy columns to avoid being captured, as they criss-crossed the plateau on their way to resupply Bir Hacheim or other units.

Rear Areas

With Knightsbridge as the forward box covering the Trigh Capuzzo, further east along the trigh was the larger El Adem Box and from there more routes north to Tobruk, Belhamed supply base and the Army Headquarters at Gambut. Both 2nd Armoured and 22nd Armoured Brigades were initially deployed in these rear areas, to be able to move towards any part of the front line. The rear areas of the battlefield remained important for various larger supply dumps linked by the trighs, especially those tracks which ran north to Tobruk and the coast road. Eighth Army set up Headquarters at Gambut, by the coast road 30 miles east of Tobruk. To head south from Gambut vehicles would head west and then south onto the Axis bypass, and then south again onto the Trigh Capuzzo. Once they had negotiated the steep escarpment by El Adem, they could drive south-west to 7th Armoured Division or onto Bir Hacheim. Even before the battle these journeys were not easy. In mid-May, Alan Moorehead visited Gambut to see the build-up and described the place as, 'a featureless stretch of tussocky plain... So many cars laden with generals and liaison officers kept driving into the camp that soon its tracks were in knee-deep fine dust. The main fighter base lay just across the main road.'[24] The need for coordination with the RAF, but also safety from roaming Axis columns had effectively distanced Ritchie from the forward area, which left Corps, Divisional and Brigade HQs on their own. This basic physical distance when added to signals problems and intermittent dust storms also contributed to command problems during the battle.

Another key problem of the trigh, was that it lay in a valley between two steep escarpments which had very few passable tracks for either tanks or trucks. This limited the choices for north-south movement, especially when some of these routes became contested by enemy columns. Secondly, the southern escarpment was high and dominated the track, so when Axis artillery reached these slopes, supply columns on the trigh were in trouble. One British officer was picked up here and he said it was

24 Moorehead, *African Trilogy*, p.313.

ludicrous that a short distance to the west was a military police checkpoint that was oblivious to the enemy column on the trigh.

Midway along Trigh Capuzzo was El Adem, one of the first defences built by Kippenberger's 5th New Zealand Brigade back in mid-February. They developed a 14,000 yard perimeter and took 19,000 mines from the Tobruk defences to make it secure. Kippenburger said this was done with full authority, a recent Army Conference had confirmed that Tobruk would not be held again, if the army had to retire.[25] Gott later told him that it was the best of all the boxes in his area. There was only a narrow entrance from the trigh through the minefield, and by May the recently arrived 29th Indian Brigade garrison added further posts along the wadis in the escarpment.[26] The XIII Corps HQ vehicles were also dispersed under camouflage amongst the wadis. Units constantly changed as the garrison for the box; 2nd Rifle Brigade moved there as a temporary garrison in mid-May and Crimp noted their position in one of the wadis, overlooked an elaborate Italian trench system on the opposite slope and also looked down on the El Adem airfield below. They guarded the engineers' compound and a nearby cold water cistern.[27] El Adem became an important centre for units to regroup from battle, along with a number of HQs creating bases within the box.

The supply bases or FMCs were also a vital part of keeping units fed, watered and fuelled. The main issue was that they added to the burden of infantry acting as garrisons, which also contributed to delays in training. 9th Rifle Brigade was digging in around an FMC north-west of Bir el Gubi by 18 May, where the sharp track junction bounded the supply dump.[28] In the rear, Tim Hely from 106th RHA anti-tank gunners was posted to a depression near Sidi Rezegh Airfield. 'Directly to the south, sloping up to the aerodrome was a depression about one mile wide from north to south, in which were sited the guns.'[29] Rear garrisons were important but Panzerarmee only reached here as they closed on Tobruk.

Southern Sector

Bir Hacheim, at the southern tip of the line, was one of the few places in this part of the desert where the higher plateau gave extended views, up to 15 miles, to the south and west. Two miles southeast was Pt.171 west. This low depression covered the trighs running east–west. The main height was along the northern edge of the deir and had similar good views to the south. To the east of Pt.171, were further low, parallel ridges, which had been selected as defensive battle locations for 4th Armoured Brigade, had

---

25 Kippenberger, *Infantry Brigadier*, p.114.
26 Moorehead, *African Trilogy*, p.322.
27 Alex Bowlby (ed.), *The Diary of a Desert Rat R.L. Crimp* (London: Pan Books, 1974), p.99.
28 TNA WO 169 5057: 9th Rifle Brigade War Diary, 18 May 1942. The C.O. attended a corps wargame.
29 Liddell-Hart Centre for Military Archives: Papers of Brigadier A. F. 'Tim' Hely, p.8.

they had time to reach them on 27 May. The 4th Armoured were to deploy between Pt.171 and the Retma Box, as their battle position Majority, with companies from 1st KRRC quite far south, beyond the armoured regiments.[30]

The southern tracks led east to a convenient junction at Bir el Gubi, continuing east again to the frontier. Twenty miles east of Pt.171 was the position at Retma, occupied by 7th Motor Brigade, which was slowly setting up a defensive box. This was sited on a height overlooking the tracks going east, and here 2nd Rifle Brigade began digging in on 19 May. A supporting battery of Rhodesian anti-tank guns arrived on 24 May. Rifleman Crimp noted it was a square position bordered by a single wire to mark the outline. After completing their truck and slit trench, he and fellow riflemen walked the half-mile to the HQ, for a Whit Monday church service given by the padre.[31] Obviously just digging in would not need that long, but more time was needed to improve the site, lay communications, add wire and more mines et cetera, other brigades had been preparing their boxes since March and were able to see off initial attacks. These three positions behind the front, Pt.171, Retma and Bir el Gubi, provided a basic line of defence to protect the left flank. Had they had more time to develop the boxes, the motor brigades might have provided a more effective barrier to delay Panzerarmee. General Tuker was critical of the whole concept of brigade groups and static boxes, had just been assigned to command this group of motor brigades. With the rapid breakthrough of 27 May Tuker did not get a chance to make his new command work.[32]

Bir Hacheim became the site of a determined defence made by the 1st Free French Brigade. Ritchie saw it as one of the main pivots of the line, along with Knightsbridge and El Adem. It was situated on a raised plateau of mostly desert scree with limestone not far below the surface. On its southern side was an old Italian fort with crumbling buildings in one corner and a small hill called the Observatoire in another. In the north, the broken water birs, or wells, created two low mounds, which the legionnaires typically called *les mamelles* (the breasts). The main advantage was that it was 20 feet higher than the surrounding desert and provided the best platform to watch for any approach from the south and west. The Free French extended the range of gun positions and dugouts begun by 150th Brigade. New observation posts were added at key points around the six-sided perimeter, and about 50,000 extra mines were laid in the immediate minefields.

Driver Susan Travers, who served with the French for much of the battle, said General Koenig placed his small caravan HQ at the centre of the box, with adjacent tents for staff and liaison officers. The men, 'set to, creating even more slit trenches, circular holes for equipment and gun pits,' larger tents were set up for the hospital,

---

30 TNA WO 169/5032: 1st KRRC War Diary, O.O. No.6, 23 May 1942.
31 Alex Bowlby (ed.), *The Diary of a Desert Rat R.L. Crimp* (London: Pan Books, 1974), pp.102–103.
32 Francis Tuker, *Approach to Battle* (London: Cassell, 1963), pp.105–106.

HQ and messes.³³ They deployed a hundred and one anti-tank guns and twenty-four 75mm guns.³⁴ Images at the Musée de l'Armée collection confirm the good observation views from Hacheim, the fort's central 'keep' was slightly higher again, adding to their ability to watch the desert. Secondly the Musée recovered one of the 75mm guns, which had clearly had its shield cut-down, giving them a very low profile in a gun pit.³⁵ The French had prepared well and gave the Axis a tough battle.

Behind the centre and south of Knightsbridge, was the Naduret et Ghesceuasc Ridge, another important area of high ground. This ridge allowed armoured regiments to regroup, leaguer, and was a key line of defence, if facing south. This area was used frequently as the armoured brigades manoeuvred and fought over the first 13 days of battle. 10th Hussars considered it a vital piece of commanding ground which enabled them to defeat the oncoming enemy on the first day.³⁶ It covered most approaches from the south and was flanked on its western side by the Hacheim track and on its eastern side by the higher plateau leading to El Adem. Overall the southern sector had some strong defensive positions, but was probably just too deep, and Axis columns were able to strike north, across the plateau to El Adem, and disrupt Eighth Army rear areas and B echelon columns.

The Gazala battlefield offered limited defensive terrain but still dictated how the army deployed, both to withstand the offensive and to find defended pivots, from which the armoured brigades might counterattack. A new doctrine was being tested from the first days of halting west of Tobruk, infantry boxes were developed, around which the armoured brigades might counterattack and defeat the Axis. If successful Eighth Army would be able to finally advance to conquer Western Cyrenaica once and for all, and enable the RAF to operate from the coastal airfields, protecting convoys to Malta.

The overriding problem for GHQ and Army planners was that the front line was too close to Tobruk and the desert supply depots. These could not be given up without crippling their logistics, and this limited Eighth Army's ability to give ground when needed. Any attempt to break-off from the enemy and making a short term retreat, would be a perilous operation even if it did overstretch a chasing Panzerarmee. The Gazala line had pinned Eighth Army and limited its freedom of movement. In addition to the terrain and deployment factors, the need for further training added to the army's ability to be ready for the next phase of operations.

---

33   Susan Travers, *Tomorrow Be Brave* (London: Bantam Press, 2000), pp.143–145.
34   Jacques Mordal, *Bir Hacheim* (Paris, Amiot-Dumont, 1951), p.86.
35   www.Musee-Armee.fr, Les Invalides, Paris, (last accessed 20 Aug 2021).
36   D. Dawnay et al., *The 10th Royal Hussars in the Second World War, 1939–1945* (Aldershot: Gale & Polden, 1948), p.60.

3

Training

> *I've learned to wash in petrol tins, and shave myself in tea*
> *While balancing the fragments of mirror on my knee*
> *I've learned to dodge the eighty-eights, and flying lumps of lead*
> *And to keep a foot of sand between a Stuka and my head ...*
>
> 'Lament of a Desert Rat'
> N. J. Trapnell[1]

The importance of further training was fully understood at all levels in the Army. The CIGS wrote to Auchinleck in January and commented on the, 'lamentable...lack of knowledge in most senior officers of the handling of armoured forces.'[2] Crusader provided GHQ Cairo with a wealth of feedback from commanders in the field. Infantry, armour, tank brigades and signals had all provided lessons from operations, with copies being sent to all commands. The notes on infantry summarised, 'thorough training before operations for both units and HQ Staffs,' and there was a, 'need for close and continuous cooperation with all arms, especially Army Tanks.'[3] Thirteen Corps lessons from Crusader were clear that all troops who fought together should be brigaded and train together.[4]

Auchinleck also blamed poor equipment, such as the inferior quality of the tank's 2pdr gun. He criticised poor leadership in the armoured formations, and said they

---

1   Selwyn, *Poems of the Second World War*, p.130.
2   Bowman, *Papers of Field Marshal Sir Claude Auchinleck, Vol. I*, p.322, Letter from Sir Alan Brooke CIGS to Auchinleck, 21 January 1942.
3   TNA WO 201/450: Cyrenaica: lessons from operations November 1941-March 1942. Lessons from Operations No.6.
4   TNA WO 201/522: 13 Corps: operations, January-November 1941. Notes on Lessons from recent operations, p.1.

had lost confidence in their equipment, which contributed to the defeats in January.[5] He was often quick to blame other factors rather than his own contributing decisions. Army formations had also been struggling to find the time to continue training. He called for a two to one superiority in tank numbers and closer tank-infantry-artillery cooperation to offset the higher quality of German equipment.

The reality of regimental training which actually took place in the three and a half months prior to battle shows a more nuanced level of readiness. Despite the best intentions there were many delays due to formations moving back to the Delta area or being reequipped with new weapons and fresh drafts of men. Many units arrived late into Egypt and needed to learn the basics of desert living, formations and navigation et cetera. Time was lost returning to the forward area, or preparing for inspections by senior officers, including the Duke of Gloucester and the King of Greece, but also the increasing frequency of dust storms as the weather became warmer. We may be forgiven for thinking that units were mostly stationary and awaiting their operational orders, while being able to train at will, but the reality was somewhat different.

Armour and artillery regiments particularly suffered from a high frequency of days spent awaiting new equipment, maintenance days, and moving to and from shooting ranges in the rear. Infantry and artillery were constantly hampered by detachments to jock columns across all brigades. Despite the lessons from Crusader and demands from GHQ Cairo, many units were still effectively sorting themselves out, rather than battle-training as occurred before Second Alamein. Some practised more than others and units became reliant on their own regimental groups, which contributed to their style of operations. From GHQ after the battle, Lieutenant General Corbett commented critically that things had been going awry, but he never had the chance to improve the army. He said that comprehensive training had just been planned, and that a start was made on new doctrine and not just 'desert folklore'. He also noted the shortages in equipment and personnel.[6]

Eighth Army Structure

Since September 1941 Eighth Army had been structured into two corps, with other units in army reserve. Now under General Neil Ritchie, this structure continued, with XIII Corps, consisting of infantry divisions and two tank brigades. The brigades were restructured into groups, to include other supporting arms, e.g. artillery, anti-tank, signals and engineers. They became self-sufficient with integral supply echelons, designed to make each unit independent and mobile. Lieutenant General W. H. E.

---

5   TNA WO 201/401: Operations: telegrams & reports, January-March 1942, to PM from Auchinleck, 30 January 1942.
6   Churchill Archive Centre (CAC): Papers of Lieutenant General Thomas Corbett, Note on Five Months as GCS MEF.

'Strafer' Gott was a highly experienced leader, having been on campaign since 1940. He remained very popular with the men and was confident and felt that the army was in good morale and ready to fight.[7]

The two forward divisions were the 1st South African, under the feisty Dan Pienaar, and 50th Infantry Division, under Major General W. H. C. Ramsden, each of three infantry brigades. Behind them, 2nd South African Division held the Tobruk perimeter with two brigades, under the more inexperienced Major General Klopper, but they played little or no part in Gazala. Supporting the infantry were 1st and 32nd Army Tank (AT) Brigades; each played a major role in the battle. Gott had difficulty with Dan Pienaar, who was a prickly and awkward subordinate, and who disliked his corps commander, so Gott was only able to offer 'advice' more than give direct orders. This contributed to the South Africans having a more static role holding the coastal sector.

The recently arrived 50th Division also had three brigades, with two in the northern sector defences, and 150th Brigade recently transferred to cover the centre at Sidi Muftah in late April. This Division was very active with jock columns and adapted well to the infantry box defence role. While the five northern brigades gave a solid base which prevented any breakthrough along the coast road, they were also 'pinned' by the Italian infantry opposite, and so could not easily be moved away to reinforce other areas of the battle.

The centre and south of the line was covered by XXX Corps, under Lieutenant General Norrie, another experienced desert hand, though Major Carver, who was Norrie's GSO2 (Operations) said he often asked Gott's opinion of any new plan.[8] Under Norrie was 1st Armoured Division, with a difficult subordinate commander in Major General Herbert Lumsden. It had two armoured brigades and 201st Guards Motor Brigade. Lumsden was fully confident of his abilities and had been pleased to get his division back from Messervy, now commanding 7th Armoured Division, whom he disliked intensely. He blamed Messervy for the defeat of 1st Armoured in January, and so was against any future plans to hand over command of his brigades again.[9] Messervy had previously commanded 4th Indian Division and was not an experienced armoured commander. Corporal Jake Wardrop with 5th RTR, said he was 'a silly old man from the Indian Army who had never seen a tank …'[10] His straight criticism was perhaps aimed at Messervy having been captured on the first day.[11]

---

7   Moorehead, *African Trilogy*, p.317.
8   Michael Carver, *Out of Step: Memoirs of a Field Marshal* (London: Hutchinson, 1989), p.97.
9   Carver, *Dilemmas of the Desert War*, p.74.
10   George Forty (ed.), *Tanks Across the Desert: The War Diary of Jake Wardrop* (London: Kimber, 1981), p.77.
11   Messervy had an unlucky battle at Gazala, escaping then but later having to hide from German patrols during the vital 12–13 June tank battle and was then sacked on 19 June, just as the battle ended.

Fourth Armoured Brigade had three regiments equipped mostly with Grants, and three motor brigades; the most experienced being 7th Motor Brigade, with three rifle battalions, under Brigadier Renton. 29th Indian Brigade formed the garrison of El Adem and 3rd Indian Motor Brigade was rushed to the front line on 26 May. Also attached was Brigadier Koenig's 1st Free French Brigade at Bir Hacheim.

Other units joined Eighth Army as the battle progressed, but most would not fight as complete formations. Instead, they were parcelled out as replacements for regiments already weakened in battle. These included 1st Armoured Brigade, 5th Indian Division and elements of 10th Indian Division. The two main brigades from 5th Indian Division arrived piecemeal and were assigned garrison and anti-invasion roles, before being concentrated for Operation Aberdeen. After that they again formed as separate brigades.

Many units were reorganised, often in late April or early May. As well as overseeing the completion of operations by January 1942, Auchinleck was determined to push through new brigade organisations to resolve a number of tactical problems. He informed London with an acidic preamble about infantry numbers and the reorganisation of divisions:

> For six months ... many of us here, whose business it is to think of such things, have been considering how to improve the organisation of our basic formations so as to ensure greater flexibility and hitting power in battle...we are all agreed that a rigid unalterable divisional composition is quite unsuited to open, quick-moving warfare.[12]

The War Office queried these plans, because they would cause problems of overall numbers of men, and would create logistical problems, if formations were transferred to other theatres.[13] General Brooke commented on the changes and shortages in tanks in North Africa as Japan widened the war. He said this would be certain to reduce the, 'flow of equipment...and make it harder than ever to complete new armoured formations...'[14] He queried some of these new plans and believed that Auchinleck's assistant, Major General 'Chink' Dorman-Smith was behind many of them. Brooke felt that Auchinleck seemed incapable of ignoring the weaker ideas and retaining the better ones.[15]

---

12 TNA WO 32/10387: Army Organisation: Tanks (Code 14(G)): Reorganisation of Armoured Formations; Proposal from Middle East 1942, C-in-C Middle East to CIGS 12 January 1942.
13 TNA WO 32/10387: Army Organisation: Tanks (Code 14(G)): Reorganisation of Armoured formations; Proposal from Middle East 1942, War Office to C-in-C Middle East, 7 February 1942.
14 Bowman, *The Military Papers of Field Marshal Sir Claude Auchinleck, Vol. I*, p.259, Letter from Sir Alan Brooke CIGS to Auchinleck, 10 December 1941.
15 Danchev & Todman, *Alanbrooke War Diaries 1939–1945*, p.224. 29 January 1942.

Auchinleck had taken Gott's advice and begun to restructure the old-style infantry and armoured brigades, into brigade groups. These contained either three armoured regiments or three infantry battalions, but also regiments of artillery or a motor infantry brigade attached to each armoured division, along with supporting services. Each brigade group, still carried out its main role, but would have direct support from other troops in attack or setting up a defensive site on which the armoured regiments could manoeuvre. If the Infantry brigades were attacking, they would have direct artillery support and supporting attached Infantry tanks, to lead them in. The C-in-C also decided that Army tank brigades would operate as single battalions under command of the infantry formations. The army tank brigadier would only have an advisory role.[16] However the experienced Brigadier Willison had already liaised with other tank brigadiers and was keen to point out that single army tank units were not strong enough to withstand an enemy tank force.[17] As the build-up gathered pace, all formations retained their Divisional HQs but worked in brigade groups. These were similar to Axis battlegroups and would be used in other allied armies. At Gazala, units were having to cope with new organisations, new working regimes and new equipment. Both commanders and their men could be forgiven for needing more time to become used to such major changes.

The new formations aided self-sufficiency, but also contributed to a dispersal of manpower and firepower. Each armoured brigade was supported by an artillery regiment of three batteries, a motor battalion and support troops. The infantry was expected to, '…hold an area vital to the manoeuvre of the remainder of the Division.'[18] Jake Wardrop noted that each regiment had, 'the same gunners, but instead of the Guards we had the 1st Rifle Brigade, a company to each tank battalion. They were a very salty motorised infantry unit and they stayed with us all the time.'[19] In 22nd Armoured Brigade, the Support Group included 4th/Royal Northumberland Fusiliers, which reorganised in March into three motor companies and one anti-tank company as 50 Recce Bn. The C.O., Lieutenant Colonel des Graz decided on three 'boxes', each with one battery, one motor company (X, Y and Z) and anti-tank guns.[20] Each allocated to an armoured regiment, creating the regimental group. Armoured regiments had to manoeuvre or pivot around a company of infantry, dug in in the open, with a battery of eight 25pdrs in the rear, giving fire support. Being sent on jock column patrols, the infantry and artillery units stood little chance of training alongside their attached armour, for an all arms battle. The weakness of the support boxes

16 TNA 169/4269: 1st Army Tank Brigade War Diary, Letter to Army Commanders, 14 February 1942.
17 TNA 169/4269: 1st Army Tank Brigade War Diary, Letter to Ninth Army HQ from 32nd AT Brigade, 8 March 1942.
18 HMSO, *Middle East Training Pamphlets*, METP No.2, Motor Battalion, 1941, p.3.
19 Forty, *Tanks Across the Desert*, p.75.
20 C.N. Barclay, *The History of the Royal Northumberland Fusiliers* (Uckfield: Naval & Military, 2009), p.78.

resulted in one being overrun on the first day, and the remaining two combined but were also overrun on 6 June.[21]

Crusader demonstrated a number of key tactics in operations. Firstly, that armoured brigades needed to be a mix of all arms and that tanks generally were no use at holding ground, this task was for infantry and anti-tank guns. Cruiser tanks should not attack enemy positions frontally, especially against known anti-tank positions, though this would happen again. Artillery should be well forward within 1,000 yards of the Forward Observing Officer (FOO) who should be with the leading squadron and at least two wireless sets to communicate with both tanks and artillery. Medium MG companies should be retained as one company rather than parcelled out in platoons. They should deploy under cover of the dust and smoke and then destroy enemy anti-tank guns with massed firepower. There were many recommended changes to counter the effective enemy tactics. HQs needed time to work with each other to be effective. XXX Corps only had three weeks before Crusader and for Aberdeen, Messervy and Briggs had one afternoon and evening to plan their attack. Questions were asked about splitting HQs into Forward and Rear HQs, during operations, as this seemed to cause delays and confusion.[22] Few recommendations were enacted during Gazala and so the problems continued.

Armoured Brigade Training

Corps HQs appreciated that units needed more time to complete training. Directives for training were issued to brigadiers at the end of March, along with updates. Lieutenant Colonel Harold Pyman, with 1st Armoured Division, signed one such update ordering further training for 8th Hussars, the Rhodesian battery with 4th RHA and a new battery with 1st RHA. In April, 1st Armoured moved east of Bir el Gubi, which enabled units to train without the usual front line wireless (radio silence) restrictions.[23]

Regimental training details showed the reality of how little time was spent in developing a combined arms approach to attack or defence. Often it was more about weapon skills and maintenance. Armoured regiments needed more time to get used to new tanks, along with a functioning supply and maintenance system to ensure full strength squadrons. Gunnery practice was often halted as dust storms increased. The 3rd CLY was unable to train on 5 May due to a very bad sandstorm and there are

---

21 Barclay, *Royal Northumberland Fusiliers*, pp.79–82.
22 TNA WO 201/450: Cyrenaica: lessons from operations Nov 1941-Mar 1942. Lessons from Ops No.8.
23 TNA WO 169/4555: 1st Royal Horse Artillery War Diary, January-December 1942, Training Conference Notes.

numerous similar comments from other units throughout April-May.[24] Experienced units wanted more time, not just to cope with new equipment, but also in brigade operations. Combined arms tactics were becoming more complex for many officers, as well as operating in the increasing difficult spring-summer desert heat.

Auchinleck had been critical of the performance of armour and wanted more training. In the January battles 10th Hussars had been reduced to just eight tanks, and the war diary wryly noted the regimental band was also reduced to Lieutenant Loney on squeezebox, QMS Dominy on the ukelele, an NCO on spoons along and a whistling Trooper Code. As they regrouped at El Adem they received fresh tanks, troops and equipment. Unit morale and regimental cohesion began to recover, with numerous football matches and other team sports. They were visited by Lieutenant General Norrie who spoke to NCOs who remembered him from when he had been Colonel. In the evenings, officers entertained fellow RAF Officers from the nearby airfield, so that the regiment soon regained its spirits to begin training again. Morale was then nearly dented again when the new formations were to be just two armoured regiments. This threatened the Hussars with transfer, though General Ritchie quickly confirmed to Lieutenant-Colonel C.B. Harvey, that 10th Hussars would continue to be part of 2nd Armoured.[25] In early March they were south-east of Sidi Muftah, sorting out new vehicles and practising for enemy attacks across the mine belt. Training intensified with six 'Hussars Group' regimental exercises and four brigade group demonstrations, sometimes on the ground they would fight across in May, e.g. at Eluet et Tamar, north of the Sidra Ridge. Attacks were also being practised by 9th Lancers, with an unsuccessful very light drill practice in March followed by another battle practice with smoke, which was judged as better and gave them some 'useful lessons learnt.'[26]

Armoured regiments had to work in replacement men with experienced crews, so gun ranges were set up for Besas and 2pdr guns, and night marches and signals exercises were practised. Moves made by Panzerarmee slowed down training during April and forced most units to wait at two hours readiness for battle. It also stopped as the supporting infantry, B battery from 11th RHA, and some Stuart tanks, were sent forward in Welcol jock column. Equipment was another problem. The 9th Lancers complained at the frequency of being ordered to hand over their good quality tanks and vehicles, receiving 'old crocks' in return. After visiting brigade, the C.O. addressed all senior ranks about the question of re-equipment, as comments were being made as to when they would receive better AFVs.[27] They certainly had the worst equipment given and little time for training, though this constant changeover of equipment took a good deal of regimental time through March-April. Crews went away in small

---

24   TNA WO 169/4495: 3rd County of London Yeomanry (Sharpshooters) War Diary, January-December 1942, May 42.
25   TNA WO 169/4489: 10th Royal Hussars War Diary, January-December 1942, February,
26   Bovington: 9th Lancers War Diary, 3 March 1942.
27   Bovington: 9th Lancers War Diary, 12 March 1942.

groups to be trained on the new Grants. In late April the Hussars participated in a divisional exercise, for a southern attack. Tanks needed constant maintenance days, which were followed by inspections by General Ritchie on 28 April, and later the Duke of Gloucester, who seems to have visited and inspected almost every regiment within Eighth Army during April-May.

The Hussars only received their first seven Grant tanks at the end of April, which gave them little time to get used to them. They moved to the ranges east of Bir el Gubi, but were delayed by dust storms which halted most shoots. The Crusaders began firing practice on 6 May and C squadron Grants only by 8 May.[28] Lieutenant Colonel Harvey created numerous regimental schemes based on their recent battle experience at Saunnu.[29] The Bays' diary is missing for May 1942, but gunner Jack Merewood of B Squadron said they received seven Grants around 1 May, along with some refurbished Crusaders and Honeys. They spent five days at Capuzzo getting used to them and another few days on the ranges, where his troop became the best shots with the new 75mm gun. He could to hit the target at 1,200 yards with just three shots.[30]

Tenth Hussars Grants continued firing practice, then the regiment returned to 2nd Armoured to the front near Knightsbridge by 24 May as a movement exercise for the group. The focus was now on an attack in the north, so the Hussars deployed facing north-west, with the Support Group and artillery two miles away. They had been reequipped and achieved some intensive training. The few brigade and divisional moves were all designed to engage an enemy attacking through the mine belt in the north. The Hussars' fellows of 9th Royal Lancers spent much of February reforming and received some new Grants and Crusaders during March. They remained in the forward area and trained quickly on the new tanks, using other brigade officers to assess their skills. They also noted the increasing number of severe sandstorms which prevented a good deal of training.[31]

22nd Armoured gained a new commander, Brigadier Carr, and refitted back in the Delta. Most of February was taken up with the return journey to Sidi Bishr base and being joined by 107th RHA and the 50th Recce Battalion (4th Northumberland Fusiliers) to form a new Support Group. March involved exchange visits to the Royal Navy and numerous inspections. The first full training TEWT took place in early April. The new deployment for support units was practised and found to be:

> the principle of employing three composite Battlegroups of all arms in advance of the Tank Regts and to form a pivot of manoeuvre appeared satisfactory. The

---

28 TNA WO 169/4489: 10th Royal Hussars War Diary, January-December 1942 and March-May 1942.
29 Dawnay, *10th Royal Hussars*, p.57.
30 Jack Merewood, *To War with the Bays. A Tank Gunner Remembers 1939–1945* (Cardiff: 1st The Queen's Dragoon Guards, 1996), p.54.
31 Joan Bright, *The Ninth Queens Royal Lancers* (Uckfield: Naval & Military Press, 2020), pp.66–67.

brigade received its new Grants by mid-April with each regiment, one squadron of 12 Grants and two squadrons of Crusaders (each 16 including 2 CS tanks). RHQ had four Crusaders and Brigade HQ another eight.[32]

They spent another month packing and moving up to Eighth Army who made more inspections. The first Brigade exercise began on 15 May and five days later they received their Honey OP tanks. The brigade was mostly involved with getting used to new tanks and making the logistical move into the forward area. The new tanks had mechanical problems, they were found to be, 'unreliable with new tracks fitted badly over old sprocket wheels, while the Grants third gear tended to jam.'[33] They were veterans but had achieved little in new training. The attached 107th RHA, which had fought at Tobruk and in Crusader, was rebuilt up to strength and given new guns in the Delta. This took until the end of April, and the process was a complex and difficult one. They were coping with new drafts, expanded formations which added major equipment shortages, along with learning brand new equipment.

The new tactics for Support Group began with a single group deployment and changed into three separate boxes. Each armoured regiment would now have its own supporting infantry and artillery battery. Major Daniel from the 107th RHA/South Notts Hussars commanded the first, the anti-tank C.O., Major Cowan, an experienced desert hand, commanded the second box; the third box was commanded by Lieutenant Colonel des Graz, C.O. of 50 Recce Battalion (4th Northumberland Fusiliers).[34] They divided 16 anti-tank guns across the group. When the fighting began the second and third boxes fought together on the first day but the first box was left isolated.[35] The theory of a pivotal support group worked less well in practice.

The 3rd County London Yeomanry (3rd CLY) spent three months near Cairo receiving new men and equipment, but only one squadron at a time went on desert training.[36] During May, they spent 15 days on maintenance and practised manoeuvres around the support box for five days. Another few days were spent moving or digging in battle positions north of Bir-el-Harmat, but on 26 May they moved east, up onto the ridge at Pt.185.[37] The brigade schemes had also been delayed by regimental training and the move to the front. The brigade said battle positions were taken up by 24 May, and like 2nd Armoured they awaited an attack from the west or north-west.

32 TNA WO169/4251: 22nd Armoured Brigade: HQ, War Diary, January-December 1942, 2 April 1942,
33 TNA WO169/4251: 22nd Armoured Brigade: HQ, War Diary, January-December 1942, 14 April 1942,
34 TNA WO 169/4563: 107th Royal Horse Artillery Regiment War Diary, January-July 1942, April 1942.
35 Barclay, *Royal Northumberland Fusiliers*, p.79.
36 TNA WO 169/4495: 3rd County London Yeomanry War Diary, January-December 1942, February-April 1942.
37 TNA WO 169/4495: 3rd County London Yeomanry War Diary, January-December 1942, May 42.

The 4th Armoured Brigade also struggled to make time for combined arms formations. Gunners in 1st RHA said they gained a higher intensity of firing by developing a new fire control system. They now had four batteries including a battery of anti-tank guns. They said they worked well with armour but there were no infantry, who were away on jock columns, which also removed individual batteries from the brigade. By April, 1st RHA was practising in the forward area, where they put on a demonstration of combined arms, with mixed results:

> The Stuart Sqn moved too far to the flank which delayed the Artillery FOO. The fire of the Grant Sqn ... was very effective indeed. 3rd RTR had concentrated on their own gunnery training ... It was unfortunate from our point of view that that the first combined exercise in which the tanks had had gunner support [was] ... a demonstration ... and mistakes in the manoeuvring can easily be corrected in future exercises.'[38]

Additional problems were noted after another exercise, 'the utter hopelessness of an armoured formation blundering across the desert without any screen of infantry scouts ahead. Two armoured battalions failed to make contact during the first three hours of the exercise.'[39] In another exercise, the artillery was better positioned but 3rd and 5th RTR were still very slow at changing fronts. Attached to them was the 1st KRRC who noted that daily training was intensive throughout April, from platoon to brigade level schemes. Each company attached to an armoured unit, or as a support battalion to protect the artillery in a box.[40]

By 11 April, the artillery was back in leaguer as they watched the Axis make their forward moves, leaving the gunners at 30 minutes notice to move, with all vehicles remaining packed. Their tone suggests frustration at being kept like this. There were continued problems in assault training. When 5th RTR attacked some mock anti-tank guns represented by screens, Chestnut Troop (1st RHA), fired a concentration, while a tank squadron went in. Afterwards, they found that none of the screens, 'had so much as a splinter.' In the debrief conference it was admitted that a 'more deliberate attack,' would have to be made.[41] First RHA spent April-May working with the brigade in attack-defence schemes only to be exchanged with 4th RHA into three jock columns operating west of Bir Hacheim with the 9th KRRC.[42] As with other

---

38   TNA WO 169/4555: 1st Royal Horse Artillery War Diary, January-December 1942, 2 April.
39   TNA WO 169/4555: 1st Royal Horse Artillery War Diary, January-December 1942, 4 April.
40   TNA WO 169.5032: 1st KRRC War Diary, 1 May 1942.
41   TNA WO 169/4555: 1st Royal Horse Artillery War Diary, January-December 1942, 19 April.
42   TNA WO 169/4555: 1st Royal Horse Artillery War Diary, January-December 1942, 13–14 May.

units they needed days for maintenance, moves and when dust storms swept in. They returned to brigade over 23–25 May, sending some personnel on leave just as the offensive began. Jock columns were proving disruptive for many units, as they moved to and fro, changing from column disciplines to regimental/brigade training.

Other, experienced units, who arrived later on during the battle, were sorting out new tanks. The 4th Hussars had participated in the ill-fated campaigns in Greece and Crete and had returned with just 160 personnel and two trucks. They were rebuilt in the Delta when it was confirmed that the Prime Minister had become their Colonel-in-Chief, and by February 1942 were being equipped with new Grants and Stuarts. They felt the Stuarts seemed weak with only a 45 mile range and 37mm (2pdr) gun. They completed six weeks training with the new tanks and left on 31 May with a full strength of 35 officers and 585 men. They arrived with the rest of 1st Armoured Brigade on 2 June, in the rear TDS area for Eighth Army.[43]

Second Rifle Brigade (2nd RB), part of 7th Motor Brigade, moved forward at the end of March and carried out three days of schemes, followed by a few days rest and some short moves. Rifleman R. L. Crimp's company went forward as part of a jock column for eight days, during which little or nothing happened, apart from being shelled by 105mm guns before they withdrew the next day. After this they provided guard duty at various dumps around El Adem, before finally moving to Retma, on the left flank by 19 May.[44]

There were new organisational changes confirmed in mid-May, e.g. such as adding six 2pdr AT guns to each battalion and making Reconnaissance Regiments up to 12 anti-tank guns. They waited to see if motor battalions really needed them because of the increase in guns to specific artillery anti-tank units. These changes added new structural problems for some infantry, as new crews needed gun-training and working out how best to deploy them.[45] Reorganisation affected the overall level of training. 1st RHA reorganised into three batteries, but this left them with one trained and one untrained troop in two of the batteries by 25 April.[46] Soon, they developed an improved fire control method, with different targets allocated to different troops, a system which they thought was practicable – but only with more training. One final brigade exercise was made before another dust storm blew in and halted everything.[47]

---

43 David Scott-Daniell, *4th Hussar. The Story of a British Cavalry Regiment* (Aldershot: Gale & Polden, 1959), pp.323–324.
44 Bowlby, *Diary of a Desert Rat*, pp.89–99.
45 TNA WO 32/10387: Army Organisation: Tanks (Code 14(G)): Re-organisation of Armoured formations; Proposal from Middle East 1942, War Office Memo HF4489, 18 May 42.
46 TNA WO 169/4555: 1st Royal Horse Artillery War Diary, January-December 1942, 25 April.
47 TNA WO 169/4555: 1st Royal Horse Artillery War Diary, January-December 1942, 5–6 May.

Another new brigade rushed to the front line was 3rd Indian Motor Brigade, which arrived from Syria in early February and began training with carriers and anti-tank guns. The three cavalry regiments were each of three squadrons. Each regiment had one anti-tank squadron of four troops totalling sixteen 2pdr guns and two squadrons of two or three carrier troops and one lorry troop.[48] Thus, they were markedly weaker than the typical infantry battalion, with approximately 500 men and fifteen officers, but were expected to carry out a similar role. For 11th Prince Albert Victors Own Cavalry (11th PAVO), equipment arrived slowly through April. They managed a five-day scheme in early May, before being sent to garrison Daba and Matruh on anti-invasion patrols around the bases. The distraction of a possible air and sea assault had worked well. They remained until 22 May, arriving at Pt.171 by 26 May. The officers and men were keen to engage the enemy but they were seriously short on personnel, equipment and training. The brigade would prove itself on the first day though, but like other units, they were given no time to prepare.

Time spent deploying and digging in affected 50th Division which was deployed adjacent to the South Africans. 150th Brigade had been at the front all winter and had to develop the first defences. They became adept at building boxes with all round defence, and new gun pits covering adjacent minefields. 'All positions were dug flush with the ground without parapet and were very hard to see.' Most dugouts had overhead cover, but only 69th and 151st Brigade had twelve 2pdrs each and the division was short of trucks. They salvaged some old 47mm Italian guns but knew these were useless against the heavier German tanks. Food, water and ammunitions stocks were set up for a three-week siege.[49] The 5th East Yorks diary states that they worked on their defensive positions from 1 March until the battle began, except for those companies sent on patrol, a period of over two and a half months.[50]

The division reorganised the battalions and sent companies out on regular jock columns. In mid-May, General Ritchie informed GHQ Cairo that the 50th Division battalions could not maintain a fourth rifle company any longer because of manpower shortages, although the unit strength returns show the battalions to be 700 strong on average.[51] In 69th Brigade, the Green Howards reformed their D Company into a new support company of 63 men, with eight 2pdrs, a carrier and a mortar platoon. The remaining men were spread amongst the other three rifle companies.[52] Unit strengths contributed to mounting problems as operations progressed, with too few men and too large an area for battalions to cover, as those in 150th Brigade found out. The 9th Durhams had 720 men and 25 officers on 14 March, but there are no other diary strength returns until September. Other battalions have strength returns noted for

48 TNA WO 169/7723: 11th PAVO War Diary, 9 February 1942.
49 Clay, *Path of the 50th*, p.51.
50 TNA WO 169/5076: 5th East Yorks War Diary, 1 March to 27 May 1942.
51 TNA WO 201/532: Eighth Army: Commanders conferences, December 1941-May 1942, 17 May 42.
52 TNA WO 169/5023: 7th Green Howards War Diary, 1 May 1942.

April and then again after the retreat from Gazala on 14 June. Much of the battalion paperwork was probably destroyed before the breakout by these units.[53]

Supporting tanks from 1st Army Tank Brigade were detached to both 50th and South African Divisions, and 42nd RTR noted in late February that 50th Division had not worked with tanks before, 'we are therefore employing our time liaising with them and teaching them the general principles of all types of 'I' Tank warfare.' Within a week infantry and tanks were working well together, and in their first joint exercise, the infantry performed extremely well.[54] The 7th Green Howards practised a scheme to capture a ridge with two companies and two squadrons from 42nd RTR in March and April, while other companies were on jock column duty.[55] They practised night defensive schemes in May and manned Robcol but did not train again with armour. Despite being an experienced unit, 42nd RTR continued to practice in schemes and defensive roles and became adept at moving out of leaguer within an hour. Their fellow 44th RTR, also trained intensively in May, though the last few days up to 26 May were noted as quiet.[56] The 32nd Army Tank Brigade had been training in Palestine for a special beach-landing operation. Moreover, it had been reequipped with Valentines in mid-April. 4th RTR arrived with only two squadrons as the battle opened and were rushed to El Adem. They had significant supply problems due to being switched around the brigades, from 32nd Brigade, 1st Armoured to 1st Army Tank and then 10th Indian Brigade by 5 June. Fortunately, they found the Valentines were mechanically sound and so they dealt directly with the supply dumps for fuel and ammunition.[57]

Operating jock columns divided units, with companies and batteries heading out for a stint in no man's land and then after returning, needing time to sort out vehicles and reorganise and return to regimental duties. 150th Brigade continued providing columns for the divisional roster even during their move to the centre at Sidi Muftah. Jock columns were tiring for the men as most observation posts, which they occupied, were constantly harassed by enemy guns night and day. Commanders remained positive that they 'blooded' the men to combat and the artillery troops gained a higher standard of fire direction, as they harassed the enemy in return.[58] Major J. M. McSwiney commanding an anti-aircraft battery attached to 29th Indian Brigade, deployed from Bir el Gubi on the left flank to a jock column, although el Gubi was not a box position or base for them. Their column, 'spent an exciting if precarious existence, Marauding Rommel's soft vehicles by day…'[59] The columns provided a challenge and excitement in this phase of the build-up, but questions remain as to their overall impact.

53 TNA WO 169/5009: 9th Durham Light Infantry War Diary, 1942, 14 March 42.
54 TNA WO 169/4520: 42nd RTR War Diary 1942, 24 February and 1 March 1942.
55 TNA WO 169/5023: 7th Green Howards War Diary, March-April 1942.
56 TNA WO 169/4521: 44th RTR War Diary 1942, May 1942.
57 Bovington: 7th RTR papers, Letter from Lieutenant Colonel Reeves, undated.
58 Bush, *150th Brigade*, p.17.
59 IWM: Doc.7004. Papers of Major J. M. McSwiney.

Armoured car regiments were providing daily intelligence and were somewhat critical of the numerous columns. With each brigade sending out units the potential for getting in each other's way was easy to see. As the enemy closed up to the front line, this squeezed the area of no man's land. The situation was commented on by 12th Royal Lancers, who wryly noted, 'It was in fact, difficult enough for anyone to move in the area, 7th Armoured Division being in the process of relieving the 1st, and columns of all descriptions 'swanning' about and rendering almost impossible the work of the armoured cars.'[60] As regiments became used to their new equipment, it was clear that the build-up of Panzerarmee was nearing completion, and training time for Eighth Army was running out. Some units were more assiduous in continued training schemes, but requirements for moves, column duty, et cetera produced a variety of experiences.

Eighth Army Equipment

Armoured brigades remained the battle-winning formations for Eighth Army, so the various tanks, artillery and anti-tank guns were vital equipment which could win or lose the battle.

As previously noted new tanks were slow reaching regiments. The much-needed Grant arrived in the spring, with some units only receiving their new Grants and 6pdr anti-tank guns in the days leading up to the offensive. Units had to make do in training and getting to know their fighting vehicle or gun, often at the last minute. There were 352 of the new 6pdr anti-tank guns (Roberts gun), with up to 425 rounds each, but they were only issued in low numbers to front line units.[61] One troop from 1st RHA returned well to the rear at Buq Buq in late April, to collect their 6pdr portees, which gave little time to return to the front and practice.[62] Valuable training time was also shortened by technical issues found when using the portee. Firing tests found that when using the Grant's 75mm gun, penetration of Mk III armour was only effective up to 1600 yards, which was nonetheless an improvement on the 2pdr tank gun. Firing at ranges beyond this was problematic being limited by, 'very small wheel corrections given by the Tk Comd [tank commander].' Equally a new, untried anti-tank crew fired the portee 6pdr at 2,000 yards but missed completely, partly due to the 'jerry-built' fittings on the portee, all of which needed to be re-welded before the gun could be run up the portee, and for new ammunition carriers to be fitted. It could take two weeks to complete the welding required to make all the guns and

---

60 P. F. Stewart, *The History of the XII Royal Lancers* (London: Oxford University Press, 1950), p.391.
61 TNA WO 201/532: Eighth Army: Commanders conferences, December 1941-May 1942, Roberts Gun, 15 May 1942.
62 TNA WO 169/4555: 1st Royal Horse Artillery War Diary, January-December 1942, 27 April.

portees effective.⁶³ Such workshop maintenance meant they were only ready by the end of May.

The 'I' tank used by the two army tank brigades, had very thick frontal armour but was slow and equipped with only a 2pdr main gun, so it had to close to 800 yards to be 'in range'. The RTR regiments were mostly fully equipped with Matildas and Valentines by May, but they already knew that they were vulnerable to German 88mm guns, despite having 78mm frontal armour.⁶⁴ In May they added one Close Support (CS) Matilda for firing smoke to each squadron and another three CS tanks to battalion HQ. The CS tanks would provide a localised smokescreen to cover the attacking squadrons as they approached an enemy position. They also gained three scout cars for reconnaissance.⁶⁵

The majority of 22nd Armoured Brigade squadrons were equipped with Crusaders, faster than the 'I' tanks but also equipped with the 2pdr gun. They received new Grants in mid-April, but found they had problems with the third gear jamming, which would need more time in maintenance.⁶⁶ The limited numbers of Grants created units with a mixture of types, the three regiments had two squadrons each of 16 Crusaders and one squadron of 12 Grants, with Brigade HQ having another 8 Crusaders.⁶⁷ The Grant's main 75mm gun was able to reach targets at longer range, with AP or HE shot, but it had a high profile, which made it vulnerable in a hull down position. Crews were pleased that the 50mm frontal armour showed it could absorb severe punishment and, in many cases, multiple hits.

The Crusader's 2pdr gun was an effective weapon at shorter ranges than most German tank guns. However, 9th Lancers found that when they carried out some test firing on the hulk of a captured Mk III tank – the 2pdr and the 37mm gun only made a small dent on the German frontal armour at 400 yards. At 100 yards the shells only penetrated the outer plates. There were also problems with capped and uncapped ammunition which often shattered when hitting Axis armour.⁶⁸ They saw the results as 'depressing' and showed them to the Brigadier and a visiting American journalist. She interviewed the 9th Lancers Adjutant, 'How do you account for the recent defeat of three famous cavalry regiments?' she asked. They showed her the Honey and then the German Mk III, she replied, 'Yes, I see.'⁶⁹ Other tests confirmed that the German frontal armour had been face-hardened and so shattered the 2pdr shell but was weaker

---

63 TNA WO 169/4555: 1st Royal Horse Artillery War Diary, January-December 1942, 1 May.
64 Playfair, *Mediterranean & Middle East, Vol.III*, Appendix 8, p.439. Valentines had 65mm frontal armour.
65 TNA WO 169/4520: 42nd RTR War Diary, 1942.
66 TNA WO 169/4251: 22nd Armoured Brigade: HQ, War Diary, January-December 1942, 14 April 1942,
67 TNA WO 169/4251: 22nd Armoured Brigade: HQ, War Diary, January-December 1942, 14 April 1942,
68 Playfair, *Mediterranean & Middle East*, Appendix 8, p.438.
69 Bright, *Ninth Lancers*, p.63.

against the heavier 75mm shell.⁷⁰ British tanks still needed to get closer to Axis armour which made crews much more circumspect in approaching enemy ridges and influenced how squadrons manoeuvred around the enemy held ridges. The light squadrons were equipped with Stuarts/Honeys. This was a popular but small, fast light tank, its weaknesses being thin armour and a 37mm gun, equivalent to the 2pdr. These had served through Crusader and regiments now used them more in a reconnaissance role.

Some units still suffered from equipment shortages, despite being at the front for some time, for example 50th Division had shortage of anti-tank guns. In March, they handed over new vehicles and were sent worn-out trucks in exchange. There were shortages of specific items, for example of tyres for 8cwt trucks. Other trucks were left jacked up in cover – their wheels were being used on the vehicles out with jock columns.⁷¹ Valuable artillery and other equipment was being sent out in jock columns, to little effective purpose, apart from giving younger officers and platoons some experience of patrol-work.

Despite the various problems and shortages, GHQ considered other matters to have the army ready for battle in a major conference on 15 May. They called for a trial of a new style of Corps HQ, with fewer administrative roles to carry out, more 'hardening' training for troops and a report on current state of morale. The recent GSI report concluded that, 'Current morale is exceedingly high. Men are convinced an offensive will soon begin and a considerable number express the opinion that this time they will finish the enemy off once and for all.'⁷²

Commanders at the time fully understood the different qualities of the opposing tanks, even before opposing tactics. In May, Lieutenant Colonel Pip Roberts from 3rd RTR provided an effective analysis of British and Axis armour and gun quality at a typical combat range of 1,000 yards. He said the German Mk III(H) 50mm tank gun and the Mk IV short 75mm gun, could not penetrate any British frontal armour, whereas the Grant 75mm could defeat their hull fronts. The British 2pdr and 37mm could only penetrate the thinner German turret armour at this range. The more powerful Panzer III(J), the 'Mk III Special', with the long 50mm gun could defeat all British tanks at 1,000 yards, but DAK only had 18 of these at Gazala. The Italian M13 tanks were vulnerable to all British guns at 1,000 yards and could defeat none of them at this range. So, the range at which each tank could make a kill affected tactics. Roberts argues that the British armoured brigades were therefore superior in quality and numbers at Gazala, 'The idea that we were out-gunned and out-armoured in this battle cannot…hold water.'⁷³

70 Liddell-Hart, *The Tanks*, p.156.
71 Clay, *Path of the 50th*, p.55.
72 TNA WO 201/532: Eighth Army: Commanders Conferences, December 1941–May 1942, Morale.
73 LHCMA: Carver papers, Comparison of British & German Armour in May 1942, Roberts, G. P. B.

In terms of comparative tank numbers, Lieutenant-Colonel Roberts summarised the following totals of tanks for both sides:

		Total
32 AT Brigade,	50 Matildas, 50 Valentines	150 Matildas
1 AT Brigade	100 Matildas,	100 Valentines
4th RTR	50 Valentines	200 Grants
2nd Armoured Brigade	100 Crusaders, 50 Grants	50 Stuarts
22nd Armoured Brigade	100 Crusaders, 50 Grants	200 Crusaders
4th Armoured Brigade	100 Grants, 50 Stuarts	700 tanks[74]

Panzerarmee sources provided Eighth Army with the following totals:

Type	15th Panzer Division	21 Panzer Division	Totals
Panzer II	25	25	50
Panzer III (H)	109	105	214
Panzer III (J)	3	15	18
Panzer IV	20	18	38
		Totals	320
Ariete Division		165 M13/14	165
Trieste Division		40 M13	40
			525

In comparison, Panzerarmee totals for 25 May, give the following:[75]

Type	German	Italian	Total	British	+/-
Panzer	340	225	565	650	-85
Scout car	65	80	145	270?	-125
Anti-tank	248	328	576	450?	+126
Light Flak	204	346	550	250	+300
Schw. Flak	34	30	64	32	+32

Panzerarmee was slightly outnumbered in tanks but had more than the British realised and would also use the 88mm Flak guns and self-propelled 76mm guns mounted on the Marder chassis, as highly effective, mobile anti-tank guns. These, as well as the towed, 50mm anti-tank guns, greatly added to the firepower for each Panzer Division,

---

74 LHCMA: Carver papers, Comparison of British & German Armour in May 1942, Roberts, G. P. B.
75 Bundesarchiv: KTB243: Panzerarmee War Diary, situation 25 May 1942,

in attack or defence. Panzerarmee had been seeking to increase its firepower with fewer troops.

There were delays to the next offensive because many units were still in the rear, or receiving new troops and equipment, or needed to be trained on the new weapons. It took time to get these units forward, moving up to the front and then acclimatise to desert daily routines again. New drafts of men had to get used to daily life and fit in with their squadrons and companies. While the new equipment needed gunnery practice or time spent in workshops, such as the anti-tank portees. The late delivery of some tanks and guns by late April, added to these individual problems.

The operational problems shown during the Crusader battles, also decided that changes were needed across divisional organisations, which created new brigade groups. These in turn became divided into regimental and battalion groups which had the effect of sub-dividing supporting artillery and therefore the firepower available to each group. There was a logic in creating a self-sufficient battlegroup, which enabled jock columns to continue. These contributed to the overall intelligence picture of the Axis forward lines and caused low level attrition, during the build-up and throughout the battle. They gave junior officers valuable experience of leadership, patrolling, navigation et cetera, and prevented troops from becoming too defensive minded. Their widespread use, across the brigades and artillery regiments, constantly interrupted other training, for a limited gain at best.

Regiments complained that training was interrupted with the warmer spring weather, which brought an increasing number of dust storms. Too much time was also lost as units negotiated brigade moves of 400 miles by rail or along road/desert tracks, up to the front. Here they were often given duties of additional garrison or anti-invasion patrols around supply dumps. The opening phases of the battle highlighted many these problems for Eighth Army.

4

Opening Battles South, 26–31 May

> *I called you once, but you were sleeping…*
> *I called you again, you were still sleeping,*
> *Pale was your face, no smile was there …*
>
> 'Asleep in War'
> John Cromer[1]

The battles which occurred on the first day were some of the most dramatic of the entire campaign up to the fall of Tobruk. They also appear to have strongly influenced commanders of both sides, as well as the troops involved, as to how the rest of the fighting might develop.

Despite weeks of planning, many units were still moved at the last minute, or did not reach their intended 'battle position' in time. Two motor brigades were rushed to the southern flank, and were not ready, they were both rapidly overrun. While the armoured brigades, which were to manoeuvre together and pivot on the flanks of the boxes, ended up fighting encounter battles with more concentrated panzer columns in mostly separated engagements, apart from the final engagement at the end of the first day. Despite all the warnings from reconnaissance and jock columns along the front line, commanders made slow decisions when faced with Panzerarmee's flank march around Bir Hacheim.

Much has been discussed about the reasons for problem of delayed command and the lack of reaction which occurred within Eighth Army HQs over the night of 26/27 May. Especially since Lord Carver published his accounts of the campaign and returned to the topic in his later memoirs.[2] As a staff officer at XXX Corps HQ, he was listening in to radio reports from 4th South African armoured car regiment, and he also noted

---

1   Selwyn, *Poems of the Second World War. The Oasis Selection*, p.66.
2   Michael Carver, *Tobruk* (London: Batsford,1964) and *Dilemmas of the Desert War* and *Out of Step. Memoirs of a Field Marshal*.

the reports passed back through 7th Motor Brigade.³ The South Africans reported Axis movements, but they could not see the scale of them at night, and he noted that warning orders were received by 4th Armoured Brigade. The watching patrols could confirm if Axis armour was heading east to the centre. Perhaps this delayed the armour being committed.⁴ Jock columns were also watching the columns of tanks and MET. One Rifle Brigade officer described their column work in the battle, how they supported the armoured car patrols as they were watching a frontage of 130 miles between them. He was adamant that the Rifle Brigade submitted 23 messages from 1530 hours to 2130 hours that evening, and another 30 reports of enemy movements overnight to 0700 hours on 27 May.⁵ This backs up Carver's own strenuous attempts to galvanise 7th Armoured Division HQ into readiness. He continued to badger the HQ and his own commander to react to these radio reports as Panzerarmee moved south and gathered ready to strike the following morning.⁶

Second KRRC jock columns also reported to 7th Motor Brigade HQ in the afternoon and evening of 26 May about Axis movements. Their July and August columns reported, 'an advance in strength by the enemy' at 1600 hours.⁷ Powerful enemy columns were driving south, towards the Bir Hacheim, which looked like the expected outflanking move. Corps commanders upwards still expected the main attack to come in the centre or the north, and Panzerarmee made diversionary attacks against the northern sector. A few tanks accompanied the mainly infantry attack, along with trucks carrying aero-engines to create false dust storms which looked like the movement of larger formations.⁸ In the south, 4th Armoured gave its three regiments, notice to move at first light. Third Indian Brigade informed them about enemy tanks forming for an attack by 0630 hours. Division ordered 4th Armoured Brigade first to the Larwood position, east of Pt.171, then a few minutes later to the Majority battle site, near the Baltets slopes just to the east. In the event the brigade never reached these pre-selected defensive sites and both 8th Hussars and 3rd RTR met the Panzer Divisions head-on, in separate encounter battles, as the main body of Panzerarmee advanced northwards.⁹

The situation reports from XXX Corps list powerful enemy columns of tanks and MET in their hundreds massed in the area map reference 3736, which was six miles south of Bir Hacheim, at both 0610 and later at 0805 hours that morning. The South Africans reported, 'much eastern movement and 13 air raids on their position,'

3   Carver, *Out of Step*, pp.102–103.
4   Carver, *Tobruk*, pp.172–175.
5   H.G. Parkyn, *The Rifle Brigade Chronicle for 1942* (London: The Rifle Brigade Club, 1943), pp.93–95. J.M.L.R., 'The Cyrenaica, Libya Operations, 7th Motor Brigade summer 1942.'
6   Carver, *Dilemmas*, p.77.
7   TNA WO 169/5033: 2nd KRRC War Diary, 1942, 26 May 1942.
8   Ian Walker, *Iron Hulls Iron Hearts: Mussolini's Elite Armoured Divisions in North Africa* (Marlborough: Crowood Press, 2003), p.112.
9   TNA WO 169/4216: 4th Armoured Brigade War Diary, 27 May 1942.

which probably added to the confusion about where the attacks were coming.[10] It is possible to see how these timings fitted with what had already occurred by 0900 hours that day…

The 3rd Indian Motor Brigade at Pt.171, 27 May

The brigade had been sent to the most southerly and exposed position, at Pt.171 and was the first to face the massed columns of Panzerarmee, as it paused to refuel south of Bir Hacheim. The commander, Brigadier Filose, had arrived earlier and made a reconnaissance as best he could. His second report, made later in conjunction with his officers, said he reached Pt.171 by 25 May, and was visited by both Generals Norrie and Messervy, who promised additional support.[11] The Brigade Major, Miles Smeeton, said they arrived late on 25 May with the majority of the Brigade arriving next day.[12] The main outcome was that they were only able to make a quick reconnaissance of the position to plan the brigade defence before units arrived on 26 May to dig in. The position was about 4,000 yards on its western side, too long for three regiments to hold, across four sides, with only about 500 men per regiment.[13] Confusingly there were two Pt.171 heights, the northern side of the box, ran about a mile either side of the western Pt.171. The southwest corner overlooked the desert well to the south. The natural defence was due to the saucer-like crater, overlooked by a 'black ridge,' to the south. Filose wanted to occupy the ridge, but they never reached it in time. Smeeton noted the lip of the depression allowed them to hide their guns and gave the anti-tank guns a chance to be on the reverse slopes, and thus not get knocked out by long range fire.[14]

Commanders had given him their appreciations of intended enemy options and HQ informed Filose that the expected plan would be codeword MAJORITY and would bring down 4th Armoured Brigade to operate between them and 7th Motor Brigade at the Retma Box. The 4th Brigade's motor battalion was intended to deploy on 3rd Indian's left flank. 7th Armoured HQ informed him they would 'probably' be attacked the next day. The continued assumption by Corps HQ was that the two Panzer divisions would most likely attempt to break through further north, and that the attack around the southern flank would only be the made by the equivalent of one Panzer Division, probably the Italian Ariete. They confirmed that 3rd Motor Brigade

---

10   TNA WO 169/4053: 1st Armoured Division War Diary, 27 May 1942.
11   TNA WO 201/380: Operations of First Free French Brigade Eighth Army, May–June 1942, Account of Operations of 3rd Motor Brigade in the area south of Bir Hacheim, 26–27 May 1942.
12   Smeeton, *A Change of Jungles*, pp.36–37.
13   TNA WO 201/2698: Operations of 2 Armoured Brigade Group, 1942 May–June, Notes on the action of 3rd Independent Motor Brigade SW of Bir Hacheim 27 May 1942.
14   Smeeton, *A Change of Jungles*, pp.36–37.

would act as a pivot with 7th Motor Brigade as a second pivot, while 4th Armoured Brigade was in the rear. Ahead of them was the recce screen provided by 4th South African (armoured cars) and behind them were the July and August jock columns from the 7th Motor Brigade.[15] In theory the newly arrived Indian Brigade would have a reasonable amount of support.

The brigade deployed with 2nd Lancers on the south face, 18th Cavalry on the west face and 11th PAVO on the north face of the box.[16] Norrie promised an additional anti-tank battery of 16 guns and a squadron of 'I' tanks, which never materialised. Brigadier Filose agreed that the position was an excellent one, once properly set up, with good views to the south and west, and had they been fully equipped with AT guns and protected by a minefield, they would have seen off most attacks, as the Knightsbridge Box was able to achieve.[17] He reconnoitred the area for only a short period ahead of the arrival of the brigade, so was given very little time and had so many tasks still to be completed, particularly planning the intended wire and minefields.

The brigade arrived in two echelons, during the afternoon and evening. They had been organised by Q branch for logistical movement, rather than in tactical units and were not complete. Each regiment had eight 2pdrs, instead of sixteen, with eight in brigade reserve, designated for future jock columns. They were able to dig the guns in, but the late arrival meant they were unable to 'net-in' on the radios, so that communications were limited next day. Only one rear link vehicle was in contact with division, and this was quickly knocked out next day. As noted, the cavalry regiments mustered only 500 men each and 15 officers, so had fewer men to cover the wide position and fewer officers to act as liaison with the supporting armoured brigades. The liaison officer sent to meet the expected 'I' tank squadron could not find them and missed the engagement. Smeeton also noted that many officers were still in Cairo gathering equipment for their units.[18] The approach march had placed the engineer squadron in the rear, so they had no chance to begin laying the 3,000 mines which had been dumped by Army that evening. For protection, B echelon vehicles were placed in the nearby hidden 'valley' between Pt.171 West and Pt.171 East. An OP officer was sent out three miles to the west to give early warning of an enemy approach. The motor company was another delayed unit which meant they were low on petrol for even basic tasks. If they had been given a less exposed defensive site, or more time, many of these issues and shortages would have been resolved. Unfortunately, the Panzerarmee timetable would not give the Motor Brigade that chance.

15 TNA WO 201/2698: Operations of 2 Armoured Brigade Group, 1942 May–June, Notes on the action of 3rd Independent Motor Brigade SW of Bir Hacheim 27 May 1942.
16 TNA WO 169/7723: 11th PAVO War Diary, 1942, evening 26 May 1942.
17 TNA WO 201/380: Operations of First Free French Brigade Eighth Army, May–June 1942, Account of Operations of 3rd Motor Brigade in the area south of Bir Hacheim, 26–27 May 1942.
18 Smeeton, *A Change of Jungles*, p.40.

General Messervy visited at 1500 hours and informed them of an impending attack. He said, "'I hope that Army are right … They are convinced that the attack will come in the north, but I'm not sure. They may come round this way…you can expect a demonstration at least. Good luck.'"[19] By 1800 hours on 26 May, Filose said it was clear that there was a large movement developing against the southern flank, and 11th PAVO Cavalry noted there were six enemy columns advancing over a front of 30 miles that evening.[20] Overnight enemy aircraft dropped flares to the south-west, and he later realised this was to enable Panzerarmee to regroup at the halfway mark. There was a good deal of noise from Axis MET throughout the night. In the early morning the OP reported a 'terrific concentration' of enemy in front of him. The 2nd Lancers verified this and Brigadier Filose made his own dawn recce from the low hill in the south-west of the locality. He said:

> Epsom Downs on Derby Day could have fitted into a tiny corner of what I saw. There were thousands of vehicles, hundreds of tanks and away to the SOUTH, a huge mass of soft stuff. They were packed tight like sardines in a tin. My first impression was, 'concentration of force' and my next was 'What an air target'.[21]

He reported to division, but not wishing to exaggerate told his Brigade Major to say, 'at least 1 enemy Armd Div.' However, Division was sceptical, so Filose made another recce. According to Miles Smeeton, who was on the radio at Brigade HQ, Filose gave an exasperated reply to the clipped queries from the 'former instructor in armoured fighting vehicles,' at HQ, who kept asking for more details, 'Tell him the that the whole bloody Afrika Korps is drawn up in front of us like a bloody review – then get up here as fast as you can.'[22] He then reported two armoured divisions and a mass of MET and asked what they intended for the brigade. Division told him, 'to remain if possible but if not – retire to a flank.'[23] So, Filose made the difficult decision to fight, rather than run, mainly to slow Panzerarmee's advance into the flank of Eighth Army. Smeeton gives a marvellous image of the Brigadier sat on the edge of a trench with his back to the enemy and a barrage already falling on the brigade. The unit commanders were crouching on one knee around him – a little lower than normal. There was not much to be said, the decision was made to hold as best they could.[24]

19 Smeeton, *A Change of Jungles*, p.37.
20 TNA WO 169/7723: 11th PAVO War Diary, 1942, evening 26 May 1942.
21 TNA WO 201/380: Operations of First Free French Brigade Eighth Army, May–June 1942, Account of Operations of 3rd Motor Brigade in the area south of Bir Hacheim, 26–27 May 1942.
22 Smeeton, *A Change of Jungles*, p.39.
23 TNA WO 201/380: WO 201/380: Operations of First Free French Brigade Eighth Army, May–June 1942, Account of Operations of 3rd Motor Brigade in the area south of Bir Hacheim, 26–27 May 1942.
24 Smeeton, *A Change of Jungles*, p.40.

The Brigade's supporting artillery was 2nd Field Regiment Indian Artillery (IA), which had been moving forward from the Delta since mid-May, and arrived late on 26 May, with just two batteries, each of eight guns. The artillery C.O. and OP joined the Brigadier for a recce, the gunners got on with digging the guns in, until late in the evening, when they were informed that large enemy forces were on the move. No.7 battery deployed with the Lancers to the south and with 18th Cavalry, while No.4 Battery deployed with 11th PAVO Cavalry on the north-western side. They noted that dawn found them looking at the whole, 'Panzer Corps on parade five miles south-south-west of the position.' The artillery opened fire at once (0625 hours) damaging some lorry transported infantry which quickly moved out of range. They then engaged more targets including a Corps HQ and some tanks, which appeared to be forming up for an attack.[25] The shelling forced the MET further away and separated the lorried infantry from the armoured attack. Their guns deployed further away which made the subsequent Axis barrage less effective and enabled the Indian gunners to engage the oncoming armour.[26]

During the next hour, Panzerarmee formed up for an attack, while they began shelling with poor effect, because they had not reconnoitred the brigade nor did they overlook Pt.171.[27] Spirited messages arrived from Division in response to the Brigade reports, '*SUB TEAK HAI MAJORITY HOTA HAI* [all is well], MAJORITY plan coming into force.'[28] So Filose expected armour to join the battle on his left flank. Smeeton and his driver headed across the Box and said that the desert in front of them was like, 'a brown soup just coming to the boil with bursting bubbles of sand and rolls of black smoke.' He and his young Sikh driver shouted, '*Sath siri akal*!' ('God is truth') swerving around the shell holes.[29]

The Axis tanks altered their facing towards the north-east, one tank column headed for the hidden valley which was full of B echelon lorries. Filose directed the eight anti-tank guns from the artillery to cover this left side and try to protect the mass of vehicles. Their standing orders were to move 'away from the fighting' and so they quickly began an 'exciting ride' north, evading the various enemy columns which later swirled around them. He believed Panzerarmee was surprised to see an enemy brigade deployed very near their intended form-up position.[30]

25 TNA WO 169/7741: 2nd Indian Field Regiment IA War Diary 1942, 26–27 May 1942.
26 TNA WO 201/380: WO 201/380: Operations of First Free French Brigade Eighth Army, May–June 1942, Account of Operations of 3rd Motor Brigade in the area south of Bir Hacheim, 26–27 May 1942.
27 TNA WO 201/2698: Operations of 2 Armoured Brigade Group, Notes on the action of 3rd Independent Motor Brigade SW of Bir Hacheim 27 May 1942.
28 TNA WO 201/380: WO 201/380: Operations of First Free French Brigade Eighth Army, May–June 1942, Account of Operations of 3rd Motor Brigade in the area south of Bir Hacheim, 26–27 May 1942.
29 Smeeton, *A Change of Jungles*, p.40.
30 TNA WO 201/2698: Operations of 2 Armoured Brigade Group, 1942 May–June, Notes on the action of 3rd Independent Motor Brigade SW of Bir Hacheim 27 May 1942.

The first attack came in from the west with at least 50 tanks and was engaged by anti-tank guns and the two 25pdr batteries with a storm of fire. The panzers advanced in a blunt arrowhead formation, with eight to ten tanks leading and more in the waves behind. They fired very inaccurately as they moved and came on very slowly. They were hit very effectively by the forward batteries and sheared away from this fire and into the path of other guns. Smeeton had to lead two anti-tank guns from PAVO across to 18th Cavalry, where he met their elderly liaison officer, the redoubtable Admiral Cowan, pacing up and down, despite the shellfire. These were soon in action, firing with a sharp crack between the thump of the 25pdrs.[31]

The enemy had still overrun the unfortunate units. They moved through the box and reformed beyond the brigade, with some tanks returning later to capture the Brigade HQ.[32] The Divisional Quartermaster, Bob Prentice, was at HQ, and pointed to the low valley behind them, where a mass of German tanks, half-tracks and towed 88mm guns was coming though, effectively turning the brigade flank. The German gunners were, 'slamming a shell into the breech, as they stopped for a moment to fire.' To the front enemy tanks were 'swarming onto our position and down the right flank too.' The Indians had the Ariete Division on its right and German tanks to its front and rear.[33] Brigadier Filose knew the outcome, as the mass of tanks waddled through the thinly deployed regiments in waves. He said 18th Cavalry and PAVO Regiments had effectively ceased to exist. One column passed through the northern – rear face of the brigade box and carried on to the north, just as a second wave of tanks attacked the southern face of the box. Colonels Bomford and Horsfield had watched and counted the enemy and agreed that this wave consisted of about 100 tanks.

The second attack overran half of the 2nd Lancers' positions in the south and all of the other cavalry positions once again. It sheered away from the continued heavy fire from Howard's battery. Indian troopers and guns accounted for a large number of tanks as they attacked the position, and the Indians put up a determined defence. With both his troop officers missing, Havildar Major Narasu had also moved from gun to gun, encouraging the gunners to keep firing, and later gathered in survivors and led them to safety.[34] Captain D. M. Reynolds of the 2nd Lancers, was awarded the MC for organising his men to fire on any exposed enemy personnel, as they attacked, and remaining behind for an hour after the brigade withdrew, later extracting the last of his squadron.[35] Dafadar Ghulam Babbani inspired his four anti-tank crews under heavy fire, and kept the two rear guns firing after the two forward guns had been

---

31 Smeeton, *A Change of Jungles*, p.42.
32 TNA WO 201/2698: Operations of 2 Armoured Brigade Group, 1942 May–June, Notes on the action of 3rd Independent Motor Brigade SW of Bir Hacheim 27 May 1942.
33 Smeeton, A Change of Jungles, p.43.
34 D.K. Palit, *History of the Regiment of Artillery. Indian Army* (London: Leo Cooper, 1972), p.71.
35 TNA WO 373/20/79: Recommendation for Award, Captain D.M. Reynolds, 2nd R. Lancers, 27 May 1942.

overrun. He later escaped after being forced to surrender, and for his gallantry he was awarded the Indian Distinguished Service Medal.[36]

The Axis infantry arrived later on, so the Brigadier ordered everyone to get out with what they could extract, as tanks closed in on the HQ. He realised later he was wrong to evacuate at that point, as he might have extracted more guns with some carriers, because there was a delay between the armour, clearly wanting to move on and their infantry arriving, to complete the mopping up process. Individual soldiers showed a determination after the fighting, not to remain prisoners. One such was Dafadar (Cavalry Sergeant) Risal Singh from 2nd Lancers, who had been forced to surrender to a tank crew, but later escaped under shell fire and commandeered a truck. He loaded it with stray troopers and towed a second full truck away – he was awarded the Indian DSM.[37] Other HQ officers collected 60 or so vehicles, formed three columns of disconsolate troops and headed east to Bir el Gubi. One engineer officer was later picked up and shouted angrily at Smeeton, 'You buggered off and left me you bastard!' Miles had forgotten about him after he had gone to attend to some wounded sappers. With so many Axis columns about, all heading for El Adem, they headed for Bir el Gubi.[38] The remaining trucks had attempted to rally on Pt.171 East, but there were too many enemy columns around, so they headed first for the Retma Box. As they approached they heard firing and then silence. The Brigadier's column moved on and reached Bir el Gubi at 1800 hours followed by odd trucks loaded with troopers, as they slowly gathered in.

The brigade had fought valiantly and paid a heavy price, but had also inflicting heavy casualties on Panzerarmee and delayed their timetable. Twelve tanks had been stopped in front of Howard's Battery and 31 more in front of K Battery, with more knocked out by various 2pdr guns. Lieutenant Reynolds commanding four 2pdrs in the south-west corner accounted for 10 more tanks, giving a total of 61 Axis tanks knocked out. Some of these were repaired but numbers of them were destroyed by catching fire. One escaped Indian trooper passed over the battlefield on 28 May and counted 41 wrecked tanks. They engaged them at ranges of 800 yards or less and had fired off all of their AP rounds and other ammunition. The Brigadier believed they had accounted for about 60 tanks before the other tank battles began later in the day.[39]

By 4 June, as the brigade slowly recovered, 2nd Royal Lancers mustered 306 men and 10 officers, but still needed another 200 to bring it up to strength. The regiment reorganised into three weak squadrons with anti-tank troops, in carriers and

---

36 TNA WO 373/20/166: Recommendation for Award, Dafadar G. Babbani, 2nd R. Lancers, 27 May 1942.
37 TNA WO 373/20/167: Recommendation for Award, Dafadar R. Singh, 2nd R. Lancers, 27 May 1942.
38 Smeeton, *A Change of Jungles*, pp.45–46.
39 TNA WO 201/380: WO 201/380: Operations of First Free French Brigade Eighth Army, May–June 1942, Account of Operations of 3rd Motor Brigade in the area south of Bir Hacheim, 26–27 May 1942.

lorries. They had been 'training all-out on 2pdrs and Roberts guns.' Brigadier Filose believed he could operate one jock column, but he was ordered back to Buq Buq to regroup in more depth.[40] They held the passes on the frontier until mid-June and were defeated again and withdrew in the running battles near Mersa Matruh on 25 June. The Royal Lancers' Diary shows that there was a good deal of order-counter-disorder over those days, so it is easy to see why the brigade might have wondered what they were supposed to achieve, as Panzerarmee headed for Alexandria.[41]

7th Motor Brigade at the Retma Box, 27 May[42]

7th Motor Brigade joined Eighth Army in early March and by 2 April KRRC was practising with its 2pdr guns. They reorganised into an HQ and four companies, each with two infantry platoons, one 2pdr anti-tank platoon and a mortar detachment. Like the brigade groups each company became a self-contained unit but with minimal firepower. In April, only one day was spent practising setting up a box, just east of Retma, before they joined the El Adem garrison, in static defences. This lack of attention to getting positions quickly set up may have contributed to the overall lack of readiness by 27 May. They stayed there, despite various warning orders that either 2nd RB or the 9th KRRC was to replace them, to the end of April. The Brigade controlled the July and August columns with 2nd KRRC and was planned to hold Pt.171 if codeword BEER was given. Rear HQ would remain at Retma as a base, and as Panzerarmee began to advance in the night, the July and August columns ran parallel with, 'the flares of the enemy column.'[43] The 9th KRRC rejoined the Box on 26 May, and found the 'defence posts incomplete…some commanded by higher ground…mines for the perimeter were still stacked unpacked in boxes.'[44]

The Retma Box was another flank guard post to the main Army and was some 15 miles to the east-south-east of Pt.171. It was not in the expected front line but was still a good distance from 4th Armoured Brigade leaguers further north. The KRRC continued to operate columns east of the wire until the end of May, then they moved west again, around Bir Hacheim, to harass the Axis supply columns. By 12 June they were briefly in reserve and then continued to harass the southern flank of Panzerarmee until 23 June when they retreated to the wire.[45] Jock columns had been providing key

---

40   TNA WO 201/380: WO 201/380: Operations of First Free French Brigade Eighth Army, May–June 1942, Account of Operations of 3rd Motor Brigade in the area south of Bir Hacheim, 26–27 May 1942.
41   TNA WO 169/7718: 2nd Royal Lancers War Diary, January-December 1942, June 1942.
42   The map denotes it as the Aghiret er Retma.
43   TNA WO 169/5033: 2nd KRRC War Diary 1942, Operational Order No.1.
44   Giles Mills & Roger Nixon, *The Annals of the King's Royal Rifle Corps Vol. VI, 1921–1943* (London: Leo Cooper, 1971), p.248.
45   TNA WO 169/5033: 2nd KRRC War Diary 1942.

intelligence and were adept at harassing supply columns. German comments said that supply was near the edge in early June. So they had impacted to a degree on the main battle but they had not slowed down the panzer groups, as they had done previously during Crusader.

The Rhodesian 6pdrs took a good toll of passing columns, but the attack turned on the Box. The enemy broke in from the west, overrunning C and D companies and the HQ within 75 minutes of the first attack. The remainder of 9th KRRC and 2nd RB withdrew to Bir el Gubi.[46] Rifle brigade gun crews had remained at their posts until wounded, killed or overrun, and had shown stoic bravery trying to stop Panzerarmee's offensive. One action was that by Sergeant G. G. Griffiths, who commanded a section of two anti-tank guns from 4th RHA. The section came under close and heavy fire during the early attack on the Box, but Sergeant Griffiths directed their fire until wounded and the guns were overrun. He escaped later that night with two others and walked the 15 miles to Bir el Gubi to rejoin his unit. He was finally evacuated after being severely wounded a second time and was later awarded the Military Medal for his exemplary conduct.[47] The 9th KRRC appeared to have lost 180 men in the battle, but many returned over the next few days and the final tally was 12 casualties and 32 missing presumed POWs.[48]

4th Armoured Brigade, 27 May

The 8th Hussars were in the eye of the storm, at their Giof el Baar leaguer. They had been warned about an attack on 21 May and had been standing-to each day for the last five days. They were ready to move, as ordered, just after first light that morning, as the enemy were on the move, although the southern move was still considered a feint. Then at 0720 hours the MAJORITY codeword was given, so they headed to their battle position, 13 miles to the southwest.[49] Within 10 minutes of moving towards Brigade, the lead squadron saw the enemy column 3,000 yards to the south. Here Major Hackett engaged them but his tank was quickly knocked out, and he changed tanks to continue directing his squadron. The two Grant squadrons formed line on either side of the light Honey tanks of C Squadron. A squadron in the south took the brunt of enemy fire and thought they had been flanked by some anti-tank guns, but continued to fire until only two Grants remained, while B Squadron continued firing until they were all knocked out and the surviving crews escaped on foot. The light Honeys in C Squadron occupied a flank and accounted for 10 tanks, the regiment believed they accounted for some 30 Axis tanks (confirmed later by a KRRC

---

46 Mills & Nixon, *Annals*, p.248.
47 TNA WO 373/20/107: Recommendation for Award for Sgt. G. G. Griffiths 4RHA, 27 May 42.
48 Mills & Nixon, *Annals*, p.248.
49 TNA WO 169/4486: 8th Hussars War Diary, 27 May 1942.

patrol). The enemy column had overwhelmed the Hussars, with the RHQ vehicles being outmanoeuvred by some Mk IIIs and knocked out.[50]

Some surviving crews made their escape. Captain Huth and other survivors from A Squadron put four Grants out of commission and walked 16 miles overnight, before being collected by some South African armoured cars. The echelon vehicles were surrounded and had no option but to surrender, some intrepid vehicles made a dash and escaped back to the regiment. The Hussars were adamant that no adequate warning had been given, despite the clear overnight reports from reconnaissance, and no other tank or artillery support had reached them in time. They were left with three Grants and the few Honeys of C Squadron.[51] The next day, C Squadron was able to collect fresh tanks and join 3rd RTR while other members of the regiment would regroup east of Gambut.

Assessing the battle, Lieutenant Colonel Roberts gave his experiences 18 months later. He said they were about nine miles north of their battle position, with 5th RTR, the gunners and 1st KRRC Motor battalion, to the east on the high ground. They were hoping to be ready in the position, adjacent to 3rd Indian Brigade, as the enemy came around the southern flank. He had been replying to an admin query from Brigade HQ, when they rang to say, 'Enemy movement towards Hacheim. Take up position Skylark,' with details of the move.[52] Robert Watt, a pre-war regular with 3rd RTR, said they leaguered about 10 miles north, and were just finishing breakfast when the order was received to move. The leading Honey squadron scouted ahead and made contact within two miles. It came under fire and was ordered to advance with all guns blazing, this forced the panzers to halt.[53] Roberts had the Honeys 2,000 yards in front, and they reported dust and vehicles three miles beyond them. As they closed on the enemy, he looked for a good hull down position, and the Adjutant reported 100 enemy tanks approaching. Roberts fed back his view to brigade, '20 in the first line, and there are six, no eight lines and more in the distance; a whole ruddy Panzer Div is quite obviously in front of us! Damn it! This was not the plan at all. Where the hell are the rest of the Brigade.' Without hesitation he quickly made a battle line on a ridge 300 yards to their front – the Honeys on the right with one troop on the left to link with 8th Hussars, who were expected.[54] The Grants were ordered to hold their fire and engage at 1,200 yards. Chestnut Troop RHA deployed behind them ready to fire. The Troop commander deployed four guns on the left flank in an anti-tank role, which placed the crews in the open. The enemy halted about 1,300 yards and the firefight began.

50   TNA WO 169/4486: 8th Hussars War Diary, 27 May 1942.
51   TNA WO 169/4486: 8th Hussars War Diary, 27 May 1942.
52   Bovington: Roberts papers, 3RTR, 'Some experiences of an armoured commander in the Middle East.'
53   Bovington: 3rd RTR, Papers of RSM Robert Watt, pp.35–37.
54   Bovington: Roberts papers, 3RTR, Some experiences of an armoured commander in the Middle East.

The new Grant tanks were a surprise to the advancing Germans. They came up into line and opened fire, their range and hitting power was a major shock to the German tanks, even if they did know about the 'American medium tank.' The Chestnut C.O.'s armoured car was knocked out and he was the only survivor. The regiment lost two Grants and would lose more later. The enemy were able to replace losses from the rear ranks, as well as sending anti-tank guns out wide on the right, forcing Roberts to fall back.[55] As the regiment began to withdraw, the Honeys moved to the flank and engaged enemy tanks, hitting the thinner side armour with their 37mm guns. However, other panzers flanked the Honeys and later attacked the regiment in flank, forcing them back, from ridge to ridge.[56] Brigade informed them that 8th Hussars had been mauled and they hoped that 5th RTR would arrive to support. C Squadron had been almost wiped out and the CO wounded, his tank had received 25 hits, but they had accounted for at least 20 German tanks. They reversed slowly for 100 yards before finally turning away to reach the high ground and get a resupply of ammunition. Roberts had two tank crews sitting on the back of his tank, which only had five rounds of 37mm left.[57] The surviving tanks needed more ammunition but the B echelon lorries were also pinned by shellfire, so they concentrated further to the northeast. They passed a wadi full of Free French trucks and had to leave a covering force to get themselves and the French away. They later refuelled one troop at a time. Out of 24 Grants there were seven remaining, with three others needing repairs to their guns.

The supporting 5th RTR history provides more of an overview of these first days, using one diary which said that one day became like one another. It generalises about combat and other events, such as the unfortunate later death of the C.O., Lieutenant Colonel Uniacke.[58] Mark Urban's regimental study confirms they engaged the mass of MET near to 3rd RTR in a two-hour battle and inflicted a good level of casualties. Driver Jake Wardrop's account was his usual laconic self, 'we gave them a good warning with the big 75. It quite shook them, I'm sure they turned and ran for it.'[59] There was a second firefight for 5th RTR, followed by the move back and an evening battle near El Adem, which left lorries burning everywhere. The regiment was largely intact, so by the end of the day this was the only viable regiment within 7th Armoured Division.[60]

---

55 Bovington: Roberts papers, 3RTR, Some experiences of an armoured commander in the Middle East.
56 Bovington: 3rd RTR, Papers of RSM Robert Watt, pp.35–37.
57 Bovington: Roberts papers, 3RTR, 'Some experiences of an armoured commander in the Middle East.'
58 Edward Wilson, *Press on Regardless. The story of the Fifth Royal Tank Regiment in World War Two* (Staplehurst: Spellmount, 2003), pp.110–111.
59 *Forty, Tanks Across the Desert*, p.80.
60 Mark Urban, *The Tank War: The British 'band of brothers' – One Tank Regiment's World War II* (London: Abacus, 2014), p.110.

The 1st KRRC, with a strength of nearly 800 men, was on the plateau along the centre line of the approach march to Majority, with the artillery HQ and engineers. One company had been detached to protect the brigade B echelon.[61] Captain Hope's C Company was further south-east of Hacheim and were tumbled out of their battle position by 30 tanks heading east with masses of MET behind. Captain Hope extracted his platoons from under the Axis' noses and drove slowly past the leading tanks, 'The commanders were standing up in their turrets. I took no notice of them, nor they of us.'[62] With so many captured vehicles being used by Panzerarmee, they never realised they had British troops next to them.

The battalion was 'comfortably' dug in on the slopes above 8th Hussar's leaguer and said they received no information to make them think an attack was imminent. Captain Hope had sent the first messages. They watched the large German column below them and to their right heading north, and they had an excellent view of the 'tank v tank battle being fought in the valley below.'[63] They were ordered to join the Retma Box, but it was overrun before they could reach it. They were then ordered east and heard that their C.O., Lieutenant Colonel de Bruyne and the entire B echelon had been captured. De Bruyne had been heading to Brigade HQ for orders.[64] So they worked their way east to Sidi Rezegh, in a confused day of fighting and retiring. They mustered with 4th Armoured and were told the tanks had been taken by surprise and suffered heavy losses. On the evening of the eventful first day, Pip Roberts was ordered to engage a German column to the south of El Adem by a XXX Corps liaison officer. They did so and shelled a few trucks and scattered their attached guns, to see them off. He'd been curious as to why Corps was getting involved and later found that Messervy had been captured.[65]

22nd Armoured Brigade, 27–29 May

The brigade was deployed facing north-west, with 2nd RGH in reserve. At first they thought the enemy were attacking elsewhere, so breakfasted, then there was a rush to remove covers and move south and soon shells were falling amongst them.[66] As the panzer columns came up from the south, some 60 tanks overran the small regimental box. The other two regiments manoeuvred south, 4th CLY on the left and 3rd CLY

---

61 TNA WO 169/5032: 1st KRRC War Diary, Field Return 23 May 1942, 37 officers and 762 men.
62 Giles Mills & Roger Nixon, *The Annals*, pp.244–246.
63 TNA WO 169/5032: 1st KRRC War Diary, 27 May 1942.
64 Mills & Nixon, *Annals*, p.247.
65 Bovington: Roberts papers, 3RTR, 'Some experiences of an armoured commander in the Middle East.'
66 Stuart Pitman, *Second Royal Gloucester Hussars, Libya-Egypt 1941–1942* (Uckfield: Naval & Military Press, 2014), p.55.

to go south and then swing west to the Hacheim track, taking the enemy in flank. By 0915 hours B Squadron's Grants engaged the enemy at about 4,000 yards. With 2nd RGH under heavy attack, 3rd CLY was ordered to fall back onto the left of the brigade, left of 4th CLY.[67]

Captain Pitman said the RGH Grants engaged the enemy at long range to enable 3rd CLY and 4th CLY to join them. The Germans concentrated all of their fire on F Squadron until they were all knocked out bar one. Four Grants retired from this first stand back to the brigade, the smoke and firing was intense with the Grants' frontal armour surviving multiple hits. Two of the four Grants ceased fire having run out of ammunition, leaving a single Grant.[68] They had given the German tanks a hard fight but lost 30 percent of the regiment.

As 3rd CLY retired, they found they were being overhauled by up to 50 Mk IIIs, who closed to 1,000 yards, so the regiment faced about, and engaged them. They knocked out 17 enemy tanks for the loss of 5 Grants and 8 Crusaders. The panzers broke off and the Yeomanry reached the rest of the brigade by late morning. For the rest of the day 22nd Armoured lined the Bir Bellefaa ridge, next to Knightsbridge, and faced the enemy columns in the south. The enemy sent a patrol in mid-afternoon but did not attack the brigade again. The RGH retreated to the ridge east of Knightsbridge, watched the Guards 6pdrs engage approaching tanks. 22nd Brigade liaised with 9th Lancers from 2nd Armoured, as that brigade moved west to engage the MET massed along the Hacheim track. In the evening, 2nd RGH were on the Raml Ridge, north of Knightsbridge, and were attacked again from the west by 15th Panzer.[69] While 3rd CLY said their left was against Knightsbridge as they faced this late threat.

The 4th CLY was effectively the reserve and moved south. The Grants along with No.3 box guns engaged the approaching MET by 1000 hours. As enemy strength grew, they withdrew under orders to the right of Knightsbridge, and stopped at B.201 to engage a new enemy column 500 yards to the south. After midday they rejoined the brigade at Bir Bellefaa ridge and refuelled. In the evening they advanced west and engaged about 12 Mk IIIs. They leaguered on the south-east side of the Guards, amongst some burning lorries.[70]

22nd Brigade crews needed to regroup the next day, but as the watching brief continued into 29 May, they were facing MET west of Knightsbridge, while to the west of these, other Axis groups were attacking the isolated 150th Brigade at Sidi Muftah. There seemed to be little likelihood of Eighth Army getting close. Both 3rd and 4th CLY watched a stationary enemy column on the Rigel Ridge, to the north, all day on 28 May and were ordered to attack them on 29 May, as 2nd Armoured was in

---

67 TNA WO 169/4495: 3rd County London Yeomanry War Diary, 27 May 1942,
68 Pitman, *Second Royal Gloucester Hussars*, p.57.
69 TNA WO 169/4494: 2nd Royal Gloucester Hussars War Diary, 27 May 1942.
70 TNA WO 169/4496: 4th County London Yeomanry War Diary, 27 May 1942.

a major battle and needed support. Later 4th CLY was ordered to attack enemy near Bir Harmat, south of Knightsbridge.[71]

22nd Brigade moved out and west, being ordered to avoid heavy casualties, and struggled through a difficult dust storm, which blew up through the day. They joined the flank of 9th Lancers near the B.230 mark, the five Grants from 4th CLY helped them engage enemy tanks. Later they joined 2nd RGH, which needed help, but lost two tanks in the storm when they ran into enemy guns they could not see. They ended up back on the Harmat-Hacheim track, but with zero visibility. That evening, they protected the flank of 4th Armoured Brigade, who attacked Pt.185, to their left.[72]

Armoured Brigades, 27–31 May

By 29 May, 8th Hussars' Honeys joined 3rd RTR to engage an enemy column some 3 miles north-west of El Adem. This would protect the Axis bypass road on the Batruna ridge. There was no contact with the enemy because of a heavy sandstorm which reduced visibility to 10 yards. Some units were able to make more effective use of their jock columns after the first day. The 1st KRRC, less one company now, made a new defensive box and sent out regular patrols and harassing groups. As 4th Armoured returned west towards El Adem, they sent a mixed column up onto the El Adem plateau, to cover the left flank. Major J. A. Hunter commanded C Company, with Ross Troop RHA, four 25pdrs and four 6pdr AT guns, two with each OP moving ahead of the infantry. They successfully shelled one enemy column east of El Adem, and then found another, using some wadis as cover. The two OP groups used fire and movement, one to pin the MET while the second pair of 6pdrs closed in to drive them from the wadis. As this action finished a large B echelon column arrived in disarray, being shelled by another Axis column using mostly British trucks. One OP group halted amidst the swirling dust looking for targets. They got off one shot before being overrun. Another ten-minute battle ensued with the new German column coming off worst and speeding away to the south-east. Hunter praised the gunner OP, Lieutenant V. Gruer, who had engaged the new enemy over open sights and controlled the excellent shooting.[73] The battalion would be sent to Eluet et Tamar for three days in June and then spent the rest of the battle operating from Naduret et Ghuscuaesc, protecting 4th Brigade flank, but making some effective harassing patrols and shoots.[74]

Both sides also used their anti-tank detachments to outflank any approaching armour or enemy anti-tank screens. At Bir Harmat on 30 May, an enemy unit of two

---

71 TNA WO 169/4496: 4th County London Yeomanry War Diary, 27 May 1942.
72 TNA WO 169/4495: 3rd County London Yeomanry War Diary, 29 May 1942; and WO 169/4496: 4th CLY War Diary, 29 May 1942.
73 TNA WO 169/5032: 1st KRRC War Diary, Report on operations by Mixed Column, 28 May 1942.
74 TNA WO 169/5032: 1st KRRC War Diary, 31 May–June summary.

50mm guns was concealed amongst some derelict tanks on the flank of some Grants. Captain R. R. Oakey from 1st RHA anti-tank battery took a section forward to drive them off with their portees. However they found six enemy guns with MGs, which put the detachment under heavy fire and set Captain Oakey's portee alight. Sergeant Cyril Cheney's portee knocked out one of the 50mm guns and a Mk III tank and using accurate fire drove off the others. He then rescued the wounded from the first portee. Their determined action had driven off the flank threat to the Grants, and Sergeant Cheney was awarded the DCM for his leadership.[75]

With the head of the German column just south of Knightsbridge on the Hacheim track by mid-afternoon, 44th RTR was ordered to attack eastwards. Three squadrons moved along the high ground, A Squadron was halted by the steep edge of the ridge, while B Squadron came under fire from a wadi ahead and had to reverse. B and C Squadrons were sent forward again and it was just C Squadron which 'got right in amongst the enemy...' and inflicted a good deal of casualties.[76] They lost 14 Valentines, but 5 were later recovered, and the battalion reformed into two squadrons.[77] The three attacks by the armoured brigades gave the panzer columns a sharp blow in their advance north. At 1700 hours, 15th Panzer Division reported that enemy tanks had broken into their right-rear on the Gebel (Rigel Ridge) and the rifle regiment had suffered heavy losses.[78] H. W. Schmidt, with 15th Panzer said they were south of Acroma, which is the Rigel Ridge where 15th Panzer spent the night out of fuel. It was his 2nd Battalion 115th Rifle Regiment which was largely overrun and captured by a mass (60 plus tanks) of British armour led by Grant tanks who defeated their 50mm guns, which could do little damage to the Grants' frontal armour.[79] Slightly confusingly, after 1600 hours, 90th Light reported that 60 tanks had attacked the right flank of 15th Panzer but that DAK's Kampfstaffel had been thrown in with its valuable 88mm guns, which knocked out 12 enemy tanks and halted the British advance. After 1700 hours the infantry from 15th Panzer had pushed ahead of the panzers closer to Acroma but had been hit in the flank by enemy tank forces and suffered losses.[80] This was the attack suffered by Schmidt's 2nd battalion.

By late morning 2nd Armoured Brigade advanced south with 10th Hussars leading, the Bays on the right and 9th Lancers on the left. The Hussars' C Squadron bumped into the enemy column on the Naduret Ridge and they knocked out various MET, guns, and one tank. They moved west to rejoin the brigade and later north. They

---

75   TNA WO 373/20/97: Recommendation for Award for Sergeant C. Cheney, 1st RHA, 30 May 1942.
76   Bovington Papers: 44th RTR, Account of action by 2nd Lieutenant K. Dodwell, 27 May 1942.
77   TNA WO 169/4199: 1st Army Tank Brigade War Diary, 27 May 1942.
78   IWM: AL833: DAK War Diary, 27 May 1942. The Kampfstaffel was a mixed unit of tanks and guns to be used as needed by the DAK.
79   Schmidt, *With Rommel in the Desert*, pp.131–137.
80   IWM: E127: 90th Light War Diary, 27 May 1942.

knocked out another two lorries and one gun, before turning right to leaguer back at the same location, the ridge east of Knightsbridge at B.743.[81] The Bays met the main column on their right-front with the Grants opening fire at 3,000 yards and doing great damage as the range shortened to 1,500 yards. Lieutenant Michael Halstead said that everything went well at first. They blew up a full petrol lorry, and he saw the enemy shells swirling past in the dust, or causing a whip-crack as they went by. Soon they were down to four HE shells each in the troop, so switched to MG fire to keep the enemy gunners down. Shortly afterwards his tank was hit, and he and the crew wounded by shellfire.[82]

The Lancers had a more successful day, switching to the right flank and combining with 3rd CLY Grants and E Battery gunners, against a line of enemy guns, including four 88mm guns. With the CS tanks firing smoke, the cruiser squadrons ran in from both flanks and overran the enemy. They knocked out all of the guns and took over 100 prisoners for the loss of four Crusaders, with two recovered.[83] The visibility worsened because of the dust and smoke, but the Grant squadron cooperated with 3rd CLY from 22nd Armoured as noted above. The Lancers said they had made their flank attack and heavily damaged the rear of 90th Light Division, getting well in amongst the infantry lorries. Many Indian prisoners were released who remained disciplined, despite having had no water, and only moistening their lips from the tankers' water bottles.[84]

The next day saw a similar advance by 2nd Armoured; however 76mm anti-tank guns were deployed on the ridge facing them, so the Hussars began losing Grants. A hasty attack was made by B Squadron cruisers from the north, supported by smoke and shelling from 11th RHA, this was very successful and they took four AT guns and 35 prisoners. The advance west continued and more enemy found near Bir Harmat. General Lumsden ordered a brigade attack with two regiments on the same lines.[85] Unfortunately, they attacked into the setting sun, after 2000 hours, with A Squadron of the Hussars swinging out too wide and ending up well amongst the enemy guns, so only three Crusaders returned, with the C.O., Major R. A. Archer-Shee and others missing.[86] The Lancers said they came under Stuka attacks, which continued for the next four days, and they could see the bombs leaving the plane racks as they pulled out of their steep dives. The Hussars had run into the Kampstaffel 88mm guns which had caught A Squadron again. The brigade ended the day resting in close leaguer on Knightsbridge.[87]

81   TNA WO 169/4489: 10th Hussars War Diary, 27 May 1942.
82   Michael Halstead, *Shots in the Sand: An Undergraduate Goes to War* (East Wittering: Gooday, 1990), pp.156–157.
83   Bovington: 9th Lancers War Diary, 27 May 1942.
84   Bright, *Ninth Lancers*, p.70.
85   Dawnay, *10th Royal Hussars*, pp.61–62.
86   TNA WO 169/4489: 10th Hussars War Diary, 27 May 1942.
87   Bright, *Ninth Lancers*, p.72.

Supply echelons also suffered as they moved between regiments and supply depots or joined the defence of a box. XIII Corps HQ appreciated that 44th RTR leaguer was on the western edge of the Sidra Ridge, but this ridge was occupied and held by 21st Panzer Division for much of the battle and at the point where 32nd Army Tank Brigade would have to assault on 5 June.

The order to 'battle-stations' went to 44th RTR at 1100 hours, leaving A echelon vehicles on Sidra Ridge to keep squadrons supplied in their forward posts. A echelon spent 36 hours, sending forward 'packets' of vehicles to them. Major Martin's A echelon followed the advance Brigade HQ, north to resupply 69th Brigade. Volunteers were asked to 'assist' to return and supply the embattled 150th Brigade. The remainder joined 1st AT Brigade echelon which retreated to the bypass junction east of Tobruk, where they were joined by elements of 44th RTR, as the 150th Brigade battle ended.[88]

On the first day Major Whitaker, C.O. of 44th RTR's B echelon, was positioned near Brigade HQ, and so were constantly chased by shellfire by approaching Axis columns. The battle position for the echelon was near Naduret et Ghesceuasc. However, with Panzerarmee now approaching from the south, they set out with six vehicles in tow, and moved north-east for eight miles, halting behind a mass of queuing vehicles. 'Congestion was terrific, all waiting their turn to go one of two ways down the escarpment.'[89] The resourceful major found another route down and held onto 12 vehicles, but the rest remained stuck behind a broken-down truck.[90] They crossed the next escarpment using the Axis road, and saw, 'smoke rising from many points' on the traffic-jammed southern ridgeline. His party was shelled again, now from the east and so they continued north into the Tobruk perimeter with 12 HQ vehicles. They were able to rejoin the Brigade two days later.

The battalion fitters also played a vital part in keeping the sabre squadrons going with working tanks. Their story gives a glimpse of the difficulties they worked under, and of their concern for the fate of the unit. They constantly followed the squadrons, tending broken-down tanks, or recovering knocked out ones, many times under MG fire. In leaguer, a workshop of four lorries was set up, with tanks arriving on transporters by midnight. Like many workshops, they worked through the night to repair the damaged tanks. Three tanks were ready at first light and a total of eleven on the second day of the battle. The workshop and leaguer were driven north as Panzerarmee took over the ridges north and east of the 150th Box, so they located with 69th Brigade. They remained busy working on many tanks needing repair. Attempts were made over 29–30 May to get fitters into the 150th Box to repair the dwindling numbers of 44th

---

88　TNA WO 169/4521: 44th RTR War Diary, May to 2 June 1942, 27 May, A Echelon Report.
89　TNA WO 169/4521: 44th RTR War Diary, May to 2 June 1942, B echelon report, 27 May 1942.
90　This was a typical occurrence at Gazala, with many columns blocked on escarpment tracks and blocked by an unlucky vehicle, often accompanied by enemy shells raining down on them.

RTR tanks. The mechanics realised that the situation did not look good for their fellow tank crews, as communication was lost. With their battalion lost for now, on 1 June they handed over their supplies to 69th Brigade and rejoined the rest of the battalion echelon east of Tobruk.[91]

It had been a dramatic first day, which threw British battle plans into chaos and heavily damaged many key units. Panzerarmee had successfully made its flank march to the south, surprised some Eighth Army formations and inflicted a good deal of damage to 7th Armoured Division units and HQ. Eighth Army units had fought back hard and inflicted a heavy toll on the vital German tanks. Rommel had pushed 21st Panzer too far north in a bid to cut the coast road, and 90th Light had been scattered in columns far to the east near El Adem, but this caused chaos amongst the numerous B echelon columns poised across the southern plateau in feeding their front line companies and sabre squadrons.

The 15th Panzer Division had been forced to halt, out of ammunition and fuel, on the Rigel Ridge, northeast of Knightsbridge, but this position divided British front line units from their supply routes along the Trigh Capuzzo. DAK said that much of 28 May included each Division reorganising to some extent. 15th Panzer said it had only 29 tanks in the early morning, the artillery was weakened, one rifle battalion had been dispersed and it was short of ammunition. XX Italian Corps was ordered to advance and make progress through the minefield, to improve the supply situation.[92] The Axis supply remained precarious, and they were soon forced to 'hedgehog' in the cauldron, to await the opening of new gaps in the minefield to get their supply echelons running again. Eighth Army, with weakened armoured regiments, would struggle to break through to the Cauldron, to save the beleaguered 150th Brigade.

---

91   TNA WO 169/4521: 44th RTR War Diary, May to 2 June 1942, Supplement to A echelon Diary, 7 June 1942.
92   IWM: AL833: DAK War Diary, 28 May 1942.

5

Cauldron

> *What did I see in the desert to-day,*
> *Where the frantic lizard runs?*
> *The song of death was shouted forth*
> *As the gunners manned the guns.*
> *The men who'd pledged for Motherland*
> *Their freedom and their lives,*
> *Swore as they sweated in the smoke*
> *To man the Twenty-fives.*
>
> 'In the Desert To-day'
> Bombardier L. Challoner[1]

The central cauldron sector of the battlefield, bordered by Tamar Ridge to the north and the Aslagh Ridge to the east, with minefields to the south and west, contributed heavily to the defeat of Eighth Army. Here Brigadier Haydon's 150th Brigade was worn down and overrun in their oversized and hastily set up box by 1 June. It was also where Panzerarmee regrouped and shortened its supply routes by opening up two routes through the minefields. Captain P. F. Stewart of the 12th Lancers, said that by 1 June, the Axis had expanded the two gaps they created into a, 'ten miles wide gash,' which contributed the supplies Rommel needed to force the demise of 150th Brigade.[2] The cauldron was also attacked on 5 June when Eighth Army finally attempted a full-scale assault (Operation Aberdeen) onto what they presumed was a weakened Panzerarmee. This attack was made by two brigades from 5th Indian Division, supported by a rebuilt 22nd Armoured Brigade. It was a failure which resulted in the armoured brigade again suffering heavy losses, while the remaining

---

1 Anon., *Poems from the Desert. Verses by members of the Eighth Army* (London: Harrap, 1944), p.13,
2 Stewart, *XII Royal Lancers*, p.393.

infantry and artillery units retreated or were overrun and forced to surrender. The defeats in the cauldron led directly to more Axis pressure against Bir Hacheim, through increased bombardment and air attacks and later more direct pressure on Knightsbridge. Panzerarmee consolidated its position in the cauldron and undermined the Gazala line, holding the Tamar and Aslagh ridges. Axis columns could also now shell the exposed Knightsbridge box, which suddenly became the 'corner' of Eighth Army's new front line. For the armoured brigades, manoeuvring around or pivoting on Knightsbridge became more difficult, as they continued to engage the Axis held ridges. The early loss of the cauldron area had undermined Eighth Army defences and given Panzerarmee time and space to reorganise before striking out once again.

This early control of the ridges and the undulating ground between them successfully isolated the 150th Brigade at Sidi Muftah and enabled Rommel to focus on its early destruction. Meanwhile Eighth Army commanders were slow to alleviate the pressure on the Brigade, leaving the armoured brigades to make fruitless attacks on the surrounding Axis ridges. If the Tamar Ridge had been held by a stronger force in the first few days, more than just the mobile reserve, Panzerarmee might have been forced to regroup further south, e.g. on the plain north-east of Bir Hacheim, in a much less favourable position for defence, and 150th Brigade would have maintained a supply link back to Eighth Army.

In late April the move by 150th Brigade from Bir Geff to the Got el Ualeb, giving them a month to prepare a new 'keep' in the centre of the mine marshes, covering both Trigh Capuzzo and the Trigh el Abd, which were approximately four miles apart. This was a demanding role for a single infantry brigade. The 4th East Yorks deployed at the Rotunda Ualeb, covering the Trigh el Abd in the south-west. In the north-west, 4th Green Howards covered the Trigh Capuzzo, leaving 5th Green Howards as a central reserve.[3] Lieutenant Dan Billany said these last-minute moves caused disruption, and his unit ended up in shell scrapes which was maddening after they had prepared so well at Bir Geff, the new site was much more difficult to dig in.[4] Lieutenant Colonel Bush said that the defences were 'fightable' by 27 May, though they struggled to get any pneumatic drills, and had little barbed wire. They managed to surround the position with additional mines, though evidently the gaps in the mine-marsh along the front line remained.[5] On the eastern side, Lieutenant Cowtan of the Royal Engineers said their sector was unprotected by wire and mines, and this caused them to be overrun during the battle.[6] After the battle the Germans praised the quality of the position, the, 'camouflage and adaptation to terrain…supported by dug in tanks, [which]…was noteworthy.'[7]

---

3   Bush, *150th Infantry Brigade*, pp.16–17.
4   Dan Billany, *The Trap* (London: Panther, 1964), pp.263–265.
5   Bush, *150th Infantry Brigade*, p.17.
6   Cowtans, *From the Gazala line*, p.41.
7   IWM: AL833: DAK War Diary, 1 June 1942.

The obvious problem was that the distance between the three battalions was too far, so that standing patrols were needed to link the flanks of each battalion and pick up Axis patrols moving in between. The battalions also remained active with jock columns patrolling aggressively to the west, harassing enemy units, taking prisoners and destroying isolated vehicles. As Panzerarmee rolled south on 26 May, the brigade jock column was forced to fire and retire south in bounds, across the brigade front, which was the clear direction of advance as far as their observers were concerned.[8]

By 0900 hours on 27 May they heard the sound of a major battle from Bir Harmat, 11 miles to their rear. The first direct Axis moves towards them were probing attacks by small units through the mine-marsh. One company of 12 Italian tanks advanced and forced the patrol from 4th East Yorks back. The Italians moved about a mile and a half into the minefield, where they were shelled by 285 Battery, which forced the crews to rapidly abandon their tanks – complete with suitcases! Brigadier Haydon then ordered a party of sappers to finish them off and Lieutenant John Cowtan led his sappers via an unmarked patrol lane in the minefield following an inner wire to the line of abandoned tanks. They placed extra mines inside the tanks, poured fuel over everything and connected them up to a single fuse. The resulting explosion looked very impressive and set off the remaining ammunition, but one tank remained largely unscathed so Cowtans was ordered back to ensure it was destroyed.[9]

In the north, near the Trigh Capuzzo, the 4th Green Howards (4th GH) standing patrol was also driven in. Captain A. P. Mitchell then led a mixed fighting patrol of MGs, mortars and AT guns out to capture a low ridge less than a mile in front of the forward platoons, which became known as 'disputed ridge' from then on, because of the tenacity of the battles for it. Keeping the Italian OPs and guns away from the ridge enabled 4th GH to hold their main position throughout.[10] Captain Mitchell's C Company engaged the enemy despite heavy shelling, and inflicted heavy casualties on an enemy company. The second in command of 4th Green Howards, Major d'Arcy Mander, said that the territorial soldiers fought tenaciously even when the Germans broke through the minefields, and this made the Axis troops hold back in the later stages of the battle.[11]

Another factor which contributed to the demise of the Brigade was the lack of re-supply mainly for ammunition. The gunners had numerous targets over the five days and yet were quickly rationed to just 30 rounds per day per gun. This meant they could often see the enemy forming up for an attack but could do little about it. With Panzerarmee holding the perimeter of the Cauldron, little or nothing could get through, though the South Africans and others did try. The Brigade also picked up numbers of Axis troops who were often lost in this confusing, undulating ground.

8 Bush, *150th Infantry Brigade,* pp.20–21.
9 Cowtan, *From the Gazala Line,* pp.38–39.
10 Bush, *150th Infantry Brigade,* p.21.
11 Darcy Mander, *Mander's March on Rome* (Gloucester: Alan Sutton, 1987), p.4.

One Italian artillery commander was picked up by a patrol and thought he was near Tobruk. The stolid Yorkshiremen thought the Axis troops at times seemed to have poor navigation skills and poor maps.[12]

By 28 May the biggest set-back was that the divisional mobile reserve had been pushed off the Aslagh ridge by a large force of enemy tanks and troops, which left the brigade isolated. The main position was shelled steadily throughout the day, which allowed some Italian units in the west to infiltrate the mine-marshes to the north of Capuzzo and south of Ualeb. Here, the two remaining companies from 4th East Yorks could not hold such an extended position and prevent the Italians from lifting the mines. By the late evening, vehicles were pouring through the southern gap to resupply Panzerarmee. Overnight, Haydon was forced to reduce the perimeter, so that all points were covered by the forward companies. The East Yorks and 286th Battery spent the night moving guns, boxes of ammunition and water cans to new positions and digging them in again. Battleaxe medium Battery ended up in a more exposed position because there was no other choice, and D Company 4th East Yorks rejoined them from the mobile reserve.[13]

In the rear, facing Bir Harmat, the mobile divisional reserve had played an important part in attacking the Panzer divisions from the west. This group was led by the HQ of 1st Army Tank Brigade, 44th RTR and B Squadron from 42nd RTR, along with 287th Battery RA and 6th Green Howards. In the morning, the Reserve occupied the Bir Aslagh ridge and shelled enemy columns heading north along the Hacheim track. By mid-afternoon the 'I' tanks attacked north-east towards 'Wriggle' ridge (Pt.166 height, west of Knightsbridge). Unfortunately, enemy anti-tank guns were already established there so they lost a number of tanks, but inflicted considerable damage on the Axis MET.[14] Later on they made a second attack towards Knightsbridge and destroyed or damaged a large number of MET and guns, but C Squadron/44th RTR came under heavy anti-tank fire and had to request smoke cover to withdraw.[15] The Reserve lost 14 Valentines and nearly 20 men, but recovered five tanks later. That night B and C Squadrons/44th RTR were combined, so the reserve now only had three squadrons remaining.

The second day was another difficult day, with 44th RTR already reduced, from first light two squadrons of 'I' tanks (A Squadron 44th RTR and B Squadron 42nd RTR) along with 6th Green Howards, they took up a position to cut the Hacheim track, near Knightsbridge. B Squadron quickly knocked out 11 enemy tanks without loss. Enemy forces were then seen gathering over on the B.100 height on the Aslagh ridge, so 44th RTR deployed facing south to receive an attack from there while 22nd Armoured Brigade were expected to strike them in the flank from the east. However,

---

12 Bush, *150th Infantry Brigade*, p.25.
13 Bush, *150th Infantry Brigade*, pp.25–28.
14 TNA WO169/4199: 1st Army Tank Brigade War Diary, 27 May 1942.
15 Bush, *150th Infantry Brigade*, p.22.

the latter were unable to cooperate, so the 25pdrs from 287th Battery, engaged Axis vehicles along the Hacheim track. By late afternoon another large enemy force moved north and attacked the Reserve in the flank. This forced the two squadrons from 44th RTR to retire north and then west along the Tamar Ridge. They noted German 88mm guns being brought forward, unusually being towed by heavy French Somua tanks. The tanks rallied west at Bir et Tamar and later rejoined the 150th Brigade in the box. The 6th Green Howards were escorted back to 69th Brigade.[16] The more powerful Axis columns had forced the mobile reserve off Aslagh Ridge. Corps HQ should have paid more attention to retaining control of these ridges, because they would be the focus of further battles and 150th Brigade was now cut-off from the rest of the army.

The following day, 29 May, was a day of major armoured battles to the northeast of Sidi Muftah. The 150th Brigade focused on repelling attacks in the west, on the disputed ridge, and in the south against 5th Green Howards. Unfortunately the supporting guns were restricted to 20 rounds per day, so the enemy simply kept out of MG range and spread out along the southern edge of the perimeter, which only had a thin layer of mines and wire. In the east, 4th East Yorks laid a new minefield 1,000 yards long to link with the right of the 4th Green Howards and the engineers watching from Pt.174, a small but important height in the middle of the cauldron. Bush said that the engineers had their own defences of mines et cetera, but Lieutenant Cowtan said they were unprotected, and their few slit trenches were open to attack.[17] Spare gunners and drivers were set up as a new platoon in the front line. The medium guns of Battleaxe Battery (4.5in guns) shelled the enemy constantly but received over 700 rounds in return on their exposed position and suffered the loss of one gun and crew from a direct hit. The 286th battery lost their C.O. to shelling, the second commander to be killed in three days. The RAF mistakenly bombed 4th Green Howards and the stolid infantry brought down the Fiesler Storch light aircraft, carrying General Crüwell, who was extracted north to 69th Brigade.[18] Major Mander interviewed him at the battalion HQ dug-out, and had to apologise to the General for being rude.[19]

Forty-Fourth RTR, plus one squadron from 42nd RTR, both provided invaluable support to the brigade. One squadron provided escort for a small supply column into the box and took the 6th Green Howards out to rejoin 69th Brigade, taking the unlucky General Crüwell with them. Later, the weary A Squadron returned by 0400 hours, 30 May. The 'I' tanks deployed around the brigade box in hull down positions for added morale and fire support. Brigadier Haydon praised them for their indomitable high morale and good spirits. The eastern side of the box remained weaker when D Company 4th East Yorks were delayed joining the forward line and they spent an

---

16 TNA WO169/4199: 1st Army Tank Brigade War Diary, 28 May 1942.
17 Cowtan, *From the Gazala Line*, p.41.
18 Bush, *150th Infantry Brigade*, p.30.
19 Mander, *Mander's March on Rome*, p.5.

uncomfortable day under heavy shellfire, trying to dig in. Other platoons were also worn out making regular night patrols of up to 10 miles. They often attacked enemy work parties, as Panzerarmee dug in their guns.

At dawn on 30 May, the brigade suffered the loss of the key Pt.174 in the east. The Axis sent in a major tank and infantry attack to capture the height from the engineers, who were caught unawares and taken prisoner. Forty-Second RTR attempted to counterattack under cover of a smoke screen but were caught moving through the minefield and were hit at long range. They halted, hull down and contested the forward slopes with gun fire. The East Yorks also put in a company attack but they failed to prevent the enemy battlegroup from achieving full observation across the rest of the box.[20] The rest of the day remained a trying one for the brigade; 4th Green Howards finally lost control of disputed ridge and the popular Major Brian Jackson was mortally wounded. In the south-west, 5th Green Howards continued a day-long duel of mortars and MG fire with enemy groups who had closed up to the wire to keep the forward slit trenches under a constant barrage. Lance Sergeant Cass was commended for fighting on until he used up all of his mortar bombs. On the east face, Axis troops attacked D Company East Yorks and this was blunted by a carrier patrol under Major Fox. He and his driver charged across the forward minefield to engage the infantry using grenades, pistol and LMG. He was mortally wounded returning across the minefield and died later in captivity. Some prisoners from 21st Panzer were taken, who made a later half-hearted attack from the south-west. This may have been to register the position of 150th Brigade guns for further attacks the next day.[21] That night, brigade morale was improved as they watched an 'I' Regiment trying to break through to them. General Ritchie sent the brigade a message, "'Well done, hit hard and hit again,'" which apparently also cheered them.[22]

Pressure on the brigade increased on 31 May which began with further heavy shelling. Enemy armour moved in from the west and in the east behind Pt.174, further attacks seemed imminent. The defenders noted that heavy artillery was being used to bombard their positions by the dud shells which fell among them. The intense shelling finally forced the 4th Green Howards off their ridge and it was difficult to get through to the forward trenches. Enemy attacks overran the 4th East Yorks' D Company, and their supporting guns from F Troop, 286th Battery and a troop of Bofors AA guns. The defenders fought valiantly until 1600 hours, with 2nd Lieutenant Farmiloe pumping 40mm shells into a Mk IV, 400 yards away, until he and his crew were hit and wounded. Both Captain Good from D Company and Captain Pybus from 286th Battery were killed and only four men escaped capture from the company position.[23] South-east of Pt.174, another enemy attack used Sdfk 251 carriers to drive right onto

20   Bush, *150th Infantry Brigade*, pp.30–33.
21   TNA WO 169/5021: 5th Green Howards War Diary, 1942, Appendix A, p.2.
22   Bush, *150th Infantry Brigade*, pp.34–35.
23   Bush, *150th Infantry Brigade*, pp.36–37.

the position. They struck the junction between A Company, 4th East Yorks and HQ Company, 5th Green Howards, where there was no minefield. The attached 25pdrs and one Bofors gun blazed away, doing heavy damage until all guns were knocked out by the massed enemy guns on Pt.174. Troops from both HQ Companies put in a later counterattack and restored the position. The 'I' tanks were rushed from one part to another repelling or making attacks. After one such attack some German and Italian tanks counter-attacked again and broke through C Company, 4th East Yorks position, who were then attacked from the front as well and forced to surrender, creating a gap in the eastern side.[24]

Fresh German tanks and troops bombarded and then attacked 4th Green Howards again after 1600 hours, taping a gap through the minefield and systematically suppressing the slit trenches; the panzers and infantry pushed through these gaps. The supporting medium MG gunners from the Cheshire regiment fought on until they were killed at close range, and the enemy withdrew. Captain Watson led some carriers forward and re-laid the mines.[25] The brigade box had been substantially undermined with the enemy on the east side, but the troops were now also exhausted and low on ammunition. There were six medium guns left and twelve 25pdrs with less than 100 rounds of ammunition, along with 13 'I' tanks. The 2pdr guns had all been knocked out, and only a few Bofors and MMGs remained. Despite the long hours and shortages of water, the troops themselves remained in good spirits.

1 June, Sidi Muftah

Overnight both sides repositioned units. Brigadier Haydon moved the various guns, tanks and companies into two defence posts, based on 4th Green Howards at Sidi Muftah and 5th Green Howards three miles south of them, holding a two-mile front, although this was still an extended position for two weakened units. Major General Lumsden had radioed earlier that morning that his plans had been countered and that his tanks, 'cannot reach you before mid-day.'[26] Though this was wishful thinking. The DAK sent in both 15th and 21st Panzer battlegroups, supported by a heavy Stuka attack at 0800 hours. The defenders remained stubborn and so 90th Light attacked from the south, and Trieste from the south-west 'The encircled enemy [British] resists stubbornly. In places positions had to be taken bunker by bunker in hand-to-hand fighting.' They took a considerable number of prisoners.[27] The Axis tanks came from the north into 4th Green Howards, and they broke into B Company's positions and then exploited left and right to overrun C Company near the mine-marsh. The

24 TNA WO 169/5021: 5th Green Howards War Diary, 1942, Appendix A, p.3.
25 Bush, *150th Infantry Brigade*, p.38.
26 Bush, 150th Infantry Brigade, p.40.
27 IWM: AL833: DAK War Diary, 1 June 42.

supporting 'I' tanks moved south-east to cut across the enemy thrusts, but were themselves hit by anti-tank guns from both flanks. Only one 'I' tank reached 32nd AT HQ to fight on from there. The northern flank was crumbling, and Brigadier Haydon told certain officers to escape north to 69th Brigade.

By 0900 hours, Major Williamson had two remaining 'crock' tanks moving and they headed for the secret gap in the west mine-marsh. He met Brigadier Haydon's party amidst all the shelling across D Company area. The Brigadier was coming across to speak to him when a shell burst very close and he was killed instantly by a splinter through the chest. Lieutenant Col. Cooper at HQ told the rest of D Company to disperse through the minefield and escape as best they could. The gunners destroyed or spiked their guns with the last few rounds, and they also attempted to break out. The enemy used shelling and MG fire to deter those trying to get away so only a few of the 4th Green Howards escaped.

Three miles to the south the troop of 25pdrs attached to 5th Green Howards was undermined by a charging group of Mk IV tanks who closed in at dawn and set the ammunition boxes and quads alight. The Germans then deployed Marders, 50mm AT guns and 20mm guns putting down a murderous concentration of fire on the Green Howards' trenches. The mortars fired until all bombs were used, the platoons fought on, being suppressed one by one. The enemy used overwhelming fire from the guns on vehicles. D Troop, 451st Battery held off the enemy from the north-east coming into the battalion rear. Captain Hook of 4th E Yorks led three carriers out to flank some anti-gun guns and was killed. The enemy used Red Cross vehicles and flags to mark the company positions. By late morning the remaining platoons were under fire from two directions. B Company held out the longest until 1400 hours. Lieutenant Bray manned the last 2pdr until it received a direct hit. Captain Dennis and 10 platoon were the last to surrender.[28]

This last battle had ranged across the repositioned dressing station, filled with large numbers of wounded, under Major Prosser. Many wounded died on the long journey west to prison camps, mainly due to lack of water. The brigade had been the focus of attacks made by Panzerarmee, from 29 May until 1 June. The South Africans and 50th Division had tried to save them with ammunition columns, but without a major attack, they failed. One column of trucks gathered early on 1 June, south of Knightsbridge, and they spent the day being passed around Brigade HQs with conflicting orders from XIII Corps. By late afternoon an escaped corporal from 4th Green Howards told them they were too late, the brigade had been overrun that morning. To add insult to injury, as the convoy and others attempted to return back through the minefield north of Hacheim, they were rounded up themselves by armoured cars from 90th Light Division. It was a dismal end to save 150th Brigade, again highlighting the lack of urgency by various HQs throughout the battle.

---

28   Bush, *150th Infantry Brigade*, pp.40–44.

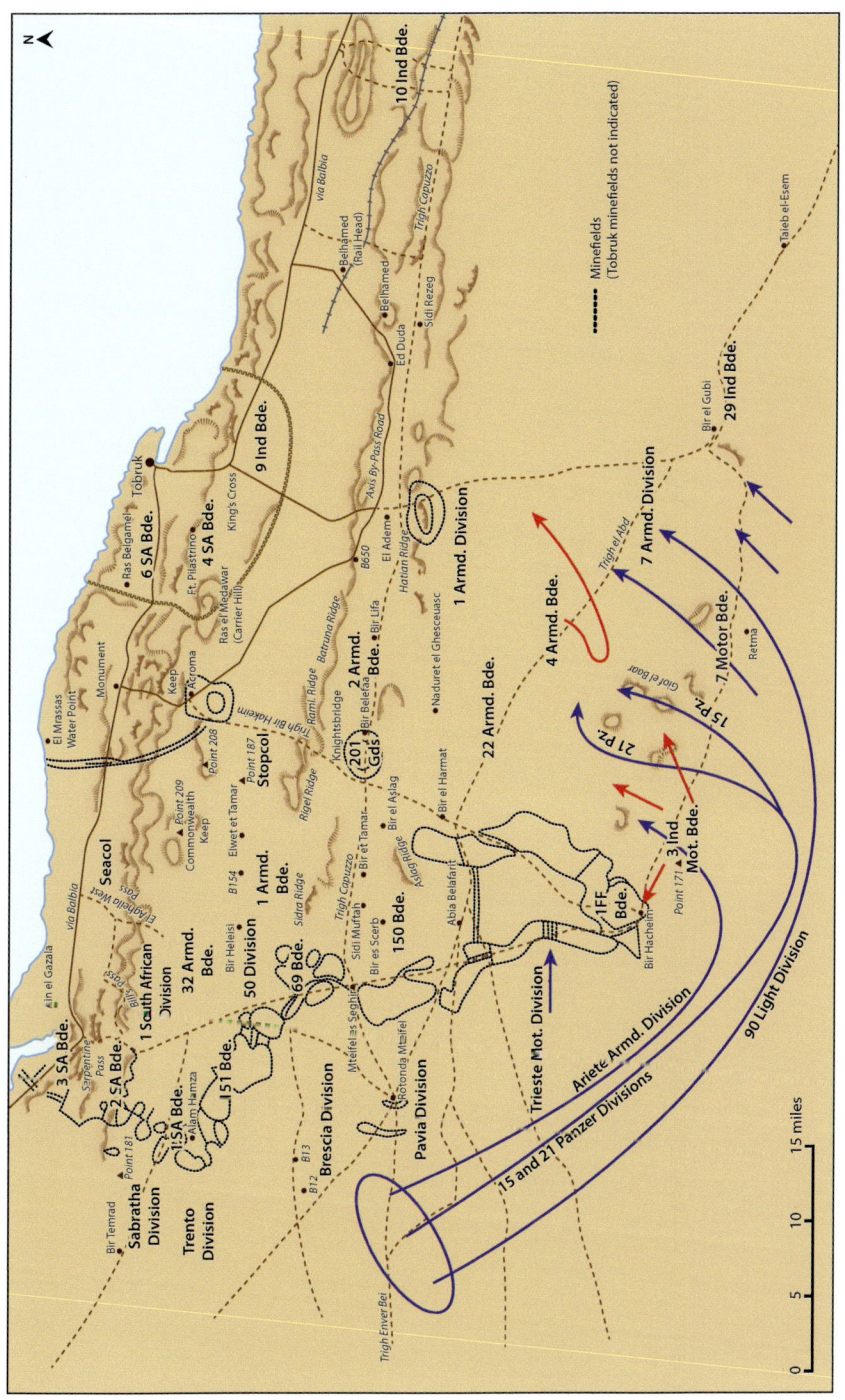

Map 1 The Gazala Position, 27 May 1942.

ii   The Tanks Are Coming Through Now

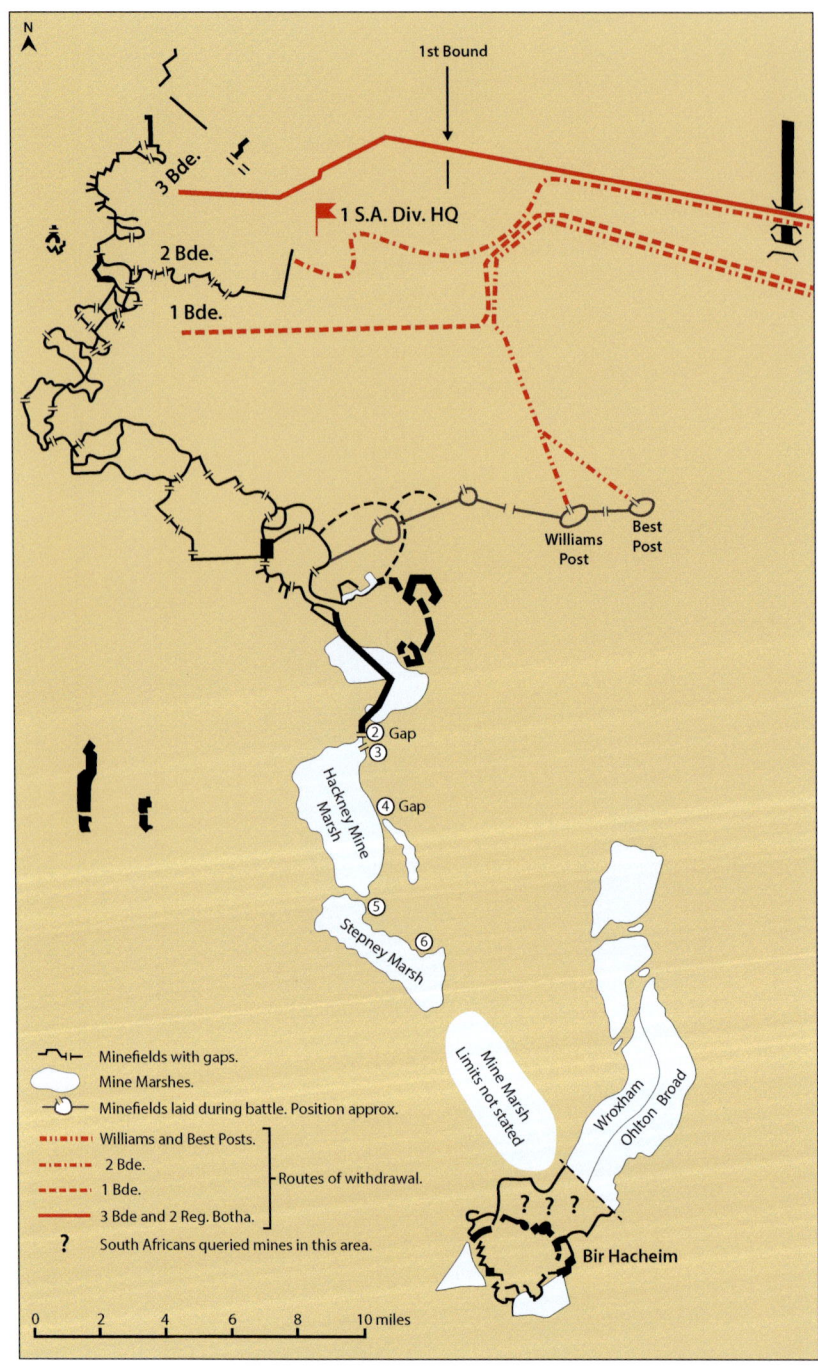

Map 2   Minefields as per South African Map, spring 1942.

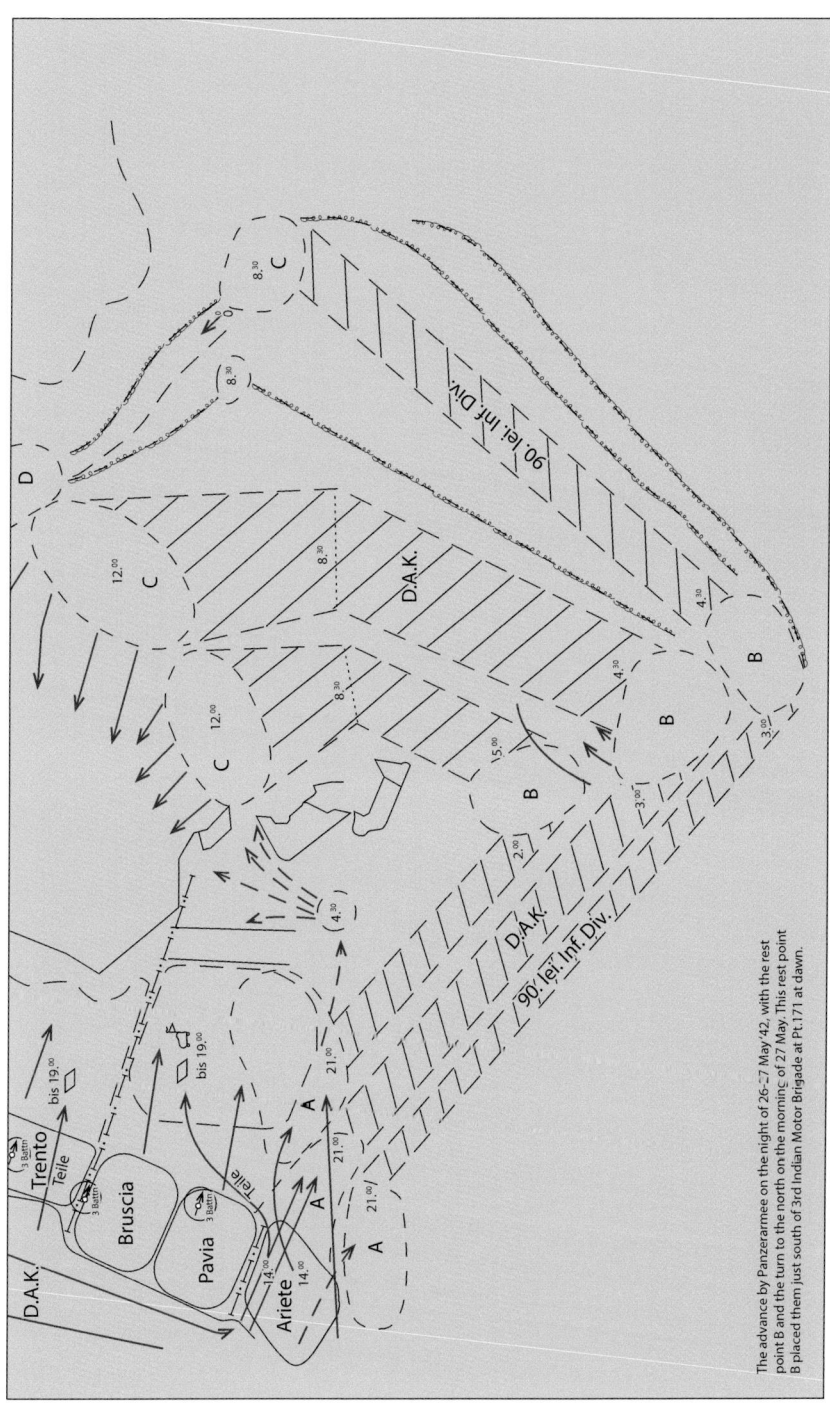

Map 3 Detail from 15th Panzer Division Sketch Map, May 1942.

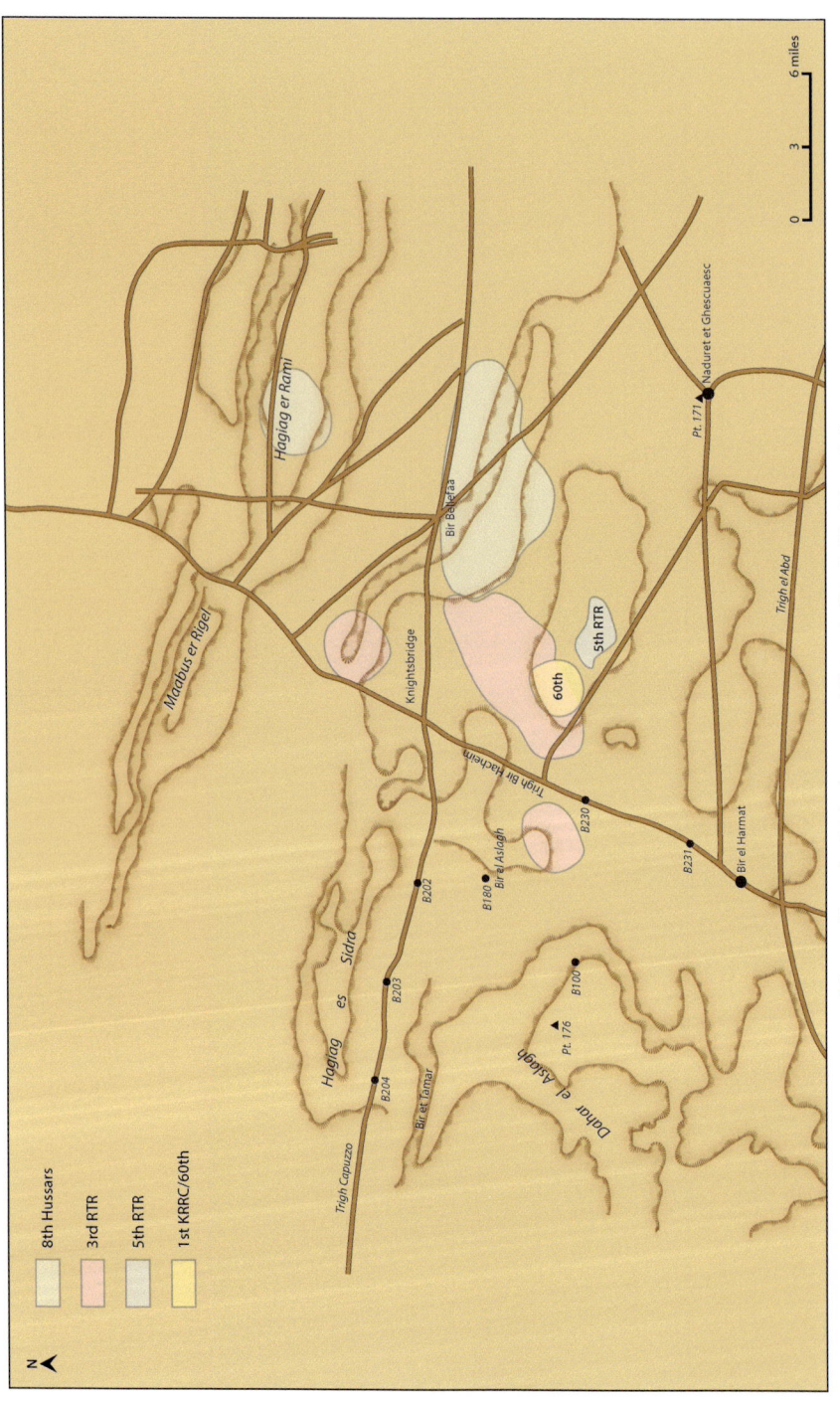

Map 4 Detail of 4th Armoured Brigade Battle Position Ack.
4th Armoured Brigade positions: 60th = 1st KRRC, 5th RTR, red, green yellow = company positions.

Maps v

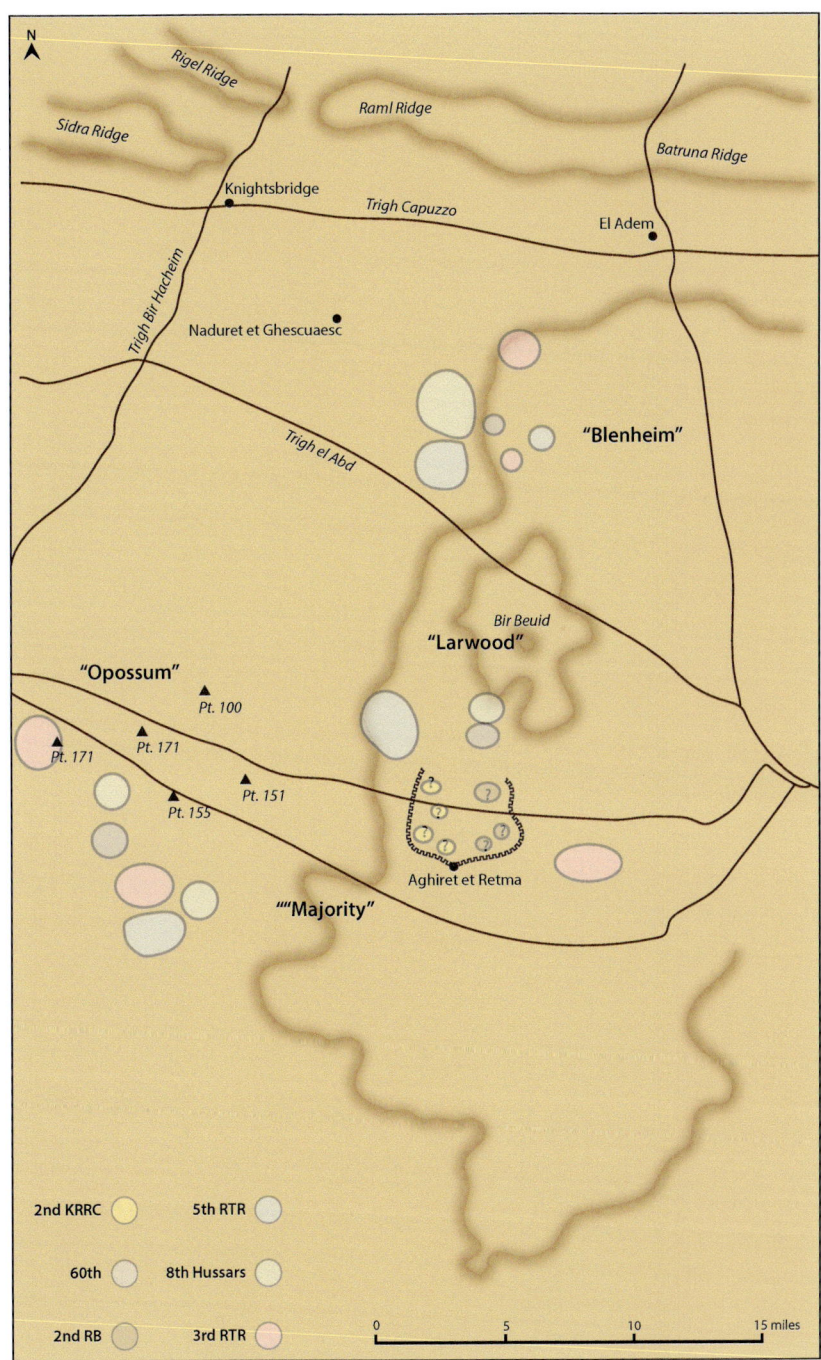

Map 5 4th Armoured Battle Positions South, 27 May 1942.

vi   The Tanks Are Coming Through Now

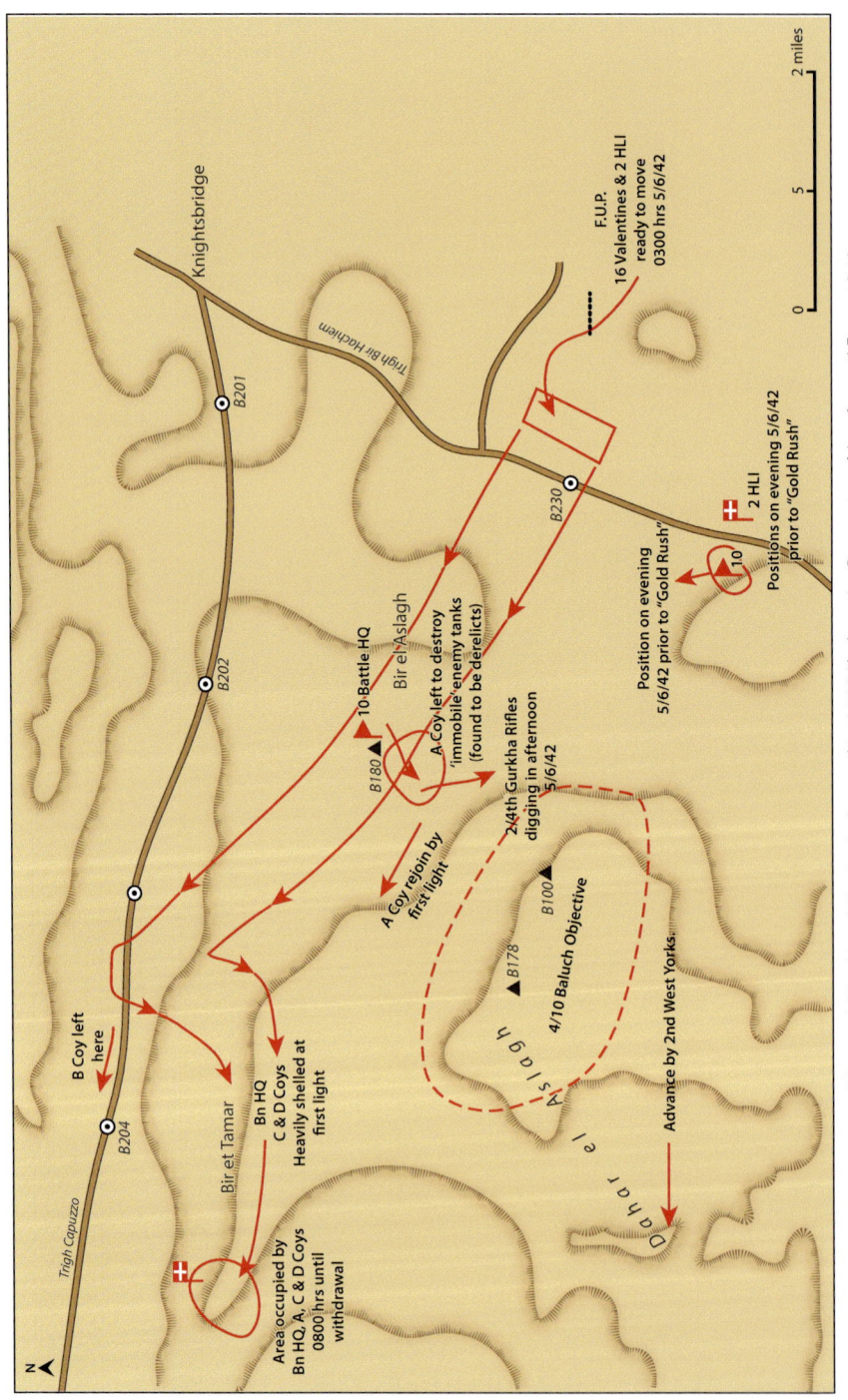

Map 6   The 2nd Highland Light Infantry (2nd HLI) Attack, Operation Aberdeen, 5 June 1942.

Maps vii

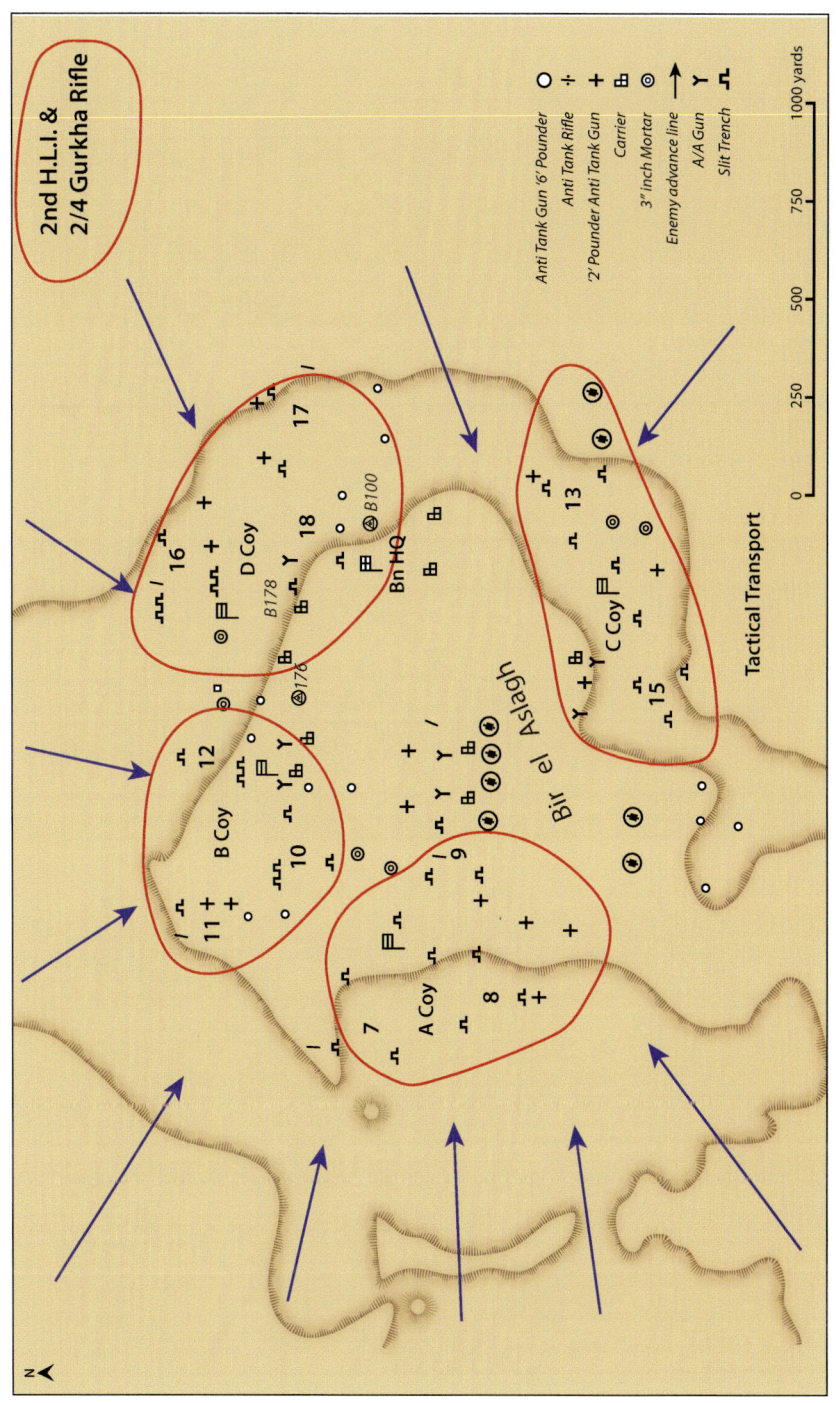

Map 7 4th/10th Baluch Regiment Position on 5–6 June, 1942.

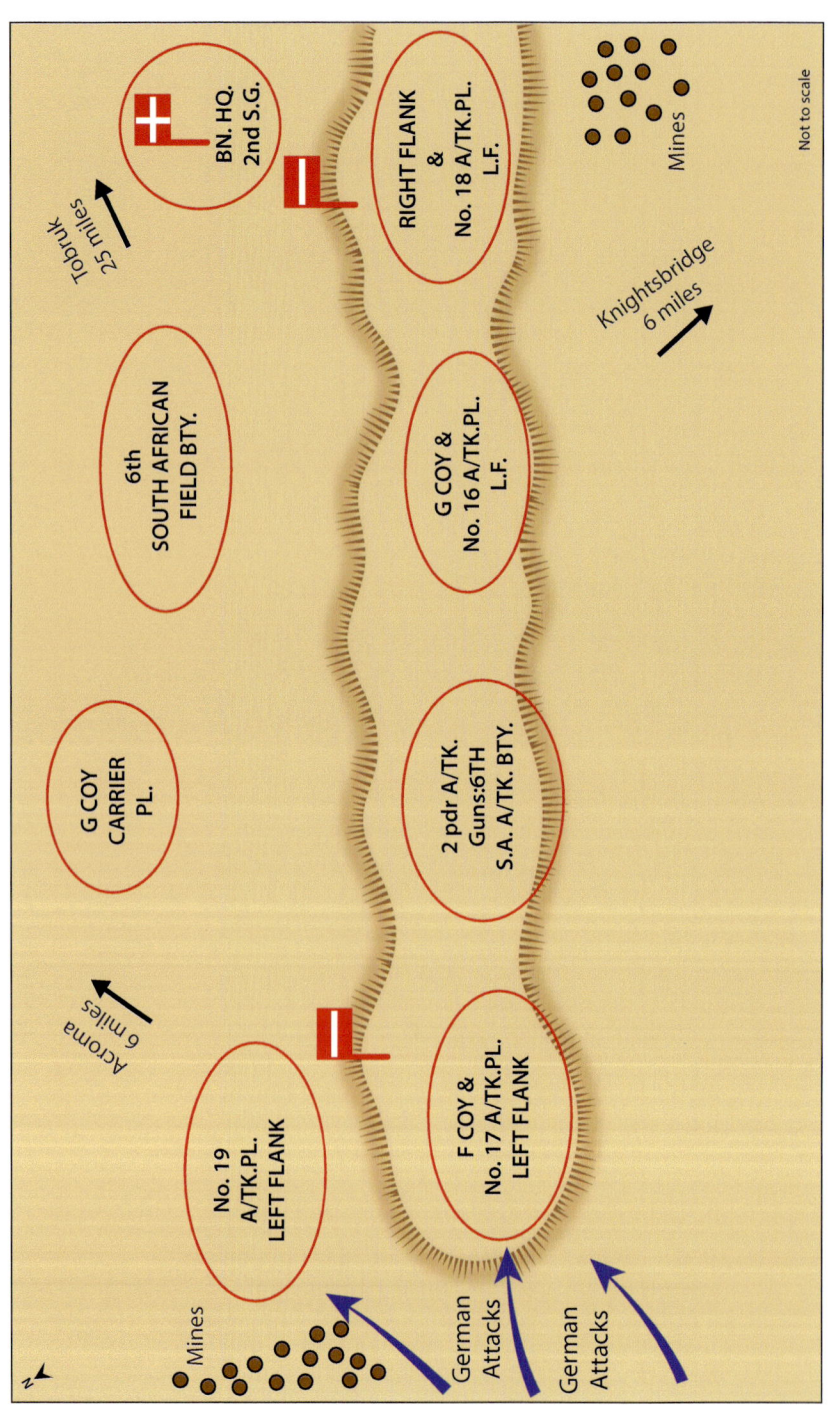

Map 8 The 2/Scots Guards locality, Rigel Ridge.

Operation Aberdeen, 5–6 June

> *The desert, mighty, void of hope, immense,*
> *Disturbed from tortured sleep by sounds of war*
> *… across her brow come men and guns to wrest,*
> *… and so the game is played on age old sands.*
> *Shades of Caesars of a bygone day,*
> *their might decayed, great triumphs turned to dust,*
> *Soon as with them, shall our deeds grow obscure,*
> *Our victories unimportant, efforts vain*
> *Defaced by time. Once more the desert reigns,*
> *Our warfare but a phase, long, long forgot.*
>
> 'Desert Warfare'
> G. Harker, Signalman[29]

Such was the importance of the Cauldron sector that by 1 June, Rommel had directed Panzerarmee to win possession of the ridges around it and he had personally led battlegroups in the destruction of 150th Brigade. By comparison Eighth Army HQ had dithered in planning various attacks to recapture these ridges and re-open the route. They didn't appear to appreciate the difficulties of the terrain or how strong Panzerarmee could be in a 'hedgehog' defence. The ever-present lengthy debates between HQs and with commanders querying orders all added to the delay in any meaningful British response. When they did agree. the main attack on the Cauldron was designated Operation Aberdeen and set for 5 June. Two fresh brigades from 5th Indian Division were brought forward and combined with 22nd Armoured Brigade to make the attack, while the 7th Green Howards would support 32nd Army Tank Brigade in an attack on the Sidra ridge from the north. The battles of 5–6 June also highlighted other problems of cooperation between all three fighting arms. The historiography commonly notes that units were destroyed, while armoured units were said to have largely left the remaining infantry groups to their own devices, but there are some nuances to this debate. The unit diaries give further details about the fate of the units involved and that 22nd Armoured Brigade, though fighting a separated battle, also remained in the Cauldron for much of the day.

Eighth Army plans were made under the misguided impression that Panzerarmee was badly damaged and struggling to hold on. Ritchie believed that one more attack would heavily defeat the 'battered' Axis divisions in the Cauldron, and enable him to, 'proceed with the counter-offensive,' that he was aiming for.[30] Unfortunately, his Corps HQs lacked the decisiveness needed and forced the Divisional commanders

---

29 Anon., *Poems from the Desert*, p.40.
30 TNA WO 201/2692: Operational reports: Western Desert, 1942 May–July, p.10,

into making a rushed plan to attack an enemy that was now firmly ensconced amongst the low ridges of the cauldron.

Operation Aberdeen was meant to be a 'pincer movement,' with 32nd Army Tank Brigade with 7th GH attacking the Sidra Ridge, while 9th and 10th Indian Brigades advanced from the east, across the Aslagh Ridge supported by 4th RTR.[31] Next the more experienced 22nd Armoured Brigade would pass through the waiting infantry/gun line and defeat the Axis armour. Planning was hasty and both corps commanders questioned the orders and then abdicated responsibility to the divisional commanders.[32] This left 5th Indian's Major General H. R. Briggs and Maj-General Messervy from 7th Armoured Division, struggling to develop an attack.[33] General Briggs took less than a day to organise the opening phase of the operation and coordinate details.[34] By 4 June 22nd Armoured Brigade had supposedly been rebuilt to 156 tanks, but 2nd Royal Gloucestershire Hussars stated that they only had 44 vehicles, not the full complement of 52. One squadron within each regiment consisted of Grants, the 2nd RGH had lighter Honeys, while 3rd and 4th CLY/Sharpshooters had Crusaders for the two cruiser squadrons and HQ vehicles.[35] Strength returns show the infantry battalions were near full strength with 700–850 men each and the two brigades had their accompanying artillery regiments of twent-four guns in three batteries. The 9th Indian Brigade consisted of 2nd West Yorks, 3/9th Jats and 3/12th Frontier Force Regiment (the Piffers), and 10th Indian Brigade had 2nd Highland Light Infantry, the 2/4th Gurkhas and 4/10th Baluchs. Additional new units would also be committed into the battle. On 5 June, 1st DCLI arrived and were sent to cover the left flank along the Hacheim track. There were numerous supply echelon columns that went forward to replenish the frontline units, though not all of these were deployed in the forward localities, and some later escaped destruction or capture.

The attacks included two of the most famous actions of Gazala, the failed northern flank attack on the Sidra Ridge by 32nd Army Tank Brigade, who lost some 50 Matildas, and the destruction of the South Notts Hussars (107th RHA) in the Cauldron.[36] Peter Mead's history shows how the other artillery regiments suffered a similar fate to the South Notts Hussars.[37] Other participants including Captain Wiberg and Major Pitman add more detail about the battle.[38] The infantry brigades

---

31 TNA WO 201/2692: Operational reports: Western Desert, 1942 May–July, p.12,
32 N.S. Nash, *Strafer. Desert General: The Life and Killing of Lieutenant General W. H. E. Gott* (Barnsley: Pen & Sword, 2013), p.178.
33 Playfair, *Mediterranean and Middle East. Vol. III*, pp.232–233.
34 Anthony Brett-James, *Ball of Fire: The Fifth Indian Division in the Second World War* (Uckfield: Naval & Military Press, 2014), pp.178–179.
35 TNA WO 169/4494: 2nd Royal Gloucester Hussars War Diary, 4 June 1942.
36 Peter Hart, *The South Notts Hussars, The Western Desert 1940–1942* (Barnsley: Pen & Sword, 2010) pp.190–219.
37 Peter Mead, *Gunners at War 1939–1945* (London: Ian Allan,1982).
38 Pitman, *Second Royal Gloucestershire Hussars Libya-Egypt 1941-1942*.

were thrust into a battle with little chance of success, and they had had no time for any combined training.

Both Messervy and Briggs had been in North Africa for much of the campaign. Briggs had successfully commanded an independent brigade in the Sudan and another brigade at Crusader and in the retreat.[39] He was appointed to 5th Indian Division in early May, as it arrived on the Libyan frontier; his brigades were still divided at first, with some battalions training or in garrisons in the rear, such as in the Tobruk perimeter.[40] Briggs had four weeks at Divisional HQ until 4 June. He said his staff were 'an HQ on ice,' because his units were constantly taken from him and used for other tasks.[41] Aberdeen was his first chance to command both brigades together.

It was Messervy who revised the initial plan, Briggs had suggested an outflanking manoeuvre to threaten Panzerarmee's supply line around Bir Hacheim, whereas Messervy decided on a direct assault. He assumed the Axis were so heavily disorganised that an attack by two infantry brigades with supporting armour would inflict severe damage. Ritchie agreed and, 'intimated…that this attack may be the decisive one of present operations.'[42] More intelligence was provided by Captain Steel from 4/10th Baluchis, who made a detailed report about enemy forces. They expected to encounter a large amount of Axis transport, with 60 German and 50 Italian tanks from two divisions, and elements of Pavia Division and 27th Brescia Division west of the minefield.[43] In reality they encountered powerful battlegroups from both 15th and 21st Panzer Divisions and Ariete Division, with their artillery and anti-tank units fully deployed.

Tactically, the infantry lacked practice in working with armour, so the brigades advanced with one battalion leading almost as a scouting force and two others in support. Mike Peyton watched 2nd HLI, 'jump out of their trucks, form into two lines, fix bayonets and start walking…their objective was the Bir Tamar Ridge about half a mile away and it seemed to take them hours to get there, all the time mortars dropping amongst them and men falling [with] the wail of the pipes, which sounded thin in the vastness of the surroundings.'[44] 22nd Armoured ended up stretched across the Cauldron in a long line between the 9th and 10th Brigades on the high ground either side. With too few troops it was a highly optimistic plan with too many forward objectives.

---

39   Lieutenant Colonel G. R. Stevens, *Fourth Indian Division* (Uckfield: Naval & Military Press, 2011) p.98.
40   TNA WO 169/7775: 3/12th Frontier Force Regiment War Diary, May 1942.
41   Brett-James, *Ball of Fire*, p.177.
42   TNA WO 169/7619: 10th Indian Brigade HQ, Diary, Operational Order No.8, 4 June 1942.
43   TNA WO 169/7770: 4/10th Baluch Regiment War Diary, Notes by Captain I. J. Steel, June 1942. Up to 2000 MET.
44   Mike Peyton, *An Average War* (Chelmsford: Maypole Press, 2014), p.75.

The advance would begin from Bir Harmat, with 10th Indian Brigade and 22nd Armoured Brigade moving west onto Bir Aslagh, one battalion would halt at Pt.176. Then 2nd HLI would advance north-west and take the Tamar Ridge. The armour would move deeper into the cauldron and 'beat-up' any enemy armour, then rally back north-east. Then, 9th Brigade would pass through 10th Brigade's line and establish three battalion boxes, two of these quite deep into the Cauldron. The supporting 'I' tanks would have to lead in 10th Brigade and then move across to lead in 9th Brigade units. Most of the movement was to be at night, using a barrel as the centre line marker, and they were to meet with a battery just arrived from Iraq and 4th RTR who would have already escorted 10th Brigade.[45] It was an ambitious plan.

Brigadier Fletcher of 9th Brigade believed the plan was 'unsound' but remained quiet because he did not want to upset Messervy, viewed as an experienced desert hand.[46] Following the orders issued on 4 June, Captain Wiberg said, 'the attack was mounted in a great hurry…there was an entire absence of detailed information about the enemy, and we were told that we would very likely meet only slight opposition. The haste was deemed necessary and justifiable…' Wiberg was proved right that the intelligence analysis was wrong, and the rushed planning multiplied the difficulties.[47] The 4th CLY noted they expected to, 'mop up the enemy' and [be] … back at B.104, west of Knightsbridge, for breakfast.'[48] Both new and more experienced commanders doubted the plans and did not expect things to be as easy as some suggested. HQs were unsure about where units were located. Major Forbes, 10th Brigade Major, noted that Divisional HQ was 'somewhat vague' about where the B.180 box was. By then they were trying to tie-in with the 50 Recce battalion somewhere just north-west of them.[49]

There was also confusion, which was exacerbated by the moves battalions made as they came into the forward area. The 2/4th Gurkhas arrived at Bir Harmat by 1 June, just in time to be shelled and strafed from nearby Axis positions and endure the nightly bombing raids. Initially, they were ordered to build a 'double battalion box' opposite the mine-gaps code-named 'Peter and Paul' to free up the armoured brigade from observing in the line. Within 24 hours they were planning for the assault into the Cauldron.[50] This attack had originally been planned for 2 June, supported by 'I' tanks and two regiments of artillery, but this was cancelled due to the severe sand-storm, which ended most operations that day.[51] Visibility was down to 20 yards and the C.O. from 4th RTR said the conditions were not suited for tanks, nor could the

---

45   TNA WO 169/7617: 9th Indian Brigade HQ War Diary 1942, Report Annex A, pp.1–2.
46   TNA WO 169/7617: 9th Indian Brigade HQ War Diary 1942, Report Annex A, p.4.
47   Brett-James, *Ball of Fire*, p.184.
48   TNA WO 169/4496: 4th County London Yeomanry War Diary, June 1942.
49   TNA WO 169/7619: 10th Indian Brigade HQ Diary, report 'Events 5 and 6 June 1942.'
50   TNA WO 169/3910: 2/4th Gurkhas War Diary, June 1942.
51   TNA WO 169/3910: 2/4th Gurkhas War Diary, June 1942, Appendix No.1.

4th RA register their guns.[52] Other units were placed in defensive roles as they arrived with no mention of an attack. Next day, 10th Brigade HQ was ordered to plan the attack for 4–5 June. Battalions sent out fighting patrols who found the enemy very alert on the Aslagh Ridge. The brigade also received a second night of heavy bombing which caused very few casualties, but kept most people awake again.

Earlier training by the infantry gave them little opportunity to practice assault tactics. Whereas 22nd Armoured had already been in action for nine days, leaving worn-out crews and tanks in need of replacement. The infantry had been part of the Cyprus garrison from early 1942: while there, 10th Brigade made two practice assaults, attacking on a two-battalion frontage. During Aberdeen they advanced with a single battalion leading and other units making for a separate objective. At Qassassin in April, Brigadier Boucher called for a stronger 'esprit de corps' exchanging British and Indian officers. He wanted tactical ideas disseminated through the use of floor models, as these were the best way for officers to learn quickly, 'it was not possible… to teach more than one method of attempting a tactical manoeuvre, [and that] units… never deployed near any 'dead ground' to avoid surprise.'[53] On Tamar, 2nd HLI ended up near some enemy held dead ground and were forced to retreat as some panzers emerged from the dead ground.

Similarly, 9th Indian Brigade carried out anti-invasion exercises at Limassol, so had not practised any desert assault training. Companies had completed some weapons training, and by the end of April, training covered practising 'cowpat' formations and some desert navigation.[54] The 3/9th Jats joined in early May from Iraq, with little chance to work together, and 2nd West Yorks were unable to practice any brigade assaults before 5 June.[55] They planned some night marches and further defensive training after 16 May, but instead they manned the Tobruk perimeter, and from there went to Bir Harmat.[56] Other newly arrived units suffered from a lack of training. 10th Brigade was joined by 2/4th Gurkhas, from Iraq, (where they had seen some fighting). Arriving at the frontier wire by 27 April they had just one month to get used to Eighth Army methods before operations began. There was some basic training with one day practising a battalion 'cowpat' and a 'brigade cowpat' in May, while platoons went on physical training or anti-tank gunnery courses. Within a week training was halted and they joined the garrison at the Gambut Airfield.[57] This was very little time for them to get to grips with desert formations and the new environment.

Units were expected to carry out new roles at or near the front, the 4th Field Regiment RA arrived on 10 April and was immediately sent forward to the defences

---

52   TNA WO 169/7770: 4/10th Baluch War Diary, 2 June 1942.
53   TNA WO 169/7619: 10th Indian Brigade War Diary, January-March 1942.
54   'Cowpats' were Eighth Army slang for battalion/Brigade defensive boxes, see de Guingand, *Operation Victory*, pp.108–109.
55   TNA WO 169/5077: 2nd West Yorks War Diary, 1942, summary for April to June 1942.
56   TNA WO 169/7617: 9 Indian Brigade HQ War Diary, 1942,
57   TNA WO 169/3910: 2/4th Gurkhas War Diary, May 1942.

at Sollum. More men and guns made it a full regiment of three batteries by May and it was expected to immediately be mobile in jock columns and joined the 4/10th Baluch 'cowpat' in the battle.[58] This regiment's diary is missing pages for May and June, so their experience is related by the Baluchs. The more experienced South Notts Hussars practised box formations in April and May, both as single batteries and as a regiment, but they noted their technical support was far too overstretched to service their 244 vehicles.[59]

Brigadier Boucher's 10th Brigade plans for more training were prevented by moves into the forward area and a lack of knowledge about likely operations. The new units lacked desert knowledge, the 4/10th Baluch discussed training in early May and asked Boucher what a 'jock column' was, as they had been ordered to prepare one. Other delays were caused by the severe dust storms and time needed to settle into garrison duties. Once in the forward area, and with the Axis offensive already underway, much of their time was then taken up with patrols between El Adem and Belhamed to prevent Axis movements along the Trigh Capuzzo. By 29 May, enemy patrols were already using 'British vehicles, with English-speaking officer [with] tin hats' to bluff their way through British lines.[60] 10th Brigade were critical of 'rumour-mongers' who were sapping morale, They noted, 'These gentry were much in evidence on 27 May and should have been liquidated.'[61] Though which gentry they were talking about is less clear. Both brigades had well motivated troops and experienced officers, but they had had little opportunity to become used to Eighth Army methods or fully appreciate what it was to face an experienced Panzerarmee.

The constant moves highlighted the confused nature of orders from Eighth Army HQ. 10th Brigade was first sent to El Mrassas fort, on the coast, behind the South Africans, then to Bir Harmat. This helped them practice desert navigation, but frequent dust storms added more confusion. Lieutenant Colonel Weallens, C.O. of 2/4th Gurkhas, was lost for a day in dust storms, as he reconnoitred the area. There was a lack of orders, so the brigade kept moving, but this cancelled the initial attack planned for early June. The journey was across unfamiliar terrain with enemy nearby. They struggled to cross two escarpments with few available tracks and avoiding Axis positions around Bir Aslagh.[62] The 3/9th Jats were rushed forward to join 9th Brigade, having arrived from Iraq followed by a spell manning the Tobruk perimeter, still new to the brigade.[63]

---

58 TNA WO169/4575: 4th Field Regiment RA, War Diary, April and July 1942; and WO169/7770: 4/10th Baluch Regiment War Diary, account of events 5–6 June 1942.
59 TNA 169/4563: 107th RHA (South Notts Hussars) War Diary, April 1942.
60 TNA WO 169/7619: 10 Indian Brigade War Diary, Summary No.2, 29 May 1942.
61 TNA WO 169/7619: 10 Indian Brigade War Diary, Summary No.2, 29 May 1942.
62 TNA WO 169/3910: 2/4th Gurkhas War Diary, June 1942.
63 TNA WO 169/7677: 3/9th Jats War Diary, May and June 1942, 'Chatty Diary,' as it termed itself.

There were training pamphlets about desert warfare although they lacked detail about the infantry role. The most recent *Notes From Theatres of War (NTW)* No.2 was available from March and No.4 arrived in May.[64] No.3 is not listed in the MLRS volume. Other doctrinal documents included the numerous *Middle East Training Pamphlets* (METPs) with No.2 part 1A covered the tactical handling of an armoured regiment. The pamphlet arrived arrived in May 1942, perhaps just too late to be fully absorbed by the armoured regiments along the frontline. The first advised infantry working with army tanks using night attacks and to keep close to supporting barrages.[65] While *NTW4* expanded on the doctrine of cooperation in battle noting that, army tanks were there, 'to put the infantry onto the objective,' and that, 'cooperation was good only when there was plenty of time to organise attacks…largely due to lack of opportunities for training together beforehand.'[66] Both brigades had no opportunity to meet or work with the supporting armour beforehand and their officers only met on 4 June. The *Notes* further explained that box defences were only effective when properly dug in, anti-tank guns were there to protect the artillery and enemy methods of attack were clearly laid out.[67] We don't know how many of these newly arrived units were given these pamphlets to help them in the coming battle.

First Day, 5 June

Control of the Tamar Ridge was considered vital for the cauldron, and more so than the other ridges, though enemy units along the Aslagh ridge running south also delayed Eighth Army's attempts to breakthrough. General Lumsden had said that controlling these heights, gave full visibility across the Cauldron.[68] Tamar was the objective for the 2nd HLI, supported by the Gurkhas and Baluchis. However, the battalions moved in different directions, towards the separate ridges which were three miles apart, with two companies forward and two in support. The HLI went further along Tamar towards the 'pinnacles', the heights Pt.202, Pt.203 and Pt.204, whereas

---

64 *Notes From Theatres of War No.2: Cyrenaica, November, December,1941*, and *Notes From Theatres of War No.4: Cyrenaica, November 1941, January 1942*, in Michael Taylor (ed.), *The Campaign in North Africa, Part 1 November 1941 to March 1943* (Buxton: MLRS, 2004), and *Middle East Training Pamphlets, Part 1* (Buxton: MLRS, 2011).
65 NTW No. 2: Cyrenaica, November, December 1941 in Michael Taylor (ed.), *The Campaign in North Africa Part 1 November 1941 to March 1943* (Buxton: MLRS, 2004), pp.9–13.
66 NTW No.4: Cyrenaica, November 1941, January 1942 in Michael Taylor (ed.), *The Campaign in North Africa Part 1 November 1941 to March 1943* (Buxton: MLRS, 2004), p.2.
67 NTW No.4: Cyrenaica, November 1941, January 1942 in Michael Taylor (ed.), *The Campaign in North Africa Part 1 November 1941 to March 1943* (Buxton: MLRS, 2004), p.19.
68 TNA WO 201/537: 1st Armoured Division Operations, May–July 1942, p.318.

4/10th Baluch were directed west to the Bir Aslagh ridge. Both C.O.s said that they quickly lost touch with their leading companies in the advance, because of the long distances involved, and both units suffered broken radio links.

The objectives were taken but there was no supporting armour and broken communications meant they never received the fire support needed to hold them. The HLI divided into separate companies across the pinnacles and came under sustained fire from enemy guns. A Company diverted to consolidate one objective, which they said had been thoroughly 'plastered' by the supporting 80 plus guns firing four rounds per minute, for 10 minutes (which is about 3,200 rounds). The advance continued, but navigation proved difficult and B Company became separated and found themselves just short of the pinnacles. They watched the escorting 4th RTR Valentine tanks spray MG tracer fire in all directions and against each other.[69] B.204 was reached and beyond it was a battery of 88mm guns with more tanks, which opened up an accurate and heavy shellfire. This stopped about 0900hrs when elements of 22nd Armoured appeared and also came under fire. The indomitable Captain Bromley-Gardner, who had already been blown out of one carrier, brought orders to withdraw the remnants of this exposed company.[70]

The other two companies also suffered heavy casualties from shelling, as they captured the birs along the ridgeline. Enemy artillery, deployed north of Tamar, fired onto the right flank of the Highlanders. The companies spread themselves across a dip on the southern side of the ridge, digging in with D Company facing west. They could see 22nd Armoured halted nearby but the tanks did not give much help to the infantry. The armour was level with C Company, but were prevented from moving forward by the 88mm guns, unfortunately much of the shellfire directed at the tanks fell into the Highlanders' positions. Lieutenant Colonel Thorburn, was wounded making repeated requests to the armour to advance, but they refused. The dip was a saucer-shaped bowl and the Axis armour soon overlooked them and directed accurate and heavy shelling, which caused constant losses. They were promised some 2pdr guns and so remained there until after midday under intense fire.[71]

Colonel Thorburn realised there was nothing to be gained by holding and ordered the battalion to withdraw, with the 2pdrs covering the retreat. C Company was enfiladed and nearly trapped as they withdrew through a 'murderous hail of fire.' By 1315hrs the HQ and few remaining men covered the withdrawal back to the B.180 box and later they returned to the Hacheim track. It had been a tough day and costly day for them.[72] Lieutenant Colonel Thorburn sited his 2pdr guns and stood on a nearby tank to act as spotter for them, despite enemy tanks firing at them from within 500

69   TNA WO 169/5024: 2nd Highland LI War Diary, Bir et Tamar Report, 5 June 1942.
70   TNA WO 169/5024: 2nd Highland LI War Diary, Bir et Tamar Report, 5 June 1942.
71   TNA WO 169/5024: 2nd Highland Light Infantry War Diary, Bir et Tamar Report, 5 June 1942.
72   TNA WO 169/5024: 2nd Highland Light Infantry War Diary, Bir et Tamar Report, 5 June 1942.

yards.[73] He was later wounded in the head; he refused at first to be evacuated but was eventually moved to the rear dressing station.[74] He was one of the last men to retreat and was awarded the DSO. Brigadier Boucher was less fortunate and was captured later that evening as he attempted to regroup the various units around the B.180 box. The rest of the HQ was forced to retire by the 15th Panzer counterattack. Boucher's capture and the retreat by Brigade HQ prevented plans to save the forward units the next day, so the two remaining battalions were left isolated.

The 4/10th Baluchs had a more successful start and captured Pt.176 quickly and began digging in. Captain Steel noted they were 'well down' by mid-morning, with slit trenches up to five feet deep. A and C Companies struggled to dig in to three feet deep.[75] They suffered a constant low level shelling all day and watched as some nearby armour lost seven tanks and had ten replacements come up. They were prepared for tank attacks all afternoon as shelling became more intense. The Baluchs were later joined by 4th Field Regiment RA and awaited the next day's events. Lieutenant Colonel Sundius-Smith, the C.O., reported the enemy attacked using four captured 25pdrs and firing from the right flank which completely overlooked their position.

Many involved were told little of what was meant to be happening in the battle. Captain M. E. Parker commanded an AT battery attached to 10th Indian Brigade. He was told very little about why they were advancing, then the navigation officer became lost. In daylight, they found they had deployed close to a strong enemy column. When the Gloucestershire Hussars swept by, he spoke briefly to Colonel Burley about the enemy threat, but Burley apologised, saying he could only take orders from brigade. In the fighting his battery was reduced to one gun and he only escaped because he was ordered to take a message to the Brigadier. He reached HQ, and he was amazed to be asked by Boucher, "'should I send in the Gurkhas?'" He replied that only tank support would save them. The remnants of the HLI got out after dusk.[76]

In the next phase, the advance was made by 9th Indian Brigade with 2nd West Yorks going forward in five motor columns protected by the overworked 4th RTR. They passed through the Baluch box and came under shellfire, so the lorries sped up across the ridge and down into the low ground beyond, their objective was the ridge-line some distance ahead. This was firmly held by Ariete and 15th Panzer Division, so they were forced to de-bus and dig in as best they could under direct fire. From now on the battle became a series of defensive actions with battalions digging in under shellfire, all of whom were too widely separated to give support. For a while they were linked by 22nd Armoured, spread across from Tamar, south-east to the Baluchs. The armoured regiments fought their own battle, supporting each other, but largely failed

---

73　TNA WO 373/21/14: Recommendation for Award, Lieutenant-Colonel D.G. Thorburn, 5 June 1942.
74　TNA WO 169/7619: 10 Indian Brigade HQ Diary, report 'Events 5 and 6 June 1942.'
75　TNA WO 169/7770: 4/10th Baluch Regiment War Diary, Collated account, Major Farrimond, June 1942.
76　IWM: Papers of Lieutenant Colonel M. E. Parker, memoirs 5–6 June 1942.

to support the infantry on their flanks. This left a bitter taste amongst the infantry, who felt they had been abandoned.[77] Brigadier Fletcher's report gave suggestions for better tank-infantry cooperation in future operations.

The 2nd West Yorks suffered a similar fate to the Highlanders. They were informed at 0620 hours that 22nd Armoured had made a, 'complete sweep of the objective and report it clear of enemy tanks,'[78] but the Highlanders were soon shelled and pinned down in a low hollow, in open ground. They were overlooked by up to 40 tanks and 12 armoured cars on the ridge ahead.[79] The two forward companies, B and D, attempted to advance on foot towards the ridge, but they were soon halted by fire. The 4th RTR squadron had to withdraw, because their 2pdrs were ineffective against the armour facing them. Heavy shellfire inflicted severe casualties on the two leading infantry companies, who quickly lost all of their officers.[80] Lieutenant Colonel Reeves from 4th RTR said they faced 188 AT guns but were re-assigned to support 22nd Armoured and spent the day in a tank versus tank battle, losing 20 'I' tanks, with most crews bailing out.[81] In the Yorkshires' D Company, Henry Foster said they advanced on foot and came under fire, their eight attached anti-tank guns were soon knocked out and from then on each company operated separately.[82] The 2pdr portees were knocked out, because their crews fired them from the back of the trucks, which became easy targets for Axis guns and tanks sitting back beyond 1,200 yards. The two forward companies were overrun by 15th Panzer and, 'more or less wiped out.'[83]

In the rear, D Company used its mortars and MG fire to repel a flank attack on their left-rear, by the armoured cars.[84] The failures of rushed planning were now being tested. Foster said communications with their artillery were cut so there was no supporting fire. The unit fell back at nightfall, as the panzers turned away to engage the 4/10th Baluch. Just south of the latter they spotted the battery from 157th Field Regt, protected by a company of 3/9th Jats, but neither joined the Baluch position.[85] The West Yorks reformed at El Adem, having taken 171 casualties out of a 762 strong unit. The 3/12th 'Piffers' were held back as they had received only one day practising

77 TNA WO 169/7617: War Diary HQ 9 Indian Infantry Brigade, 1942, Brigadier Fletcher's report.
78 TNA WO 169/5077: 2nd West Yorks War Diary, 5 June 1942.
79 TNA WO 169/5077: 2nd West Yorks War Diary, 5 June 1942.
80 Brett-James, *Ball of Fire*, pp.184–185.
81 Bovington: 4th RTR Papers, Letter from Lieutenant Colonel Reeve to Lieutenant Colonel Wetherall, n.d.
82 Henry Foster, A4175732, *BBC Peoples War* <https://www.bbc.co.uk/history/ww2peopleswar/stories/19/a4531619.shtml> (accessed 8 August 2017).
83 Brett-James, *Ball of Fire,* pp.184–185.
84 TNA WO 169/5077: 2nd West Yorks War Diary, 5 June 1942.
85 TNA WO 169/7617: 9th Indian Infantry Brigade HQ War Diary, 1942. 'Operations on 5 June' report.

box formations, and because of the strong enemy defences ahead. They were ordered back to El Adem in the evening.[86]

The attached artillery had a similarly tough time. With 10th Indian Brigade was 28th Field Regiment, which advanced to the B.180 position at first light with a forward HQ. They were intermittently shelled through the day but their B echelon trucks got through in the late afternoon. As dusk fell a column of 25 enemy tanks came up from the south-west and cut off communications with brigade and rear HQs. For support, B echelon joined the Gurkha box overnight. Then Lieutenant Colonel J. Needham ordered the artillery HQ back out of the danger area, which they complied with, but vehicles became scattered in the darkness, although they eventually regrouped at El Adem. The guns remained in the box and were mostly captured the next day.[87]

The South Notts Hussars had been in action on 27 May when 520 Battery was attacked by enemy tanks. Captain C. W. Bennett extracted one troop under heavy fire, the remaining troop fought to the last and was overrun. Major P. G. Birkin was killed along with eight others and the remainder became POWs. The survivors joined Support Group and spent the next few days 'standing firm', being shelled and exchanging fire.[88] They remained in position for Aberdeen to give fire support, and so were not properly dug in. They were overlooked by enemy tanks on higher slopes and were soon under direct attack, with the battery positions surrounded, the guns exposed, their crews suffered from MG fire and the guns ran short of ammunition. The panzers manoeuvred to outflank the group. Captain Pringle was angry that HQ did not understand their predicament, and Brigadier Carr explicitly ordered Major Daniell to fight to the last man and last round.[89] Alongside them 50 Recce Battalion suffered a heavy day of shelling, on a lower ridge, also overlooked by the Axis guns.[90]

22nd Armoured Brigade

The role of 22nd Armoured Brigade during the attack has been seen by some as controversial, there was certainly a lack of understanding between armour and infantry. The commonly held view is that the brigade advanced through the infantry, moving fast but came under heavy fire from guns and tanks, so it rallied back according to orders, having lost some 60 tanks, mainly due to mechanical problems, despite the heavy fire.[91] However, unit reports tell a different and a much more nuanced story with the armoured regiments remaining in the Cauldron for much of the day. The 2nd Gloucestershire Hussars reached B.178, on the north-eastern edge of Bir Aslagh

---

86   TNA WO 169/7775: 3/12th Frontier Force Regiment War Diary, June 1942.
87   TNA WO 169/4581: 28th Field Regt RA, War Diary, 5–6 June 1942.
88   TNA WO 169/4563: 107th Regt RHA, War Diary, 27 May–5 June 42.
89   Hart, *South Notts Hussars*, pp.205–208.
90   Barclay, Northumberland Fusiliers, p.81.
91   Ken Ford, *Gazala. Rommel's Greatest Victory* (Oxford: Osprey, 2008), p.55.

ridge, when they were stopped by heavy anti-tank fire from guns dug in further along the ridge. Along with 4th CLY, they veered north and halted a mile from B.203 on Tamar Ridge and faced west. They saw 2nd HLI pinned down by heavy shelling and had held off two attacks from tanks and infantry guns by mid-afternoon. Their Grants later returned to help 3rd CLY at the Baluch B.100 position by evening, where they accounted for another four Mark IVs.[92] The 2nd RGH were saved from the worst of the anti-tank fire by the rising sun behind them, and dust created by heavy 150mm shellfire. Major Pitman remembered sweltering in their tanks in front of their own guns; they repelled two attacks on the Tamar Ridge.[93]

The 4th CLY moved north-west across the Cauldron after the first contact on Bir Aslagh. They attempted to advance towards Sidi Muftah but encountered more guns and 15 tanks, and so rallied back south of the ridge, and returned to Bir Aslagh to support the Baluchis. They found a 25pdr battery under heavy fire and moved it back 1,000 yards. Then they returned north to B.178, to help the hard-pressed 3rd CLY. They held this line, between the 3rd CLY and the minefield, until nightfall. The enemy made two attempts to get around their left flank, but then darkness fell.[94] Third CLY advanced into a thick mist and contact was soon lost. They rallied south of Tamar Ridge with the other regiments and spent the day engaging enemy tanks. Towards evening the enemy attacked again and the brigade was ordered to withdraw and rally just south of the Knightsbridge Box.[95] Oddly the 3rd CLY failed to mention the nearby 4/10th Baluch position in their war diary whereas 4th CLY gave much more detail about the day's events. There was a general confusion over the position of the regiments and any adjacent infantry positions. One can only imagine exhausted officers trying to keep such reports properly updated, often late at night with a mass of daily tasks still to be checked and completed. It is no wonder that unit diaries vary in quality and detail.

Brigade HQ said that by late afternoon regiments needed more ammunition and were facing fresh advances by enemy armour. By 1600 hours a wedge formation of enemy tanks gathered, including six Mk IVs, began to threaten 4th CLY's flank, but 2nd Armoured HQ said they were nearing the B.100 position and would support them. After an hour only one squadron of 4th RTR arrived and slotted into the line between the RGH and 4th CLY. Some 6pdrs were also sent to reinforce the line, but radioed to say they needed a guide. By the mid-evening, 4th CLY were still under fire and threatened by the panzers, while 2nd Armoured Brigade were still two miles away. They halted and offered artillery fire support.[96]

By the evening of 5 June, different columns from 15th Panzer Division advanced through the gaps in the minefields and then swung to the north, overrunning the

---

92 TNA WO169/4494: 2nd Royal Gloucestershire Hussars War Diary, 5–6 June 1942.
93 Pitman, *Gloucester Hussars*, pp.68–69.
94 TNA WO169/4496: 4th County London Yeomanry War Diary, June 1942.
95 3rd RTR War Diary, 5 June 1942 <http://www.warlinks.com> (accessed 9 August 2018).
96 TNA WO 169/4251: 22nd Armoured Brigade War Diary, 5 June 42.

unlucky 1st DCLI, and scattering division HQs, B echelons, and many reforming units. Subedar-Major Khan from 4/10th Baluchs stood fast with his cook wagon, whilst tanks and vehicles from 15th Panzer Division swept past him, one column consisted of seven tanks and 40 MET carriers came through. Khan watched the passing British HQ vehicles, who were 'retiring back at considerable speed' into the rear that evening.[97] Next day he watched the demise of his battalion. Most of the rag-tag of HQ groups and supply trucks ended up running eastwards to El Adem, to avoid capture. This sudden thrust cut the Hacheim track and prevented 22nd Armoured Brigade from returning to save the Baluchs and Gurkhas the following day.[98] All of the rear echelons, forward HQs and oddments of units drove north or east. Some rallied at Bir Belefaa ridge and the situation there was said to be confused. Panzerarmee columns had caused panic in the rear echelon areas and left the forward units isolated.

The 1st Duke of Cornwall's Light Infantry (1st DCLI) was part of 21st Indian Brigade in 10th Indian Division. The Battalion had been ordered forward from Iraq on 17 May, ten days before the battle. They arrived at Gambut Airfield by 1 June, a journey of over 1,500 miles. They moved into the Tobruk perimeter on 2 June and were ordered forward again to join 5th Indian on 4 June, as divisional reserve. Three junior officers attended the 5th Indian Aberdeen planning meeting after four that afternoon. At first they were given the northern mine gap to be blocked with new mines, but Lieutenant Colonel Dean reminded Major General Briggs that the battalion was still in Tobruk and could not reach the start line for first light the next day.[99] So they were ordered to arrive at Harmat and block the southern mine-gaps of the inner minefield.

They gathered their eight 2pdr guns, used borrowed trucks and suffered a confused night march, being sent to first to barrel B.722, south of El Adem, where a staff officer from XXX Corps was supposed to explain their role to them, but he did not appear. Such night moves were difficult for units who knew the area, but for newly arrived units this was an almost impossible task. They had not received any radios, so the recce group could not inform HQ of the route. They were separated at times but managed to regroup at 5th Division HQ, near Naduret, at dawn on 5 June. As the massed tanks of 22nd Armoured swept past them in swathes of dust, the GSO1 from 5th Indian pointed to the west and ordered them to, '"Drive for about nine miles and see what you can do,"' which brought them to near Harmat.[100] Lieutenant Colonel Dean placed two companies to cover the mine-gaps, with C Company facing south and A Company in

---

97 TNA WO169/7770: 4/10th Baluch Regiment War Diary, report by Subedar Major Nawab Khan, June 1942.
98 TNA WO 169/3910: 2/4th Gurkhas War Diary, 1942. Report of 5–6 June, by Brigade Major.
99 E.G. Godfrey, *The Duke of Cornwall's Light Infantry 1939–1945* (Malvern: Images,1994), pp.98–116.
100 Godfrey, *Duke of Cornwall's Light Infantry*, pp.120–121.

reserve. Because of the ground, the troops could only dig in about 18 inches to make shell scrapes. The battalion had to use runners to liaise with each company.

Hacheim was 16 miles south but he was told not to worry about an approach from that direction, as British armour patrolled the area. To be safe, a carrier platoon patrolled south. The platoon leader, Captain Jobson, made three patrols, and spotted a column moving west to east, and a new gap in the minefield. Both HQ and a passing recce subaltern brashly dismissed this as false, and that the column seen was only soft vehicles. The carriers stumbled onto a group of enemy tanks lurking in a fold and made a hurried exit under heavy fire. The DCLI realised enemy armour was forming up to their south.[101] 5th Division HQ repeated that this was not correct, so Colonel Dean sent C Company and carriers on a reconnaissance in strength. They were caught in flank by various enemy columns, proving that 15th Panzer was near them. He reported this again to HQ and requested artillery, they promised an OP officer, who never arrived and soon after the telephone line went dead, so further links were lost as the enemy columns surged north between them and HQ.

In a very short time, a strange group of Bren carriers drove rapidly into the battalion HQ area and began firing on the trucks and nearby troops. The men wore British helmets, so it was a 'coup de main' to disorganise their defences. Across the slope, A Company was also quickly overrun so Major Petre with D Company decided to counterattack to drive them from the HQ position. It was a gallant charge, coming over a low rise only to be met by a hail of fire from the dismounted troops and nearby tanks. Major Petre was killed while using his truck to create a dust-screen for the troops to advance behind. Very quickly the separated B and D Companies were forced to surrender, and some newly arrived tanks rounded up the other companies, although the battle continued until after dark. While some men got away in the confusion, several hundred were taken prisoner and gathered in with 9th Indian Brigade and tank crew prisoners from further west, they were marched south-west next day. The German general leading the column told the DCLI, 'it was a good fight, and but for your bad 'war luck' you might have won.'[102]

Attack on the Sidra Ridge, 5 June

The 32nd Army Tank Brigade was to attack 21st Panzer holding the Sidra Ridge. The brigade was 42nd RTR, 7th RTR and one squadron 8th RTR totalling about 90 'I' tanks. The battalion was positioned south of the 151st Brigade box at B.157 since 1 June. One attack was planned for 2 June, but then cancelled. The enemy strength on Sidra was unknown, because sufficient reconnaissance had not been carried out.[103]

101 Godfrey, p.122.
102 Godfrey, *Duke of Cornwall's Light Infantry*, pp.124–126.
103 TNA WO 169/4520: 42nd RTR War Diary, 2–4 June 1942.

Infantry support would be 7th Green Howards and supporting artillery behind provided smoke cover to close with the enemy.[104] The unit supported 4th Armoured on 4 June, but this attack did not develop so they returned to leaguer. The tanks were ordered not to proceed onto the ridge, i.e. let the infantry go in. Major Tatum said he knew the ridge was not easily discernible as a slope.[105]

On 5 June, the brigade advanced with 42nd RTR with 32 tanks on the right and 7th RTR at near full strength on the left, with 8th RTR in reserve. They followed a line of telegraph poles well to the east of the minefield, so could not have run onto it later.[106] C Squadron led the battalion, then A Squadron, then BHQ. The bombardment began with HE and then smoke, the Germans added smoke on their left flank. Visibility was very poor with just a few enemy tanks at 1,000 yards. The Axis began using 105mm guns and the fire became very heavy. The left flank was hit by accurate anti-tank fire and 25 tanks were spotted on the right at 2,000 yards. The fire affected 7th RTR, who swerved right across the C Squadron front. This stopped the advance and those at the front were milling about amidst the heavy fire.[107] Three HQ tanks were damaged and believed they'd hit a minefield. The CS tank was hit and the crew machine-gunned as they evacuated. Major Kent's tank, the acting C.O., was seen to move back northwards and the 7th Green Howards came under shellfire and sustained heavy losses.[108]

Germans tanks then threatened and attacked the brigade right flank, so Major Tatum's A Squadron engaged these and halted the advance. The brigade lost about 70 tanks and the rest rallied in some confusion about 1,500 yards in front of the artillery, with five tanks from C Squadron and 10 from 7th RTR, while the infantry dug in. They exchanged fire with enemy tanks until about midday, and watched the Germans blow up their knocked out vehicles on the Sidra slopes. The battalion became a composite 42nd Squadron of seven tanks under 7th RTR. Brigade ordered them to retire and regroup.[109]

The Second Day, 6 June

The Baluchis, Gurkhas and their supporting artillery were all overrun by Axis attacks, though enough remaining troops from these units escaped to be reformed later on.

---

104 7th Green Howards diary pages are missing until 11 June. The 42nd RTR's Major Tatum's letter to Liddell-Hart says 6th Green Howards would attack, but later 7th Green Howards' carriers were picking up wounded. The Battalion history by Powell says 7th Green Howards took part in the assault.
105 Bovington: 7th RTR Papers, letter from Major Tatum, A Squadron 42nd RTR, n.d.
106 Bovington: 7th RTR Papers, letter from Major Tatum, A Squadron 42nd RTR, n.d.
107 Bovington: 7th RTR Papers, letter from Major Tatum, A Squadron 42nd RTR, n.d.
108 TNA WO 169/4520: 42nd RTR War Diary, 5 June 1942.
109 Bovington: 7th RTR Papers, letter from Major Tatum, A Squadron 42nd RTR, n.d.

The main weakness was that their temporary dug-in positions were isolated and lacked support. Secondly the ridges themselves – as was found time and again across Libya and Egypt – were almost impossible to dig-in below a varied but shallow layer of sand. On Bir Aslagh, at B.180, Havildar Thapa said the Gurkha box was extremely rocky across the position and they could only dig slit trenches to a depth of about two feet.[110] While the Baluchs deployed across mixed ground, allowing 'slitters' (slit trenches for infantry) of 3 to 5 feet.[111] In contrast the Knightsbridge Box was a 'base of operations', in a shallow depression, and where vehicles were dug in to roof level.[112] Overstretched recce parties, hurriedly searching new sites, probably never had the time to check how deeply they might be able to dig-in if at all, yet this became a serious consequence in their ability to hold on.

In the battle around the Baluch box, there were many acts of inspired leadership and courage. Major Farrimond and Captain Steel provided cool-headed leadership, Captain I. J. Steel had just returned from brigade on the evening of 5 June and he gave a clear account of the battle. At 0920 hours on 6 June, Captain R. H. Farrimond (acting major, and C.O. of C Company), heard the A Company Commander tell the Baluch Colonel, 'The tanks are coming through now' – Farrimond assumed he meant British tanks. About ten minutes later the colonel rang him and said, 'Get your company out now Farri...whilst the goings' good.' Farrimond was able to extricate his company, and although he was briefly captured himself, he quickly managed to evade the harassed Germans, trying to round up various groups of British and Indian soldiers, who were equally trying to evade and escape back to the east of Bir Harmat. Jemadar Punnu Ram returned with just 15 men.[113] Many units had suffered serious losses but a core from most of these units survived and were rebuilt later.

Some new gaps in the minefield were added by 90th Light Division, which provided 15th Panzer Division with options to move through them and outflank and surprise the forward HQs and B echelons who were near the Hacheim track. Some writers confuse these with the earlier gaps, made either side of 150 Brigade. We know that 5th Indian Division infantry had to watch over two gaps in the inner minefield by Bir Harmat, so the confusion is logical. The 2/4th Gurkhas sited their cowpat positions opposite these these just prior to the advance, the 'Paul' gap being about 1,000 yards west of Bir Harmat.[114] Comparing intelligence, the Tenth Brigade Brigade-Major said there was a good deal of confusing comment about the failures from those who returned. Most agreed it was the rocky nature of the ground which prevented units

---

110 TNA WO169/3910: 2/4th Gurkhas War Diary, 1942. Statement of 7071 Havildar Puransing Thapa.
111 TNA WO169/7770: 4/10th Baluch Regiment War Diary, Collated account, Major Farrimond, June 1942.
112 Mead, *Gunners At War*, p.44.
113 TNA WO169/7770: 4/10th Baluch Regiment War Diary, reports by Major R. H. Farrimond and Captain I. J. Steel, June 1942.
114 TNA WO 169/3910: 2/4th Gurkhas War Diary, June 1942.

from digging in, along with the heavy enemy shelling which prevented the infantry and artillery defending themselves, and this contributed to them being overrun.[115]

On the northern edge of the Aslagh ridge, at B.180, the 2/4th Gurkhas suffered a similar fate to the 4/10th Baluchis. In the early morning they were heavily shelled, but their gunners maintained a good return fire, despite having many wounded. The unlucky 2pdr guns were soon knocked out, probably being too exposed on their portees. The heavy shelling prevented movement around the position so the Gurkha riflemen continued to fire until they ran out of ammunition. After 1400hrs the shelling increased and machine gun fire poured into the position from all directions. The last of the 25pdr guns were either destroyed by shellfire or by the gunners. About 1700hrs tanks and infantry approached the battalion HQ, the Gurkhas fired on these with the last of their ammunition. The Germans ordered the Gurkhas out of their dugouts under further MG fire, gathering up most of B and C Companies. Havildar Thapa was unable to see what happened in A and D Companies and he thought probably only a few stragglers escaped.[116] The battalion lost a some hundreds of men either as casualties or mostly as POWS. Lieutenant-Col. Weallens was seen with the men after capture.[117] So another battalion new to the desert had been overrun, but enough groups and various individuals made it back to enable the battalion to be reformed later. Two companies returned to the Delta, and by autumn the battalion strength had again reached 646 men.

The 4th Field Regt with the Baluch box, and 28th Field RA with the Gurkhas, regiments also suffered because they were unable to dig in properly. There are few diary records for 4th Field Regt between May and July 1942. They noted they had received 200 rounds per gun, and this was buried 'one box deep near the troop positions.' It was these loosely covered boxes which easily caught fire from the intense shelling, so most of the ammunition was lost despite the guns still being in action. The regiment fought on until only two guns remained firing. Most of the surviving crews were taken prisoner, but their C.O., Lieutenant-Col. Truscott, and a few other men escaped by truck. The regiment also survived and was later reformed near Alamein.[118]

The battered 22nd Armoured leaguered south of Knightsbridge that night and were ordered by Messervy next day to focus on the 50 enemy tanks and 400 MET to the south, so there was no mention of aiding the units still in the Cauldron.[119] The Gloucestershire Hussars, who watched them from the Pt.185 ridge to the south, said they could see 25 tanks and guns (probably elements of 15th Panzer Division). Later

---

115 TNA WO 169/3910: 2/4tth Gurkhas War Diary, 1942. Report of 5–6 June by Brigade Major.
116 TNA WO 169/3910: 2/4th Gurkhas War Diary, 1942. Statement of 7071 Havildar Puransing Thapa.
117 TNA WO 169/3910: 2/4th Gurkhas War Diary, June 1942. Report of 5–6 June by Brigade Major.
118 TNA WO 169/4575: 4th Field Regiment RA, War Diary, and Administrative notes.
119 TNA WO 169/4251: 22nd Armoured Brigade, War Diary, 6 June 1942.

the Hussars lost 2 Grants and one Honey in an artillery exchange, before they were ordered eastwards. Unfortunately, they were fired on by 88mm guns and suffered more losses including Lieutenant-Col. Burley, their C.O. They ended the day north of Knightsbridge at the blockhouse on the Hagiag et Raml Ridge.[120] The Brigadier had earlier requested Messervy to allow the Support Group boxes still in the cauldron to retire. Messervy replied not to worry because 4th Armoured Brigade, which had been reinforced and refuelled ready to the northwest, would go to their support. Brigadier Carr then visited Brigadier Richards at 4th Armoured HQ, but the diary concluded, 'help did not arrive in time.'[121]

Major R. B. T. Daniell escaped from the cauldron debacle and left a sketch map which shows the Support Groups placed north of B.180, with the Baluch box to the west, and 28th Field Regt RA to their right (south-east). The Jats were in the south and 4th Field Regt placed between them and the Baluchs. He noted the whole group of units and guns were surrounded by 'enemy tanks'.[122] The regiments of gunners and Indian battalions were spread out so widely across the western side of the plateau that the South Notts believed they were isolated. Their battle again showed the methodical doctrine used by the Panzer groups. Gunner Mayoh remembered how the approaching tanks weaved and changed direction to avoid direct fire. The gun layers, like himself, waited until the tank turned or came over a rise, to hopefully cripple the vehicle. The tanks turned away from the gunners' heavy fire, leaving them to clear the empty shells and await the next attack.[123]

The Hussars Colonel was asked by an HQ over the radio, to hang on for 12 hours and replied, 'A fat lot of f****** use that's going to be.'[124] He spent the day moving around in his Honey tank, until it was hit, and unfortunately he and his wireless officer were both trapped and died.[125] The guns were soon low on ammo, with only 20 AP rounds left. Their B echelon trucks endeavoured to bring in more shells, but 12 of the 15 trucks were shot-up. The Axis guns resumed their shelling and there were more attacks by Stukas, before another tank attack came in. Sergeant Ray Ellis managed to hit a Mk IV tank despite the hail of MG and shellfire, but soon after his gun was hit and he was knocked out. The medical staff struggled to deal with such large numbers of badly wounded gunners, before they were injured themselves. Major Daniells organised scratch crews of gunners to man the remaining 25pdrs. Then he mistakenly ordered one troop to form a 'British-square' – putting the guns back-to-back as the tanks closed in. These guns and crews were also badly shot-up, so Captain Pringle ordered his remaining guns to stay put. He blew them up with his last two

120 TNA WO 169/4494: 2nd Royal Gloucester Hussars War Diary, 6 June 1942.
121 TNA WO 169/4251: 22nd Armoured Brigade, War Diary, 6 June 1942.
122 TNA WO 169/4251: 22nd Armoured Brigade, War Diary, 6 June 1942. Sketch map by Major Daniells, RHA.
123 Hart, *South Notts Hussars*, p.209.
124 Hart, p.211.
125 Hart, p.212.

rounds. Another officer leapt onto a tank but was gunned down, so Pringle pragmatically surrendered.[126] There was nothing more the South Notts gunners could do. They had fought their own battle and were completely overrun. All guns were knocked out and had at least 26 men killed and 539 as POWs. The few remaining troops later formed a new battery in the Delta.[127] Lieutenant Colonel des Graz from 50 Recce (Northumberland Fusiliers), manned the 2pdr guns with his men to the last. One Jat officer saw him drive up to a nearby 2pdr and got the crew to begin firing again. They hit a tank but with no effect. The tank returned fire from 100 yards and hit the 2pdr gun twice, silencing it and killing des Graz.[128] The remnants of his motor battalion was all either killed, wounded or captured.

Eighth Army had been seriously defeated during Aberdeen and the others cauldron battles. Armour and Infantry had been thrown together and HQs assumed they would work well together. Later battles would show the training time needed for infantry and armour to understand each other. The magnitude of the failure has contributed to a wider negative historical view, which undermines the hard-fought efforts by Eighth Army to defeat Panzerarmee. The losses were said to be one and half brigades of infantry and four regiments of artillery, along with their supporting arms, totalling some 4,000 in casualties and POWs.[129] John Masters believed his old battalion, 2/4th Gurkhas, had been wiped out, and equally the 1944 propaganda booklet *Eighth Army* described two battalions as, 'fighting to the last man.'[130] The South Notts Hussars, the Northumberland Fusiliers (50th Recce Battalion), 2/4th Gurkhas and 4/10th Baluchis all suffered the most losses during Aberdeen. The realities of their separated battles give a more nuanced conclusion about what occurred on those stifling hot days in June.

One might imagine the remaining Infantry might be thoroughly demoralized by their recent experiences, however 9th Indian Brigade remained optimistic about achieving better cooperation with armour in future.[131] They also developed new tactics to knock out armour. The brigade intended to allow the panzers to close up on the infantry, who awaited them with ammonal bombs. The West Yorks demonstrated a new defence called the 'human minefield…using 1 man pits sited in lines, 20 yards apart, with each man having an anti-tank grenade or Molotov cocktail to attach as the enemy tanks rolled over them. Placed 500 yards behind this minefield, would be a line of Bren MGs, to force the panzers to close up their hatches, and enable the anti-tank grenades to be attached.'[132] Therefore some Indian troops remained determined to take on the panzers again and find some way to defeat them.

---

126 TNA WO 169/4563: 107th RHA War Diary, June 1942.
127 TNA WO 169/4563: 107th RHA War Diary, June 1942.
128 Barclay, *Northumberland Fusiliers*, p.82.
129 Playfair, *Mediterranean and the Middle East, Vol. III*, p.238.
130 HMSO, *Eighth Army*, p.45.
131 TNA WO169/7617 9 Indian Brigade HQ War Diary 1942, Report Annex A, p.4.
132 TNA WO 169/7617: HQ 9 Indian Infantry Brigade, War Diary 1942.

6

Armoured Battles, 29 May–13 June

> *Now in my dial of glass appears*
> *The soldier who is going to die.*
> *He smiles and moves about in ways…*
> *The wires touch his face; I cry*
> *NOW. Death, like a familiar hears*
>
> 'How to kill'
> Keith Douglas[1]

The last days of May involved some heavy fighting by the Armoured Brigades as they sought to push Panzerarmee out of the Cauldron. They were also trying to prevent the Panzer divisions from breaking through at Eluet et Tamar and Acroma, towards the coast, so it became more vital to hold the front line in the northern sector, to prevent a breakthrough along the coast road towards Tobruk. For the armoured regiments, the continued poor leadership at Division and Corps levels led to more patrols, recovery and some inactivity, often due to rapidly changing orders. When out of action they constantly had to fetch replacement tanks and crews, keep on with much-needed maintenance and being exchanged across brigades for just a few hours or days at a time. All of these problems added to the need to defeat Panzerarmee. Meanwhile the Axis battlegroups had eliminated the isolated 150th Brigade box and were pressing the Free French at Bir Hacheim.

The commander of 2nd Armoured Brigade, Brigadier Raymond Briggs, sent a message on 21 May; he said indications were that the enemy were likely to attack in the next few days, 'By attacking, the enemy lays himself open to violent resistance from our forward troops…and to decisive attack by our armoured formations. By

---

1 Ted Hughes (ed.), *Keith Douglas: Poems selected by Ted Hughes* (London: Faber, 2006), p.39. Douglas was writing about Alamein or later in the campaign but gives a clear image of a tank crew's experience.

destroying his tanks we will destroy his armies… We have all been waiting for this moment…we have been re-equipping…and training for it, we welcome it.'[2] As we have seen, far from being ready, 9th Royal Lancers had received their last few Grants after reaching Bir el Gubi on 12 May, with the last one arriving on 22nd May.[3] Its fellow unit, the 10th Hussars, received seven Grants at the end of April, and began test firing the 75mm gun on 8 May.[4] Range practice after this was intense, and their ability to be fully ready was a close run thing.

Most of the armoured actions during late May were attempts to breakthrough to 150th Brigade at Sidi Muftah. Ritchie and his corps commanders then paused to discuss a renewed attack on the Cauldron, which became Operation Aberdeen. This was followed by another phase of daily skirmishes and regrouping of brigades, which culminated in the evacuation of the Free French from Bir Hacheim by 11 June. Panzerarmee then concentrated to attack Eighth Army holding the ridges on each flank of Knightsbridge. Once the weakened British armour had been defeated, the Panzer divisions pushed towards Acroma and the western side of Tobruk but also east, along the Trigh Capuzzo to isolate El Adem. In trying to stem these new advances, Eighth Army deployed single infantry battalions to make isolated, defended localities. These would suffer the same fate as the full brigade boxes. So the defeat of the armoured brigades also undermined the northern sector of the Gazala line which was now outflanked. This meant that in the end 1st South African and 50th Divisions had to retreat, to avoid a similar fate to 150th Brigade.

In a sense there was a slight chance that just one of the defended localities might cripple either 15th or 21st Panzer Divisions, enough to slow or even halt their offensive. All of them fought hard and damaged the battlegroups. If they had been fought to a standstill, this might have forced Rommel to think again, as had occurred during Crusader in the previous winter. Rommel, however, remained tenacious over the possibility of reaching the prize of Tobruk and the supply bases nearby, so he pushed his tired divisions onto one more battle. They had developed a logical assault doctrine and were confident in their ability to break down any renewed armoured attack or overcome a defended locality. British armoured brigades were now a 'rump' of their original strengths after suffering heavy casualties, and presented a weaker threat than on 27 May, so now, for Ritchie and his corps commanders, only the defended localities might offer a more robust defence.

2   IWM: Doc.8109. Box RB2/5: Private papers of Major General Raymond Briggs, 1942.
3   Bright, Ninth Lancers, p.67.
4   TNA WO 169/4489: 10th Royal Hussars War Diary, 1942. April-May 1942. The Regiment was out of action by 30 May and sent back to Sollum by 8 June.

29–30 May, Armoured Battles near Knightsbridge

There were heavy engagements west and north-west of Knightsbridge on 29 May. 22nd Brigade had a limited day of operations against enemy groups around Bir Harmat which were inconclusive and halted by a worsening sandstorm. They suffered from continued shelling and were without good intelligence on what strength they were facing, so operations were halted.[5] There were problems with cooperation between brigades which remained difficult to coordinate, and regiments were directed towards different objectives. The Royal Gloucestershire Hussars operated two squadrons, one supported the brigade against enemy columns who attacked northwards towards Knightsbridge, while H Squadron and HQ moved south and intercepted another column coming up from Harmat. The 4th CLY arrived in support, but the afternoon dust storm stopped all movement until the weather cleared that evening, which allowed the renewal of some shooting.[6]

In 4th Armoured Brigade, the remaining 8th Hussars now fought as a reequipped C Squadron attached to 3rd RTR to create a more viable tactical unit. Major 'Shan' Hackett had finally handed over command due to his burn injuries from 27 May. This composite regiment moved west to engage an enemy column near Bir Harmat, but a severe dust storm prevented contact. Cyril Jolly said this storm was 'doubly unpleasant' and they struggled to move west in the afternoon to join the 2nd Brigade battle.[7] Later on, they engaged another column to the south-east, but nightfall ended operations.[8] This often meant a difficult night march back to leaguer positions followed by re-fuelling and rearming tanks, so crews were fortunate to get two hours sleep before stand to. After a long night resupplying his regiment, Major Lomax steered his empty trucks gingerly around Knightsbridge. He spotted two sentries and confirmed it was the Guards Box, 'Thank goodness, another few yards and we would have been in the minefield.' They replied, 'On the contrary sir, another few yards and you will be out of it.'[9] Both brigades were still weak and had been engaged in limited contacts with enemy columns. They were frustrated by the afternoon dust storm and were unable to properly support 2nd Armoured Brigade.

Meanwhile, 2nd Armoured was positioned west of Knightsbridge, and came under heavy attack from both the north and from the Cauldron, across the Aslagh ridge. They were deployed in a semi-circle 400 yards from the crosstracks at Knightsbridge, facing the Rigel Ridge to the north. They began the day weak in numbers of tanks and were supported by their Rifle Brigade motor battalion and B Battery, 11th RHA (HAC). All units successfully held off a series of heavy attacks by up to 150 enemy tanks, 80 of which were Italian. It was the hardest battle for the Brigade and its

---

5   TNA WO 169/4251: 22nd Armoured Brigade War Diary, 29 May 1942.
6   TNA WO 169/4494: 2nd Royal Gloucester Hussars War Diary, 29 May 1942.
7   Cyril Jolly, *Take These Men* (London: Constable, 1955), p.299.
8   TNA WO 169/4486: 8th Hussars War Diary, 29 May 1942.
9   Bright, *Ninth Lancers*, pp.72–73.

commander, Brigadier Raymond Briggs, said it was the most effective brigade group battle fought during the campaign.[10]

The regimental battles show how difficult the day was for 2nd Armoured Brigade. The 10th Hussars stood their ground all day in what they saw as their fiercest battle. They had had little sleep, Trooper Gilbert Wilson noted, 'We had a terrible night, planes were over continually from 10.30pm till about 4am machine gunning and bombing the whole area. Planes also came over during the next day.'[11] They fought as a regimental group on the flank of the brigade and lost 4 Grants, 16 Crusaders and 50 casualties, being reduced to just 4 tanks, which went to the Ninth Lancers.[12] Most of the Hussars and remaining crews returned to A echelon near Brigade HQ and later back to Sollum by 8 June. The second in command, Major J. P. Archer-Shee remained with a small group who went forward and discovered some of their abandoned Honeys near Bir Harmat where the crews had been taken prisoner.[13] Second Armoured was also now reduced to two regiments.

The 9th Lancers also suffered heavy overnight shelling which continued as they deployed early and moved to the right to assist the Bays. The gun line to their rear was attacked, so the Colonel sent in A and C Squadrons (Cruisers) with the Grant Squadron providing fire support from a nearby ridge. This stopped the enemy but also cost the regiment heavily, leaving just 11 cruisers. The Germans sprayed the position with heavy MG fire as they replenished ammunition from A echelon trucks under cover of smoke, which caused further casualties, including the popular 2nd Lieutenant Heycock. They remained observing until dark, while their attached battery engaged in an artillery duel with enemy guns to the west. The exhausted crews leaguered on the battery guns nearby. They reformed with two troops of guns, one each side of the Grant squadron, with the depleted cruisers behind. They found themselves surrounded by derelict enemy tanks the next day and believed they had knocked out at least 13 if not more.[14] The regiment now had 11 Grants, 4 cruisers with 3 more unfit for battle.

Saturday 30 May was another frustrating day for armour. All three armoured brigades were to attack west and north-west, towards a wide area of defended ground either side of B.230. Panzerarmee defences were noted as resolute, and large number of enemy tanks were spotted two miles to the south at Bir Harmat. The enemy withdrew though and before 9am the B.230 area was in Eighth Army hands. 9th Lancers now faced north watching a large group of Italian M13 tanks and other MET. They could see another screen of light tanks, on the ridge west of Bir Aslagh (Tamar Ridge), which were fairly spread out and a potential target. The Brigadier viewed the position

10 IWM: Doc.8109. Box RB2/5: Papers of Major General Raymond Briggs, letter of 29 July 42 & address June 1943.
11 Gilbert Wilson, 29 May 1942, A207869, *BBC People's War* <https://www.bbc.co.uk/history/ww2peopleswar/stories/97/a2078697.shtml> (accessed 14 August 2017).
12 Dawnay, *10th Royal Hussars*, p.63.
13 TNA WO 169/4489: 10th Royal Hussars War Diary, 29–31 May 1942.
14 Bovington: 9th Lancers War Diary, 29 May 1942.

and ordered an attack, the 9th Lancers leading and the Bays, with just 16 tanks, the 10th Hussars being in reserve with just three runners. The Lancers advanced up the slope with the Grants in the centre and the few cruisers on either flank. As they crossed the final ridgeline they were hit by, 'all kinds of heavy fire…the leading squadron pushed on and the 75mm guns…were very busy.' Realising they faced a far superior weight of fire, the Colonel ordered them to retire under cover of smoke from the CS tanks, as the Grants needed more ammunition.[15] They still had 11 Grants and a few cruisers, but they found out later they had taken on 36 tanks and 90 guns. However, a second attack was ordered. General Lumsden said to the C.O., after the first attack, 'Well done Ronald, just once more and we've got them.'[16] Which was wishful thinking but typical of the optimism from higher commanders that somehow Panzerarmee was near collapse by then. The 150th Brigade a few miles to the west had a rather different view.

For this second attack they were joined by the two remaining squadrons from 22nd Brigade. The CRA arrived to register fire support from 60 guns, laying smoke. The guns laid a 'beautiful' smoke screen, but 10 minutes too early, so the top of the ridge was as clear as day as they crossed it a second time. The 2i.c. gave up his tank, with a working radio, to the C.O., whose set had just failed at that moment. With reports coming in of a new enemy flank attack, this second attack was forced to withdraw as well. The enemy maintained the pressure with heavy Stuka attacks for the rest of the day.[17] They caused numerous casualties amongst the A echelon trucks, medical trucks and to personnel.

Support from 4th Armoured Brigade was also largely ineffective. They operated east of Bir Harmat again, towards the beleaguered 150th Brigade still hoping for some support in their battle. The composite 3rd RTR advanced west with C Squadron, 8th Hussars' Stuarts scouting forward towards the B.180 height, on Bir Aslagh, from nearby Naduret et Ghuscuaesc. Unfortunately, even before they reached the Hacheim track, they encountered nine enemy Mk IVs with anti-tank gun support. One troop commander was knocked out; his fellow troop leader, 2nd Lieutenant Carter, went forward under heavy fire and towed the stricken tank out of the line of fire. With 5th RTR also arriving, the Brigadier made preparations to attack. Unfortunately, the advance by the weakened 4th Brigade was stopped by the visible enemy tank gun line on the Aslagh ridge. The Stuarts made a reconnaissance further south and successfully shot up some German trucks.[18]

The following day, 31 May, 3rd RTR group advanced again to B.230 on the Hacheim track. Patrols were sent out to the north-east towards Knightsbridge, rather than west towards the Aslagh ridge. The rest of the day became an artillery duel

15   Bovington: 9th Lancers War Diary, 30 May 1942.
16   Bright, *Ninth Lancers*, p.76.
17   Bovington: 9th Lancers War Diary, 30 May 1942.
18   TNA WO 169/4486: 8th Hussars War Diary, 30 May 1942.

which forced the enemy to withdraw because of the heavy shelling.[19] It was the crucial day for getting a breakthrough to save 150th Brigade. 22nd Brigade spent the day observing the Bir Aslagh ridge and, 'nothing of note occurred.'[20] This was another lost opportunity for Eighth Army to put pressure on Panzerarmee, though the reality was the armoured brigades needed fresh tanks and crews. Third RTR continued to observe the enemy to the north-west and were then withdrawn to leaguer and maintain their vehicles near Naduret. The watch was taken over by 4th RTR 'I' tanks.

The 22nd Armoured were to support 2nd Armoured and their account is less positive than the comments made by Division. The 3rd Sharpshooters (3rd CLY) were to link on the left flank, while 4th Sharpshooters had to stay in touch with 4th Armoured in the south. They were trying to outflank a group of 17 tanks, east of Bir Harmat, while the other two brigades would strike north-west, towards the high ground at B.202 and 'Wiggly Ridge' west of Knightsbridge.[21] This was not exactly a concentration of armour, because these objectives were some miles apart, east and west of the Hacheim track.

Command problems continued as squadrons from 22nd Armoured were also moved in and out of command of fellow regiments within 2nd Armoured. Attacks were 'going in' and then 'not going in' as the morning went on. The 2nd RGH suffered further losses for no gain while 3rd Sharpshooters knocked out seven panzers. It was a frenetic and confused morning of fighting. The Gloucestershire Hussars provide a brief summary about helping 4th Armoured in an attack on Harmat and that some anti-tank guns were destroyed but that the ground was not held, the regiment suffered three wounded and was now 'very tired.'[22] As with all crews they had been leaguering at midnight and with reveille at 0430 hours, these were long days on duty or in combat.

By 30 May, one of the causes for British optimism about the state of Panzerarmee was that it appeared to be in retreat, when up to 1,500 MET were spotted retreating through the minefields in long columns, although 15th Panzer still held the Maabus et Rigel Ridge. The Stop Jock column was directed to harass this retreating MET.[23] One onlooker said the vehicles looked like the riders at the starting gate, so Eighth Army HQ might be forgiven for thinking that the Axis was on the run and could be driven from the sector. Rommel had certainly ordered the supply units to get themselves sorted out and what had been seen from 150th Brigade and Tac-R was just the empty lorries queuing to get through the minefield.[24]

---

19 TNA WO 169/4486: 8th Hussars War Diary, 31 May 1942.
20 TNA WO 169/4251: 22nd Armoured Brigade War Diary, 31 May 1942.
21 TNA WO 169/4251: 22nd Armoured Brigade War Diary, 30 May 1942.
22 TNA WO 169/4494: 2nd Royal Gloucester Hussars War Diary, 30 May 1942.
23 TNA WO 169/4053: 1st Armoured Division War Diary, Operations 30 May 1942.
24 IWM: AL833: DAK War Diary, 28–30 May 1942.

1–2 June, 4th and 22nd Armoured Brigades

This was another quiet day for 22nd Armoured Brigade, apart from constant changes of command for most units. The brigade had 59 'runners' so was at regimental strength, and only 4th CLY received new tanks, the Hussars returned to the TDS to fetch more new vehicles. Plans were made to take over the tanks from 2nd Brigade but these plans were later cancelled.[25] Now that 150th Brigade had surrendered, Panzerarmee was able to reorganise itself. The heavy scale of the fighting since 27 May had also affected Axis troop morale, so that some Italian and German troops crossed the front line to surrender.[26] To the east the Bays again took up battle positions at dawn facing the Aslagh ridge. They fought all day, suffered Stuka dive bombing attacks and buried their dead. Later that day, 10th Indian Brigade arrived, but it was too late for an attack on the ridge that night.[27] It was also too late now for 150th Brigade, which had surrendered that morning.

A series of heavy dust storms prevented any attacks on the Aslagh Ridge the next day, 2 June. Armoured regiments continued to be switched between brigades for different tasks, which added to the delays. Meanwhile Panzerarmee sent one battle-group each from 15th Panzer and 21st Panzer Divisions to make an early attack towards the British held ridges. The Afrika Korps had been ordered by Rommel to make feint attacks against the armoured units near Harmat, while 90th Light and Trieste Divisions went south again to attack Bir Hacheim. These feints would also protect recovery (of tanks) operations, in the Cauldron.[28]

The 15th Panzer battlegroup advanced four kilometres when both groups came under heavy artillery fire and were threatened by enemy forces of unknown strength from the south. Colonel Bayelein at Panzerarmee HQ ordered them to make another attempt that afternoon. 21st Panzer would move north towards Eluet et Tamar with 15th Panzer in support. The dust storm became more intense and visibility was reduced to 30 yards. The commander of 21st Panzer suggested they delay moving until midnight, to avoid units being scattered in the swirling dust, but Rommel insisted on the 1500 hours deadline, although he agreed to let DAK HQ make the final decision. By then, 21st Panzer reported that the storm had become much worse, so they could not advance before 1800 hours. Rommel decided to wait and agreed for the advance to start in the evening.

Later that afternoon, 21st Panzer reported an enemy tank attack which had 'bumped into them.' Panzer Regiment Nr5 had moved to counterattack and the enemy had retreated to the north-east.[29] This was the engagement with 3rd RTR and 5th RTR in which the latter's Lieutenant Colonel Uniacke was killed. Cyril Jolly with 3rd RTR

---

25   TNA WO 169/4251: 22nd Armoured Brigade War Diary, 1 June 1942.
26   TNA WO 169/4251: 22nd Armoured Brigade War Diary, 2 June 1942.
27   Bovington: The Bays War Diary, 1 June 42.
28   IWM: AL833: DAK War Diary 1942, 1–2 June 1942.
29   IWM: AL833: DAK War Diary 14 May–1 Aug 1942, 2 June 1942.

described their part. The regiment had no heavy tanks so engaged the four 88mm guns on the Sidra Ridge to their front with Stuarts. He and his gunner were in a cat-and-mouse firefight with his tank bracketing an enemy gun to get a hit, while the German gunners scrabbled at the ground below their gun to depress the barrel further. In the end Jolly's gunner won and scored a direct hit, causing the ammunition to explode. They knocked out another 88mm and the Germans scrambled to evacuate the ridge. This enabled the battered 5th RTR to retire through the covering 3rd RTR.[30]

The severe storms hampered the advances made, and supplies failed to come to the regimental leaguers in time. The Gloucestershire Hussars were at the TDS being reequipped and found 6th RTR with 1st Armoured Brigade newly arrived at the Capuzzo Delivery point. However, this fresh brigade received orders to hand over all tanks to 4th Armoured. They moved forward to the next TDR at El Duda, leaguering with just their personal weapons for two days.[31]

Meantime, the Bays deployed in the same battle position and watched the Aslagh ridge, but the heavy dust storm lasted until 1800 hours and prevented any fighting in their sector. Later they were sent north-west to support the 4th Armoured Brigade attack on the Sidra Ridge, where 50–60 enemy tanks had been seen. The Bays reached the Maabus et Rigel Ridge by 2100 hours, but they made no contact with the enemy. In the darkness they watched the many flares which always surrounded the Axis leaguer positions at night.[32]

Both sides used the next couple of days to reorganise and reequip units. There was a stand-off, north of the Sidra Ridge on 3 June. DAK intercepted messages that both 2nd and 4th Armoured brigades would attack again, and so ordered the divisions to prepare.[33] However, 4th Armoured, which now only consisted of the weakened 3rd RTR, was told to reoccupy Eluet et Tamar, arriving from the north-east, at Pt.208. 2nd Armoured was to support them. Having spotted 80 plus tanks and numerous MET to the south, they awaited what looked to be a German advance.[34] With 22nd Armoured south of Knightsbridge, the three armoured brigades were not strong enough to take on DAK frontally.

Meanwhile preparations continued for 22nd Brigade to support 10th Indian Brigade in their attack into the cauldron. The brigade regrouped on the high ground at Naduret et Ghesceuasc facing west. By nightfall on 4 June, the brigade was back up to strength with a mixture of 156 Grants, Crusaders and Stuarts, and plans were received for Operation Aberdeen the next day. As we have seen, their objective was to destroy the enemy opposite them on the Aslagh ridge, next they would enter the Cauldron as far as B.174 in the centre of the depression, then they would turn right or north across Tamar Ridge, then east to Pt.166 and leaguer on the Sidra Ridge.

30   Jolly, *Take These Men*, pp.304–307.
31   TNA WO 169/4509: 6th RTR War Diary, January–December 1942, 2–3 June 1942.
32   Bovington: The Bays War Diary, 2 June 1942.
33   IWM: AL833: DAK War Diary, 1942, 3 June 1942.
34   TNA WO 169/4216: 4th Armoured Brigade Diary, 3 June 1942.

Despite fresh armoured regiments arriving in the forward area, they also suffered from being used in piecemeal fashion and were constantly split up and divided under different formations, 6th RTR had already handed over its original tanks at the rear TDR. The crews from C Squadron were later equipped with tanks at El Duda TDR with other squadrons following to await fresh tanks. As the attack on the cauldron began, 6th RTR moved to just east of Acroma, gaining two squadrons of 12 Grants and an RHQ with four more by 6 June. This was the same for 6th RTR, which suffered from these constant changes, first to 1st Armoured Division, then moved to 4th Armoured Brigade under 7th Armoured Division.[35]

Following the disaster in the Cauldron, and the flight of numerous B echelon columns, there were two aspects to the long hot days to 12 June. Firstly, armoured regiments operated on both sides of Knightsbridge to hold Axis forces in the Cauldron. Secondly, the constant changes of orders and commands must have caused a good deal of confusion, but units seemed to accept they would have different commands for different operations. Eighth Army again faced renewed threats of an advance towards the coast road. In the west, 22nd Armoured Brigade retired from Sidra Ridge and reorganised at the blockhouse east of Knightsbridge. Later they moved to Eluet et Tamar alongside the 9th Rifle Brigade, to stiffen the defences there. Next day they advanced to protect the Scots Guards at Rigel Ridge, but little occurred there for the next two days. On 10 June, they were ordered to act with 2nd Brigade, but these orders were later cancelled.[36] East of Knightsbridge, 4th Armoured Brigade was aligned along the ridge, and in the evening 1st and 3rd RTR again attacked towards Bir Harmat. The two Grant squadrons from 6th RTR covered their flank to the south, where they could see up to 50 panzers, in case of attack.[37]

The attacks were not very well coordinated at this point. Panzerarmee countered that afternoon when Ariete and 15th Panzer advanced and forced some deployed artillery to retire. Later on, 2nd, 4th and 22nd Brigades attacked both formations, but it was a 'halting attack with negligible artillery support.' Within an hour the British withdrew.[38] Attritional losses, worn-out crews and inexperienced new crews were having an effect on the armour's offensive capability. Jock Watt remembered, 'orders from Brigade would send us scurrying off to a new map reference. We would spend most of the day crouched in the turret, searching the horizon til sunset,'[39] Whereas Peter Roach recorded his experience of being in a newly arrived crew. They arrived in the forward area and had been given a Stuart tank to join the Gloucestershire Hussars:

> We sat on a flat stretch, to one side the lip of a depression sloping down to the battle area, to where the Germans should have been contained but weren't, for

---

35 TNA WO 169/4509: 6th RTR War Diary, January-December 1942, 6 June 1942.
36 TNA WO 169/4251: 22nd Armoured Brigade War Diary, 7–11 June 1942.
37 TNA WO 169/4509: 6th RTR War Diary, January-December 1942, 7 June 1942.
38 IWM: E127: 90th Light Division War Diary, 7 June 1942.
39 Bovington: 3rd RTR, Papers of Robert Watt, RSM, p.41.

they were busy breaking out at the south end…we could hear the firing and at times see the tracer… On our other side sappers were steadily laying a minefield in spite of constant attacks by dive bombers. We sat and waited, unknowing and unwanted…on the next day we were told to take the tank back to Tobruk, because the regiment was coming out of the line. Unknown to us they had suffered very severe casualties and were…joined to a sister regiment soon after.[40]

Some regiments were already being withdrawn from the battle. After Operation Aberdeen, 2nd RGH was reduced to one squadron which became the 'patrol squadron' for 22nd Armoured Brigade. By 11 June it was sent to 7th Motor Brigade to operate with the July column.[41] By mid-June the regiment was back at the railhead, heading for the Delta. From 5–8 June 10th Hussars collected stray crews in the rear, before being sent back to Bardia. Two troops of Grants rejoined 9th Lancers who still had two squadrons. By 18 June, there were attempts to form a composite regiment with 3rd CLY, but there were not enough tanks and so regimental personnel returned to Sidi Barrani.[42] Brigades were operating with just one or two units each.

Defence of Knightsbridge, 8–11 June

Even though 12–13 June are considered the decisive battles for the armoured brigades, 8 June was another difficult day of battle for some. The relatively fresh 6th RTR, with 4th Armoured Brigade, took up position at Pt.167 outside Knightsbridge, expecting an attack from some MET to the south-west. More enemy vehicles were then seen to the north-west. They were joined later by the Stuarts from 3rd RTR, who patrolled west towards the Hacheim track. By noon, more enemy batteries, some with up to 150mm guns, were deployed on the Aslagh ridge.[43] In the evening 6th RTR attacked westwards, with fire support from a single battery of RHA guns and covered by 1st RTR on their left flank. They came under very heavy shellfire from both guns and tanks but the supporting RHA fired an effective concentration on the Aslagh ridge, and believed they knocked out three tanks and some gun crews, but standard procedures meant they retired three miles to leaguer for the night.[44] The opening attack during Operation Aberdeen had been on the same ridgeline. The next day 6th RTR moved forward again and engaged in long range fire with various targets, again

---

40 Peter Roach, *The 8.15 to War. The Memoirs of a Desert Rat* (London: Leo Cooper, 1982) p.45.
41 TNA WO 169/4494: 2nd Royal Gloucestershire Hussars War Diary, 1942, 8–15 June 1942.
42 TNA WO 169/4489: 10th Hussars War Diary, 5–18 June 1942.
43 TNA WO 169/4053: 1st Armoured Division War Diary, 8 June 1942.
44 TNA WO 169/4509: 6th RTR War Diary, January-December 1942, 8 June 42.

supported by the RHA battery. In the evening they regained their own A squadron and the Stuarts returned to 3rd RTR.

While the armoured brigades continued with these minor attacks against more powerful enemy defensive positions, Rommel now focused his attention on Bir Hacheim. The French were finally forced to evacuate by 11 June, Panzerarmee returned north again, to increase the pressure on Knightsbridge and the adjacent British armour. Units were regrouped into more viable squadrons across regiments, the Bays initially had 11 Grants and 10 Crusaders and 1 Stuart remaining, with 6 Grants from the 8th Hussars. Next day a full squadron of Grants arrived from 4th Hussars under Major Knight and later A Squadron rejoined with another 11 Crusaders, under Viscount Knebworth. On 11 June, 4th and 8th Hussars moved to 2nd Armoured Brigade and later in the day the Bays moved to 7th Armoured Brigade.[45] This left 4th Armoured as essentially 3rd/5th RTR combined in one regiment. The 2nd RGH was ordered to be a regimental group, operating west of the minefield, as a jock column, which considering enemy concentrations of static Italian divisions in that area was optimistic for one squadron of Stuarts and a battery of 25pdr guns.[46]

Typical of the ongoing battles against the Aslagh ridge, 6th RTR made another attack on Panzerarmee positions, with the lighter Stuarts from A Squadron covering the flanks. They received heavy 88mm fire into their left flank which knocked out four Grants within a few minutes. The regiment pulled back slightly until these guns could be engaged. On the left, 1st RTR was attacked by a group of panzers, so 6th RTR's C squadron Grants moved around them to give fire support. This effectively halted the 6th RTR's own attack. These daily battles added to the constant attrition in numbers of tanks; the regiment lost another three Grants and two Stuarts, as always with some or all of their unlucky crews. The Grants remained a particular target, so with only 12 tanks in each squadron even those units which had received replacements were being constantly weakened. With the attack halted, they spent the rest of the day recovering the knocked out Grants, and later on some of the remaining crews walked in. Any opportunity to destroy knocked out vehicles was taken by both sides, and some Italian infantry came forward to destroy the Grants and some remaining crews were taken prisoner. The weary tankers retired under moderate shellfire to leaguer three miles back.[47]

Meanwhile 6th RTR occupied the ridge line south of Knightsbridge and completed some much-needed maintenance. Large enemy columns were then seen some miles to the south at El Igela, so by mid-afternoon they were ordered to patrol south of Naduret. As the Stuarts pushed forward to contact, Lieutenant Knott's tank was hit and he and two crew were killed. In the evening the reduced 4th Armoured, now with 1st and 6th RTR, continued south-east towards B.727 where they encountered

45 Bovington: The Bays War Diary, 8–11 June 1942.
46 TNA WO 169/4053: 1st Armoured Division War Diary, 9 June 1942.
47 TNA WO 169/4509: 6th RTR War Diary, 1942, 10 June 1942.

another 30 panzers. They turned half-right to engage them in line with 1st RTR on the right, and the Bays came up on the left, with an RHA battery in support. First RTR was unlucky to advance over the crest line at Naduret and beyond only to be hit by anti-tank guns at short range, losing nine Grants quickly and leaving them in disorder.[48]

As always, the enemy column halted just out of range and fighting died down in the afternoon. In the evening C Squadron went forward to engage them and knocked out one tank at last light.[49] Effectively, 4th Armoured Brigade had been drawn south a few miles from Knightsbridge by 12 June and encountered more powerful enemy columns than their own supports, on almost the same ground as the first day. The early morning mists uncovered some 70 panzers with supporting 88mm guns, which quickly knocked out one Grant. The next two days' battle would prove to be a testing one for the regiment.[50]

With Hacheim evacuated, and fresh MET columns moving up towards Knightsbridge, 22nd Brigade (3rd/4th CLY) were joined by 4th Hussars' Grants for added firepower and positioned left of the Guards with 2nd Armoured extending to their left, watching the Naduret et Ghesceuasc Ridge. The Hussars had arrived with 1st Armoured Brigade in early June, but were split up and used as detachments across other regiments. B Squadron had given over its new Grants to others and was given 10 old Grants and 1 Crusader in return. It was attached to three different regiments in as many days, fighting on 10 June with 3rd CLY. The rest of the regiment sat frustrated on the El Duda ridge, listening to the heavy fighting in the west. Lieutenant Colonel Kidd on his own initiative decided to get some tanks from the nearby TDS depot and returned with six assorted vehicles to bolster the defence.[51] Regiments now had daily changes of command, 4th CLY moved from 22nd Brigade to 2nd Armoured command, and returned the next day. They observed both 2nd and 4th Armoured in battle on 12 June, from Bir Bellefaa ridge, and became involved in the battle into the afternoon.[52]

Armoured Battles of 12–13 June

The defeats of 12–13 June are seen as another key turning point in the battle. Panzerarmee forced the armoured brigades to retreat north and so the evacuation of the Knightsbridge Box became inevitable. With Bir Hacheim also evacuated, the original Gazala line had been undermined as a defensive position. In the north, both 50th Division and 1st S.A. Division had the unenviable task of retreating through

---

48   TNA WO 169/4216: 4th Armoured Brigade War Diary, 10 June 1942.
49   TNA WO 169/4509: 6th RTR War Diary, 1942, 10–11 June 1942.
50   TNA WO 169/4509: 6th RTR War Diary, January-December 1942, 11 June 1942.
51   Scott-Daniell, *4th Hussar*, p.325.
52   TNA WO 169/4251: 22nd Armoured Brigade War Diary, 12 June 1942.

Tobruk, around the rear of Panzerarmee, or face being trapped. For Eighth Army it was the beginning of the end of the battle, with 90th Light Division roaming south of the exposed El Adem Box; any new defensive 'lines' would be likely to unravel under further attacks.

There were further poor command decisions and unfortunate delays. On 12 June Messervy was caught out again, this time travelling to meet Norrie at XXX Corps, and was forced to take a wide detour, before hiding down a well to avoid 90th Light columns. There were also further arguments about what to do on the second day of heavy battle. Meanwhile, the armoured brigades were being defeated in detail and pushed northwards.

In comparison to British command delays, Rommel was at his forward HQ, in full contact with DAK and his three divisions. Nehring was with 21st Panzer HQ and all Panzerarmee HQs coordinated well. In the evening of 10 June, Rommel ordered his commanders and intelligence chiefs to meet him at 0600 hours next day for new orders. The forward HQ was sited north of Bir Hacheim, where he coordinated the attacks around Knightsbridge.[53] General Ritchie was 45 miles away at Gambut. He believed that both sides were still evenly matched in overall tank numbers, therefore Eighth Army was right to defend the ridges on either side of Knightsbridge to wear down Panzerarmee as it made costly attacks. However, Axis attack doctrine continued to be highly effective in wearing down British armour. These two days left them worn down, despite replacement tanks, to weakened regiments by 14 June. Troops had been holding the line for 16 days, with constant night marches back to leaguer, refuel and rearm. Panzerarmee was equally worn out, with 15th Panzer complaining of being under more strain by 9 June.[54] Yet they had achieved more success so far, and retained a higher morale, as the advances came closer to Tobruk. Ritchie's policy of getting fresh armoured regiments to simply hand over their tanks to the exhausted crews also did not help British morale. John Verney noted how pleased the Yeomanry Division was going forward to fight:

> The Free French, on their way back from Bir Hacheim, drove past and we cheered them. Our General paid us a call. A pep-talk. You are the finest Division in the world and you have been kept waiting all these years for this one moment to strike the decisive blow…we waited, poised, to strike the decisive blow…Within days we were ordered to hand over their tanks to the battle-weary troops, 'What's the matter with you chaps?' One of them said with understandable asperity, 'Can't you fight?'[55]

---

53   IWM: AL833: DAK War Diary, 10 June 1942.
54   IWM: AL833: DAK War Diary, 9 June 1942.
55   John Verney, *Going to the Wars: A Journey in Various Directions* (London: The Reprint Society, 1957), pp.121–122.

One subaltern of 4th Hussars who arrived with 1st Armoured on 2 June – his regiment was at full strength equipped with Grants and Stuarts, trained and ready for battle – said the Brigade was shocked to learn they would be handing over their tanks to the battle-weary units. He commented that he would have received 'nought out of ten' for making such an order in his promotion exams.[56]

In the two days prior, both Ritchie and Auchinleck made appreciations on the battle so far and Ritchie suggested the likely moves ahead. He estimated that both sides were roughly equal in numbers of tanks, guns and brigades. Auchinleck also updated the Prime Minister on 10 June, on the battle up to then, sending estimated casualties and remaining strengths in tanks, guns and aircraft. Churchill saw the overall situation as being positive, and praised Ritchie for his, 'dogged and resolute fighting' though he privately queried the high numbers of British POWs, (based on 150th Brigade and Operation Aberdeen losses). He told Auchinleck that an attritional battle would be more harmful to Panzerarmee with Eight Army reinforcements arriving more quickly. These fresh units, along with Eighth Army's own recovery rates for equipment, that Ritchie had predicted, meant that they would be successful.[57] The commanders remained confident, Gazala would end with Eighth Army still forward of Tobruk, and an exhausted Panzerarmee left battered and hopefully forced to retreat again.

He reported that the Free French escaped Bir Hacheim overnight on 10/11 June although with losses, and all of their heavy equipment had to be abandoned. Ritchie wanted Panzerarmee to be contained in the cauldron, but Eighth Army would now avoid direct attacks on this area. It would continue operating jock columns attacking enemy supply lines west of the minefield, which he hoped would draw off enemy forces. DAK had reported that the supply situation remained precarious by the evening of 9 June, and the supply track needed protection.[58] So 7th Motor Brigade columns were having some effect.

Auchinleck visited Ritchie on 12 June, as Panzerarmee renewed its attacks around Knightsbridge. Connell argues that by now he and Ritchie no longer saw eye-to-eye on operations, noting Auchinleck's numerous queries of Ritchie's appreciations to him from 9–11 June.[59] He left a day later just as the armour was defeated. De Guingand travelled with him as DMI, but stayed for two extra days. He later considered the dilemmas for both during this phase of the battle. Auchinleck had interfered in all plans either by telegram, letter or by visiting Ritchie, while the latter always had to await a response to any new plan he came up with, which, in the DMI's view, caused vital delays. For GHQ, this was now the main battle on which the defence of the whole Middle East theatre hinged. Therefore, Auchinleck felt that if all decisions

---

56 Scott-Daniell, *4th Hussar*, pp.324–325.
57 Winston Churchill, *The Second World War, Vol. IV: The Hinge of Fate* (London: Cassell, 1951), pp.326–327.
58 IWM: AL833: DAK War Diary, evening report, 9 June 1942.
59 John Connell, *Auchinleck* (London: Cassell, 1959), pp.556–558.

were left with Eighth Army, he would appear to be ignoring his responsibilities as C-in-C.[60] Back at GHQ his assistant, Major General Dorman-Smith, had never been a fan of Ritchie as Army commander. He blamed the failure to gain a victory on GHQ for keeping Ritchie and that the, 'Auk may have to pay a high price for his loyalty to a man [Richie]…who…is a very ordinary occupational soldier.'[61]

In comparison, German command remained near the front and decisive. On 11 June, Rommel issued a verbal summary of the attack to his commanders, then he discussed the orders in detail with 15th Panzer's C.O. Meanwhile Nehring was to liaise in person with Group Baade, brought up in reserve, while DAK battle HQ would be positioned on the Hacheim track near the minefield-gap, with only essential vehicles.[62] As they advanced northwards, DAK battle HQ was in close contact with 15th Panzer HQ where further measures and personal opinions were exchanged on 'several occasions.'[63]

Panzerarmee advanced north on 11 June and crossed the Trigh el Abd, where 15th Panzer observed 50 enemy tanks on their left flank but received only weak shelling from the British guns. Eighth Army tanks gave way after a short battle. Radio intercepts were picked up that 4th Armoured refused to attack towards the south-east (into them).[64] 4th Armoured reported a strong thrust towards their left flank as they took up a battle position on the Naduret ridge. The situation became critical and they requested a regimental group from 22nd Brigade, which arrived quickly. Lumsden then ordered the rest of 22nd to join them on the Naduret ridge.[65]

On 12 June the main attack was made by about 100 Axis tanks and supporting guns. Two points occur here; firstly, the defending armour was spread across nine miles of ridge line from Naduret, to the pinnacle near B721. Secondly, that British Y intercepts picked up that Panzerarmee would be thrusting northwards, now that the Bir Hacheim battle was over. The main weight of the thrust was against the British left flank, at B721. By the afternoon, the British line was under pressure from losses and had retired slowly to the northern edges of the Naduret ridge, with Pt.169 in the centre. With 6th RTR reduced to four Grants, 3/5th RTR was ordered back to cover the pass at B652, north of the Bellefaa ridge. The brigade rallied north of the Batruna ridge, and had been shelled by German guns, which had followed them.[66] This meant the panzer columns were now east of the Scots Guards, further along the ridge at Rigel, and Knightsbridge was more isolated now.

---

60 Francis de Guingand, *Operation Victory* (London: Hodder & Stoughton, 1947), pp.117–119.
61 Lavinia Graecen, *Chink A Biography* (London: Macmillan, 1989), pp.198–199.
62 IWM: AL833: DAK War Diary, 11 June 1942.
63 IWM: AL833: DAK War Diary, 11 June 1942.
64 IWM: AL833: DAK War Diary, 11 June 1942.
65 TNA WO 169/4216: 4th Armoured Brigade War Diary, 11–12 June.
66 TNA WO 169/4216: 4th Armoured Brigade War Diary, 12 June.

In 22nd Brigade, 3rd CLY had been joined by the 4th Hussars' Grants, who moved south to engage 20 Italian M13s. Faced by the more powerful Grants these quickly withdrew, but the squadron did not hear the recall order, and continued south to be ambushed by some 88mm guns, who knocked out the entire squadron.[67] The British were losing their best tanks at an alarming rate. They knew the enemy was pushing towards El Adem which was affecting the resupply routes along the Trigh Capuzzo. On the right, 90th Light columns were directed towards El Adem again, but again lost contact with DAK. In between, linking the two, were the light reconnaissance groups.[68]

The evening before, Nehring had visited 15th Panzer to give instructions for an expected British attack on 12 June. He ordered 15th Panzer to receive the attack on the southern ridge, before counterattacking, with 21st Panzer making a thrust into the enemy rear. Rommel arrived later and agreed to the plan.[69] Next morning Rommel adjusted the plan slightly when the attack did not appear, so 15th Panzer was ordered to attack with the main effort on the right towards Bir Lefa (to the left of Knightsbridge) and then to Pt.176 (B.652), the pass heading north to Tobruk on the Hagiag et Raml ridge.

DAK began the advance and counted up to 100 British tanks opposing them; soon the defensive fire forced the DAK attack to falter. Nehring watching from a nearby ridge, believed it was because the panzers were too spread out and thus losing momentum trying to protect their right flank. To regain the momentum, 115th Rifle Regiment was sent in on the right, but were too far to the north-east. The British were still holding the escarpment, but some gave way on their left, which made Nehring push for an enveloping movement from his right flank. The Panzer Division could not discern which units were opposing them – 2nd or 4th Armoured Brigades.[70] Both divisions were slow to get going and it took a visit by Rommel and Nehring to galvanise their attacks. 4th Armoured were out on a limb to the south-east of Knightsbridge, facing 15th Panzer to the east and 21st Panzer to the west. The main attack still faltered in front of the British line which was found to be strong along the ridge, with 115th Rifles advance having no impact. Confusingly for 15th Panzer, some British units fell back slightly to the north;[71] these may have been replenishing ammunition to the front line tanks.

The brigade position was heavily shelled in the evening.[72] The 4th Hussars were ordered to attack a force of armoured cars but were themselves ambushed, with only

---

67   TNA WO 169/4251: 22nd Armoured Brigade War Diary, 12 June 1942.
68   IWM: AL833: DAK War Diary, 12 June 1942.
69   IWM: AL833: DAK War Diary, 11 June 1942.
70   IWM: AL833: DAK War Diary, 12 June 1942.
71   IWM: AL833: DAK War Diary, 12 June 1942.
72   TNA WO 169/4251: 22nd Armoured Brigade War Diary, 12 June 1942.

Lieutenant A. Cartmell's tank getting away. This was a cruel blow to the regiment which had arrived at the front fully equipped just 10 days previously.[73]

4th Armoured, with the Bays on the left flank, was now facing large numbers of panzers and support fire from 88mm guns. Heavy shelling caused 6th RTR a trickle of minor casualties before the enemy began to occupy higher ground, so the regiment was allowed to pull back slightly to align with the Bays. The afternoon brought further sniping by anti-tank guns hidden in the afternoon haze, and heavy shelling as the B echelon trucks came forward to resupply the tanks. The pressure forced them to make a steady withdrawal northward and they passed Knightsbridge and onto the Raml Ridge at Pt.176, the only narrow track down the steep escarpment in that area. This was partially blocked by enemy shellfire, but the tanks were able to negotiate it. They were ordered north again to rally at Pt.190, on the ridge next to Acroma – they arrived having lost another three Grants.[74] 28 panzers were on the Batruna ridge west of Raml by the evening and were being engaged by 4th Armoured to their west.[75]

6th RTR had suffered similar losses of Grant tanks over the last few days, but do not state their current strength by 13 June. That day they operated north of the Raml ridge line, onto which the enemy had established itself, with anti-tank guns. They saw the overrunning of the Scots Guards position to the south-east. They leaguered adjacent to Pt.187 position for the night, having run onto an unmarked minefield, but appear not to have been in contact with 1st Worcesters who were rapidly preparing it for defence from an expected attack the next day. This lack of communication shows the fluid situation which added to the confusion across Corps and Army HQs. By the late evening, as darkness fell, the panzer column was in possession of the high ground along the Raml-Batruna ridge, and 4th Armoured said they were struggling to hold them there.[76]

During the night Lumsden appreciated that, so far, the enemy was being held to the west of Knightsbridge, with the Scots Guards to the right at Raml. The enemy were in strength to the east and south of the Guards Box. There were no orders from Corps, so he decided to hold Knightsbridge for another day. By early morning 20 panzers were pushing west towards 22nd Armoured. North of them, 30 panzers and four 88mm guns were pushing west towards B.652, and the beleaguered 2nd and 4th Armoured. At 0800 hours, Norrie was informed that all brigades were weak and struggling to hold the valley behind Knightsbridge and up to the Raml Ridge. Norrie said he would speak to Ritchie. At 1015 hours the 1st Armoured Division was ordered to hold its present positions.[77]

The two main attacks came from noon onwards. At Bellefaa they were shelled from the south, while 80 tanks and more MET came along the ridge from the east, pressing

---

73 Scott-Daniell, *4th Hussar*, p.325.
74 TNA WO 169/4509: 6th RTR War Diary, January-December 1942, 12 June 42.
75 TNA WO 169/4053: 1st Armoured Division War Diary, 12 June 1942.
76 TNA WO 169/4053: 1st Armoured Division War Diary, 12 June 1942.
77 TNA WO 169/4053: 1st Armoured Division War Diary, 13 June 1942.

22nd Armoured. North of them, 30 panzers moved west towards Rigel, and the Scots Guards. Both 2nd and 4th brigades were to make a joint attack the ridge from either side. By late afternoon there was a heavy sandstorm and 2nd Armoured said they were waiting for the 4th to attack. By 1830 hours the Guards Rigel position had been overrun. In the evening columns of enemy tanks and MET moved north and south of the Raml ridge area, while 22nd Armoured fought to keep the route open from Knightsbridge. The guns were extracted after 2200 hours and the Guards withdrew during the night.[78]

The 22nd Armoured report said that they remained in battle positions next to Knightsbridge on the Bir Bellefaa Ridge, to the right and extended to the Bays in 2nd Armoured on their left.[79] As the Bays were forced to pull out to refuel and rearm, enemy panzer began to work around their left flank to enfilade their position. They had to pivot backwards into the valley with 32nd Army Tank Brigade coming in on the left. The line was being forced north to the Raml ridge and Knightsbridge had become untenable and so orders were given for its evacuation that night. They had to protect the flank of the Guards Brigade as it retired along the track to Acroma, and then rally themselves at B.674, the southern point of the small minefield dividing the valley. They did so but 4th CLY suffered heavy casualties from some deployed anti-tank guns.

North of Rigel Ridge, 4th Armoured were on the Acroma slopes facing south and west. They were told that 40 panzers were moving east along the Rigel Ridge to their south, but visibility was reduced to 200 yards due to the dust and smoke. Both brigades were urged to move south and west to support the beleaguered Scots Guards at the western end of Rigel. Unfortunately, they were unsure of the ground in this area, and the attack was slow to begin. As visibility improved they made progress and knocked out 11 panzers for no loss, but not in time to save the Guards from being overrun. They rallied back towards Acroma, and 6th RTR reported the loss of two tanks to minefields at Pt.187.

The battle continued the next day for 22nd Brigade near the B.652 pass, where a tough rearguard action was fought by 4th RTR and 3rd CLY.[80] The Sharpshooters were reduced to a composite squadron and 4th RTR returned to 32nd AT Brigade, the Guards sent a grateful thanks for covering their exit from Knightsbridge. Meanwhile 4th Armoured, with some infantry and 6pdrs, covered the northern gaps in the minefield near Acroma, though they were not informed about the Worcesters' battle nearby. They were directed to counter the evening thrust to the Pt.208 feature, where a major battle took place at last light.

From the very beginning of Gazala, the armoured brigades had fought too many separate battles. Occasionally they received fire support from their group battery or

---

78 TNA WO 169/4053: 1st Armoured Division War Diary, 13 June 1942.
79 TNA WO 169/4251: 22nd Armoured Brigade War Diary, 13 June 1942.
80 TNA WO 169/4251: 22nd Armoured Brigade War Diary, 13 June 1942.

regiment, or they pivoted on Knightsbridge, which had become the bulwark position for the army's centre. Regiments were weakened by these daily attacks and forced to spend long days observing Panzerarmee from adjacent ridges before going forward again. The crews and support echelons suffered from fatigue and battle stress but carried on doggedly. Ritchie had decided to filter in replacement tanks and crews, rather than deploy fresh regiments, which, judging from the comments made at the time, was a major blow to morale of both the worn-out and fresh regiments, who had trained together and wanted to fight as a unit. The defeats of the remaining armoured units on 12–13 June was the culmination of these earlier difficulties.

7

Infantry Battles

Think at this time of the patient Infantry
Far from your comfortable, lit rooms,
Where you sit talking about victory
And listening to gramophones.
Outside-oh, not in the books you read!
Is the legend of wounds that bleed,
Story of the Sower and
The Dragon-seed.
It is the harvest-time in no man's land,
And the big granary is being made,
The yawning, open grave
For casualties,
Who will be wrapped in blankets
When death puts out their eyes.

'Think at this time'
G.O. Physick[1]

As the battle reached a middle phase, Ritchie believed the more dominant Axis armoured forces could be held, by creating a defensive line running from Acroma down to El Adem and east to Sidi Rezegh. In between would be further localities held by battalions which would again inflict heavy casualties, should they be attacked. These positions would protect both the southern approaches towards Tobruk and the Trigh Capuzzo. If Tobruk could be held long enough, fresh units could be built up on the frontier, combined with a counterattack from a refreshed armoured force towards El Adem.[2] This could force Panzerarmee into an over-extended flank of over

---

1 Anon., *Poems from the Desert*, pp.39–40.
2 TNA WO 201/379: Notes on Operations in North Africa, May–June 1942, Ritchie, p.13.

50 miles, from south of Tobruk, with its forward elements facing Eighth Army along the frontier. The Panzer divisions might be overstretched again, as they had proved at Crusader with their infamous 'dash to the wire'. The main problem with this plan was the dislocation of existing Eighth Army formations as they struggled to extract themselves from the Tobruk sector. Secondly, Ritchie also intended to hold the Axis, along the, 'western side of Tobruk and south from there.' at Pt.187 and Acroma in the west.[3] So the loss of Pt.187, and later the evacuation of El Adem and Sidi Rezegh boxes, meant that the potential of this defended line was left in ruins, cutting off Tobruk from the frontier.

This defensive plan was in one sense a logical method of covering key positions in a loose outer ring of sites beyond Tobruk in order to halt Panzerarmee; by forcing attacks on these positions one after another, they might just suffer enough heavy casualties to come unstuck. The Worcesters believed 15th Panzer's final assault on their locality at Pt.187 was a timid affair, directly because of the earlier heavy casualties suffered attacking the position.[4] However, they were just smaller versions of the brigade boxes in the Gazala line. Panzerarmee applied its rigorous assault tactics on the localities. First they would knock out the guns and MG posts, before sending in the engineers under a smoke screen to create a pathway wide enough for the panzers and motorised Axis infantry to close in amongst the slit trenches; there was little the defenders could do, except evacuate or surrender.[5] Having broken the front line brigades and much of the armour, these subsequent localities were within striking distance of Tobruk and the adjacent supply bases, so the prize for Rommel and Panzerarmee was just too great an opportunity to halt their offensive. Casualties received in these attacks would have to have been crippling to save Tobruk.

From 151st Brigade, 9th Durham Light Infantry (9th DLI) were detached to the south on 1 June, along the British side of the minefield, to occupy a position which overlooked the cauldron. This was west of Eluet et Tamar and helped to fill in the gap between Tamar and the mine belt, where they dug in a locality and held it, despite being shelled by artillery or strafed by passing fighters. From there day and night patrols gained valuable intelligence on Panzerarmee in that sector.[6] They evacuated the position at dusk on 14 June and with the rest of the 50th Division moved west through the mine-gaps. This was typical of higher HQs breaking up brigades into individual battalions, to be sent out to hold new defences in an attempt to slow Panzerarmee. Other units were less fortunate in their defence.

3   TNA WO 201/379: Notes on Operations in North Africa, May–June 1942, Ritchie, p.14.
4   Lord Birdwood, *The Worcestershire Regiment 1922–1950* (Aldershot: Gale & Polden, 1952), p.40.
5   War Department, *German Methods of Warfare in the Libyan Desert* (Buxton: MLRS, 2004), p.3.
6   TNA WO 169/5009: 9th Durham Light Infantry War Diary 1942, 1–14 June.

Knightsbridge, 27 May–13 June

The position at Knightsbridge became the most important 'pivot' for Eighth Army, yet was conceived quite late on in comparison to other defensive boxes. Reconnaissance parties from 2nd Scots Guards and 3rd Coldstream Guards only went forward on the 19 May to select a position for, '…a defensive box in flat area' near Bir Bellefaa.[7] The place chosen covered the cross-tracks for the Trigh Capuzzo and Hacheimtrigh running north to Tobruk. The Scots Guards were part of the line initially but as they moved out to Rigel, their posts were taken by the Sherwood Foresters. No.4 Company of the Coldstream deployed one motor platoon each side of the eastern gap of Capuzzo. On the first day, the box appears to have been attacked from two sides. Tanks appeared near the southeast face but were engaged and four were knocked out by 25pdrs and 2pdrs. No. 2 Company portees arrived and dispersed, but unfortunately the Axis guns focused on them with heavy fire and knocked out five portees. The remaining German tanks withdrew at last light.[8]

In the late afternoon the Box received some shelling, then three Mk IVs approached the southwest corner opposite No.3 Company. They turned and drove along the outer wire, spraying the slit trenches with MG fire. The Coldstreamers fired back with their two pounders. By nightfall there were five Mk IVs and 20 vehicle derelicts on the edge of the Box.[9] This was followed by a number of quiet days. The enemy used a derelict Grant as an OP post. The Guards sent out a patrol to knock out the nearby artillery but the patrol leader, Lieutenant Stobart, was wounded and failed to return. A fresh attack was made on 7 June, by mixed armour and infantry, using their standard tactics of heavy shelling and MG fire. The artillery batteries returned fire and kept the enemy at a distance, though the gunner OP was wounded. More 'quiet' days followed from 8 to 12 June, apart from heavy shelling from Axis guns, while Panzerarmee dealt with Bir Hacheim. The shelling increased on 13 June, and that evening orders were received to vacate the Box by midnight, leaving nothing.[10]

With Panzerarmee in the centre of the Cauldron-Knightsbridge sector by 28 May, RAF bombers and fighter bombers made heavy attacks on the concentrations of Axis MET along the Rigel Ridge, north of Knightsbridge. Next day there was heavy firing near to Knightsbridge, then the battle moved further west, with the enemy holding a line from Eluet et Tamar down to Bir Harmat. Panzerarmee engineers widened gaps in the minefield near Sidi Muftah and Ualeb but were shelled by artillery and attacked by the RAF at these choke points.[11]

Like other brigade boxes, Knightsbridge Box was being weakened, reduced from three battalions down to being garrisoned by 3rd Coldstream and their supporting

---

7   TNA WO 169/4983: 2nd Scots Guards War Diary, 1942, 19 May 1942.
8   TNA WO 169/4982: 4 Coy/3rd Coldstream Guards War Diary, 27 May 1942.
9   TNA WO 169/4982: 3 Coy/3rd Coldstream Guards War Diary, 27 May 1942.
10 TNA WO 169/4982: 3 Coy/3rd Coldstream Guards War Diary, 13 June 1942.
11 TNA WO 169/4983: 2nd Scots Guards War Diary, 1942, 28–30 May 1942.

gunners. By 5 June, 9th Rifle Brigade had moved to hold Eluet et Tamar, and 2nd Scots Guards moved to dig in on the Rigel Ridge, along with detachments from Knightsbridge. As enemy columns deployed around Knightsbridge from 11 June, batteries and companies were being switched in and out of the Rigel locality. At last light 2nd RHA battery and one company of 9th RB arrived, but at 2300 hours were moved on elsewhere.[12] As the battle coalesced around Knightsbridge, there appeared to be a lack of grip at division, corps or army level command.

The 2nd Scots Guards at the Rigel Ridge, 2 to 13 June

The battalion had only rejoined 1st Armoured Division 10 days before the offensive, arriving at the divisional rear area near El Adem, It was a motor battalion with five companies, HQ, Left Flank, Right Flank, F and G companies, and had sent jock columns to the west occupying the Ualeb Box since February.[13] One company went forward to dig in at Bir Bellefaa adjacent to Knightsbridge, and on 21 May, the rest of the battalion was ordered to defend the 'passes' on the steeper end of Hagiag et Batruna Ridge, which had very few crossing places for vehicles. They began setting up a box to cover the crossing points at B.650 and received orders to 'stand to' at 0820 hours on 27 May, as the offensive began. There was fighting all around them by the late afternoon, with 90th Light reaching west of El Adem. The battalion anti-tank gunners aided the defence at Knightsbridge, knocking out three Mk IVs with their 2pdrs, in their first action.[14]

Changes in orders showed continued uncertainty. On 31 May the Guards were sent to the Hagiag et Raml Ridge to start a new box, along with a column heading west with 2nd RHA to attack the enemy in the cauldron, unfortunately this group suffered heavy losses with 51 men missing. The battalion was shuffled back to B.651 and then returned again to the Raml Ridge on 2 June. Almost immediately they were moved west, along the ridge, to occupy the Rigel position, shaped like a hind leg pointing north at the 'toe'. They were joined by the remnants of I Battery of 2nd RHA (3 guns) and for a while by 339 Battery of 104th RHA (8 25pdr guns and eight 6pdrs) and 6th S.A. Battery (8 25pdr guns and eight 2pdrs). The South African gunners supported them when attacked by 21st Panzer on 13 June. From 2 June, they were finally digging in and F company began to lay a minefield by night.[15]

Battalion HQ made a full appreciation of the ground they had been allocated, to prevent Panzerarmee from driving northwards. They saw the position as a temporary defence which could not be established as a fully defended locality, though higher

---

12   TNA WO 169/4983: 2nd Scots Guards War Diary, 1942, 5 and 11 June 1942.
13   TNA WO 169/4983: 2nd Scots Guards War Diary, 1942, 17–21 May 1942.
14   TNA WO 169/4983: 2nd Scots Guards War Diary, 1942, 27 May 1942.
15   TNA WO 169/4983: 2nd Scots Guards War Diary, 1942, 2 June 1942.

commanders may have thought otherwise.[16] By 10 June, as enemy columns moved back around the Rigel Ridge, the C.O. made another recce for a new site back at B.651 and B.652, where they had originally come from.[17] From Rigel they had a good view to the south across Knightsbridge, but they were overlooked by the higher Hagiag et Raml Ridge to the east. To the south was Pt.166 which overlooked the entire ridgeline and which could be used by enemy OPs.[18] The physical terrain of Rigel affected the strength of the position and created problems for the battalion. The north and west sides had more gentle slopes, whereas the southern side of the ridge was more convex, up 150 feet high, steep-sided and cut by wadis. This meant the forward companies were under direct enemy observation, and some of the enemy held ground was not visible. Most of the gun pits had to be blasted out, because there was only one pneumatic drill which the Indian Sappers refused to use under shellfire. Additional features, such as crawl trenches to allow movement under fire, were never completed nor were the minefields extended. The Guards saw this position as a delaying action, and not as a fully defended locality, to be combined with an armoured counterattack, but this never happened.[19]

The locality also extended west of the ridge by 1,000 yards, as well as being on the ridge, this was quite extended for a single battalion.[20] The plan shows an extended line of companies and anti-tank gun platoons rather than a more compact defence. The numbers of guns attached also kept altering, but when attacked, they had only eight guns with them. The anti-tank crews were also given little time and only one practice shot with the new 6pdr guns and criticised their late delivery on 3 June. The Guards believed their guns would have lasted longer, if they had kept their old 2pdrs, which had been camouflaged in and had a lower profile. The gun pits blasted and drilled out of the ridge had been made for them, not the larger 6pdr guns.

Artillery OPs were sent to nearby heights and watched the events of the attacks on the cauldron. After the Aberdeen battles, the sector became quiet and the next day there was also a failed advance towards Knightsbridge by an enemy column. The quiet period continued to 9 June, which allowed them to lay a new minefield south-east across to Knightsbridge, only stopping work early on 10 June as enemy vehicles approached. Hostilities resumed with an exchange of shellfire that day which resulted in some German vehicles being knocked out.[21] They heard the large-scale tank battle on 12 June and found that the Panzerarmee had surrounded El Adem and was on the Raml Ridge to the east, overlooking the Scots Guards.[22] Typically they received four compressors and two bulldozers to aid their digging in, but these had arrived too late to help improve the defences.

16 Erskine, *Scots Guards 1919–1955*, p.100.
17 TNA WO 169/4983: 2nd Scots Guards War Diary, 1942, 10 June 1942.
18 TNA WO 169/4983: 2nd Scots Guards War Diary, 1942, 3 June 1942.
19 Erskine, *Scots Guards 1919–1955*, p.100
20 TNA WO 169/4983: 2nd Scots Guards War Diary, 1942, 3 June 1942.
21 TNA WO 169/4983: 2nd Scots Guards War Diary, 1942, 7 June 1942.
22 TNA WO 169/4983: 2nd Scots Guards War Diary, 1942, 12 June 1942.

In the afternoon of 13 June the Guards endured a rapid and heavy direct assault. They watched a large enemy column of 29 tanks move up from the west to attack, with another column consisting of eight panzers and about 200 MET to the south, with infantry and guns. To the north the Worcesters at Pt.187 observed the battle from 1400 hours, and by late afternoon the enemy had broken into the Rigel defences.[23] The Scots Guards made a determined defence of their position. For some reason the approaching tanks were not engaged by artillery and so panzer commanders were standing on their turrets and spotting for the edge of the minefield. They peeled off left and right and began machine gunning the Guards' slit trenches on the ridge. One group of tanks attempted to advance through a mine gap but were hit by 6pdrs and direct fire from 25pdr guns, which knocked out two or three Mk IIIs. The flank platoon, commanded by Lieutenant Calvocoressi, also hit another tank, and lost one 6pdr knocked out. Having been repulsed the enemy held back and shelled the ridge-line and gun positions behind.[24]

The second attack was made from the south-west, where the enemy had spotted a gap of 2,000 yards with no minefield to protect the ridge. After pressing this sector with heavy shelling and MG fire from both tanks and infantry, all of the remaining guns were knocked out. Army artillery had been allocated by DAK, as the battle developed.[25]

More panzers appeared from the south and closed in, effectively rolling up the company positions. F and G Companies were suppressed by heavy shellfire and machine guns zeroed in on those attempting to return fire from their slit trenches. As this was taking place, tanks from 2nd Armoured Brigade were approaching from the east but halted near the battalion HQ, on the left flank. Their liaison officer met with the HQ and 'with great confidence' promised that with 4th Armoured moving down from the north, they would counterattack and destroy the enemy panzers on the Rigel.[26] Yet, as already described, 4th Armoured reported that they were cautious because they lacked knowledge of the terrain in this sector of the battlefield. The two companies had no protective minefield for the anti-tank guns and they were overrun and eliminated in succession. G Company only had two guns and at both sites the guns fought to the last, knocking out tanks as they closed in. DAK noted the attack was continued only after the infantry, 'have been thrown in.'[27] The German infantry mopped up after that, while the remainder of the Guards headed north to escape. Tragically they were bombed by the RAF and artillery as they withdrew, while the South Africans sacrificed their battery to save most of the Guards. The 21st

23 Birdwood, *Worcestershire Regiment*, p.36.
24 TNA WO 169/4983: 2nd Scots Guards War Diary, 1942, Appendix A Maabus er Rigel battle, 13 June 1942.
25 IWM: AL833: DAK War Diary, 13 June, 42.
26 TNA WO 169/4983: 2nd Scots Guards War Diary, 1942, Appendix A Maabus er Rigel battle, 13 June 1942.
27 IWM: AL833: DAK War Diary, 13 June 1942.

Panzer reported 20 tanks destroyed in a tough battle.[28] The loss of Rigel, added to the defeat of the armoured brigades on the other flank, compelled the abandonment of the Knightsbridge Box, and so the rest of Gazala. Rommel praised the, 'tremendous courage and tenacity' of the Guards that held these positions.[29]

Knightsbridge, 13–14 June

On 13 June, No.4 Company of the Coldstream Guards was approached some enemy armour. They were seen off by the Sherwood Forester guns and later the 25pdrs. In the afternoon a severe dust storm blew up. Under cover of this the Germans lined the perimeter with heavy weapons – AT guns, mortars and armoured cars. These sniped at the Guards when they could see them. Infantry also appeared to be working through the minefield but were engaged by the Coldstream MGs, as visibility allowed, inflicting about 70 casualties. After dark they made ready to evacuate the Box. They were the last to exit by the northwest gaps, and walked with the rest of the battalion to Acroma.[30] No.3 Company also left on foot, all their stores and guns had been destroyed. They watched the armoured screen around them being attacked but this did not stop the Guards moving towards Acroma.

The 1st Worcesters at Pt.187, 14 June

The El Adem Box was garrisoned by 29th Indian Brigade for much of the battle. As the threat to the rear of 50th Division increased, battalions were taken from these brigade boxes and deployed to cover key features, and 1st Worcesters was one of these units, thrust into the line at Pt.187 in another last minute change. They had already spent three days of early June, developing a new box at Sidi Rezegh, before being sent on a confused series of moves first to Belhamed, and were finally ordered from 8 June to hold Pt.187. Each locality had a battalion, a troop of 25pdrs and the promise of further armour and artillery nearby for support. The low hillock of Pt.187 was due east of Eluet et Tamar, which had halted earlier Axis advances reaching the coast road behind the line. It overlooked the plain for four miles south to Rigel Ridge. Two miles to the north lay Pt.208 and east to the Acroma Box, on the escarpment which overlooked the coast to Tobruk.[31]

The locality was a rough hexagonal shape with each flank being approximately 1000 yards long, the position had strengths and weaknesses. Second Lieutenant J.

---

28 IWM: AL833: DAK War Diary, 13 June 1942.
29 Liddell-Hart, *Rommel Papers*, p.222.
30 TNA WO 169/4982: 3 & 4 Companies, 3rd Coldstream Guards War Diary, 13–14 June 1942.
31 Birdwood, *Worcestershire Regiment*, p.35.

J. 'Chota' Horton said the position was like a large crater.³² The minefield was laid in a density of one mine per yard, with two dummy minefields projecting out from each southern corner, to discourage the panzers from moving around the flanks. The battalion's eight anti-tank guns were dug in on the forward slopes, with B Battery, 95th Anti-Tank Regiment and the 3rd Light AA Battery covering the flanks and rear, and a 25pdr battery deployed behind.³³ Fortunately, some of the ground included soft sand patches, which enabled the gun pits to be bulldozed out. Most platoons were also well dug in but pneumatic drills were needed to break the rock which was below a thin layer of sand on the forward slopes. D Company slit trenches had an average depth of only 12 inches. The box was to be supported by armour if attacked.

Having dug in, they were visited by Lieutenant General Gott on 11 June and he explained the seriousness of the situation. Two days later, they witnessed the 2nd Scots Guards being overrun on Rigel Ridge, and soon stragglers arrived at Pt.187. However, the Worcesters had poor radio links and received no intelligence from their new higher command at 2nd S.A. Division. Their battalion radio net was not working either, so communication across the site was difficult.³⁴ The stragglers from the Scots and Sherwood Foresters also gave confused reports about the evacuation of both Rigel and Knightsbridge Boxes, but by 14 June, it was obvious that Pt.187 was now under direct threat.³⁵

The attacks began at 1000 hours. Following a bombardment, there was a heavy frontal attack by 50 tanks and supporting infantry, with German sappers lifting mines, using their tanks as cover. 15th Panzer reported they were held up by a strongpoint and waited for the infantry to come up.³⁶ Over the next two hours, the panzers manoeuvred, staying out of range and picking-off the 2pdrs one by one. The flanking dummy minefield kept the tanks on the front face of the box for quite a while. The Worcesters used two effective tactics; firstly, the anti-tank gunners held their fire until the panzers were very close, so that a good number were immediately knocked out. Although they could not touch the Panzer Mk IVs at long range, the 2pdr was still an effective gun at close range.³⁷ Captain F. N. Lynes kept up the morale of his gun crews, despite heavy fire, and Major D. H. Nott also showed exemplary courage, when he dashed forward under heavy fire and got a Bren MG working again, which inflicted heavy casualties on the German infantry crossing the minefield. The panzers added to the natural dust storm, by making rapid turns outside the wire, which made the visibility worse. In the midst of the firefight an intrepid B echelon column arrived under heavy fire and distributed fresh mortar bombs and beer.³⁸

32 *Tobruk 1942* <www:worcestershireregiment.com> (accessed 20 November 2021).
33 Birdwood, *Worcestershire Regiment*, p.35.
34 TNA WO 169/5074: 1st Worcesters War Diary 1942. The Diary states it was compiled from memory as the original was lost after the surrender of Tobruk on 21 June.
35 Birdwood, *Worcestershire Regiment*, p.36.
36 IWM: AL833: DAK War Diary, 14 June, 1942.
37 As one quietly unassuming veteran told me during a local talk.
38 Birdwood, *Worcestershire Regiment*, p.37.

There was more supporting fire from the rear guns at 62nd Battery, who effectively targeted enemy tanks and MET, with support from other batteries. However, the assault continued remorselessly with panzer OPs directing their artillery from hull down positions, while their engineers made a second attempt to lift the mines and break in. By 1400 hours another attack was building and they could see more heavy guns being deployed, the Worcesters requested air support and artillery fire, as there were many excellent targets. At 1545 hours a message was received from General Ritchie expressing his 'admiration for their defence, and to evacuate the present position tonight.'[39]

Under cover of an increasingly bad dust storm by the late afternoon, the Worcesters were heavily attacked again. Engineer mine clearance parties were making gaps in the minefield. Behind them over 65 tanks approached and pinned the defenders with heavy fire. The thick dust caused the Bren guns to jam and the defenders suffered badly from thirst. On the forward slopes, D company were unable to enjoy the beer which had been delivered, but Lieutenant Colonel Knight heartened morale, by coolly disregarding heavy MG fire in his visits to the front line.[40]

There was a controversy over some confused radio messages received from 2nd S.A. Division. The Worcesters said they received a 'garbled' radio message in cipher – to withdraw, 'noted at 1730 hours,' which said, '500 leave immediately.' The C.O. replied that this was impossible, due to the enemy attacks breaking into the minefields at that time, but 30 minutes later he decided to withdraw while still able to do so. They used the dust storm as cover and before the panzers could overrun their slit trenches.

The forward companies executed a model withdrawal under fire, followed by the remaining platoons. The German infantry also advanced using the storm as cover, but Lieutenant J. J. Horton laid out lines of booby traps across his trenches which wiped out the first waves of infantry coming in and this discouraged the Germans from following too closely.[41] The wounded were evacuated by carriers and ambulances, while two platoons covered the withdrawal and fought to the end. The retreating troops were surprised to find some British tanks in their rear as they retreated towards Acroma, and this may have been a cryptic comment as to why there had been no armoured support.[42] They had knocked out about 20 tanks with at least 8 being permanently destroyed, as well as other armoured cars and numerous MT. DAK spent much of the day pushing both 15th and 21st Panzer to cut the coast road, so 15th Panzer reported that they had broken through the division, 'thrusts through the minefield to the north.'[43]

The battle for Pt.187 had been another dogged defensive battle by infantry and gunners. Yet despite Eighth Army's determined efforts to inflict heavy casualties

39 TNA WO 169/5074: 1st Worcesters War Diary 14 June.
40 Birdwood, *Worcestershire Regiment,* p.38.
41 Birdwood, *Worcestershire Regiment,* p.40.
42 TNA WO 169/5074: 1st Worcesters War Diary, 14 June.
43 IWM: AL833: DAK War Diary, 14 June, 42.

on the attacking Panzer divisions, they failed to halt their offensive. They certainly delayed the attempt to block the coast road on 14 June, which enabled 1st S.A. Division to retreat through Tobruk. Auchinleck said that they had escaped primarily because of the tough defence made by 1st Worcesters. He also complimented the efforts of 1st Armoured Division south-west of Tobruk, which DAK had reported alongside the Worcesters battle.[44] As with the Scots Guards at Rigel, they found the debris of the battle still visible a year later, along with 120 German and some 60 Worcesters, still unburied.[45]

The Worcesters later reported on the battle and suggested a number of improvements for future defended localities to highlight what could have enabled them to hold on for longer: the links to 2nd S.A. Division were not good enough, they needed to be under a local command, to obtain the right support quickly. Secondly, the 25pdrs needed to be in an anti-tank role as the panzers cruised just out of range of the 2pdr guns. They needed more medium machine guns to suppress the assaulting engineers and infantry who were lifting the mines. Finally, they believed that heavier casualties had been avoided because they had been well dug in, with the company positions being 'doubled' (in depth), so that despite the heavy enemy shelling, heavier casualties were not sustained.[46] The South Africans stated that 1st Armoured Division had provided support, but the Worcesters had not been informed that armour was nearby. 6th RTR reported that they were on the Rigel Ridge on 13 June, before retreating to refuel, but that they had later run onto, 'an unmarked minefield near Pt.187 and stayed there overnight.' Next day they were ordered east to Pt.190 ridge but the visibility was very bad due to a dust storm.[47] This period of the evacuation of Knightsbridge, followed by Panzerarmee's thrust north on 14 June, had added to the confusion of the retreat from the Gazala line.

The demise of Knightsbridge and the armoured units left a few defended localities along with the El Adem Box south of Tobruk, which became the focus of Eighth Army's new defence line. However, Auchinleck's constant and confusing advice to Ritchie contributed to the failures to hold this new defensive line. As the situation across the battle became more critical and with Tobruk under serious threat, he demanded action to stabilise the line. On 15 June, Auchinleck made it clear that the southern flank of Tobruk must be held. Ritchie signalled that Tobruk might be 'invested for short periods.' They agreed that the defended locality at Belhamed was vital to keeping the door open to Tobruk, and that El Adem should be held to cover Belhamed. In addition, he was trying to reinforce El Adem with, 'additional artillery, but this had not been possible due to the tactical situation there.'[48] On 14 June, 90th

---

44 TNA WO 201/405: Operations, June 1942, CS/1265. Mideast to Troopers, 16 June 1942.
45 Birdwood, *Worcestershire Regiment*, p.41.
46 TNA WO 169/5074: 1st Worcesters War Diary 1942, 14 June 1942.
47 TNA WO 169/4509: 6th RTR War Diary June 1942, 13–14 June 1942.
48 TNA WO 291/405: Operations: telegrams & reports, 1942, 04477 to Mideast from 8th Army, 16 June 1942.

Light Division, on the far right of Panzerarmee's advance, had reached El Adem, while on the left 21st Panzer lost contact with the enemy facing them and all British armour was concentrated against 15th Panzer near to Acroma.[49]

The approach of enemy columns to the rear army areas forced key HQs to move out and this added to continued command delays through 16 and 17 June and contributed to the collapse of this southern flank. Enemy activity had already forced Norrie's XXX Corps HQ to move that day, and Ritchie said Eighth Army HQ would be moving from Gambut to the, 'bottom of Halfaya Pass, which he recognised would leave his communications disrupted for a period. Meanwhile Auchinleck reported to London that El Adem was the pivot on which Eighth Army manoeuvred and prevented the enemy from advancing east.[50] He believed that the Axis did not have enough forces to invest Tobruk *and* to mask Eighth Army on the frontier and wanted the army perpendicular to its supply line, not fighting parallel with it. The defended localities were to be supported by jock columns operating on the flanks and rear of the enemy forces.[51] He did not consider the defensive line to be a continuous one, but that the enemy should not establish itself east of the line.[52]

Achieving an increase in firepower was another issue as the Infantry Training Manual (1937) showed a normal layout for a defensive locality was sited with forward and reserve companies, deployed to offer mutual fire support. They were meant to be a defence in depth, ideally supported by anti-tank and artillery fire support and additional MMGs.[53] For single battalions only half the firepower was available against any one approach, front or flanks. Of the four defended localities across the south of Tobruk, two were overrun and two were evacuated at the last moment. Numerous battalions were badly mauled and many men were captured in their attempts to escape towards the frontier.

El Adem, 14–17 June

In defending the surrounding area, El Adem Box was considered to be a strong defensive position, situated on the ridge overlooking the Trigh Capuzzo. The garrison had been reduced to two battalions, the 1/5th Mahrattas and 3/2nd Punjab Regiments. Other units were sent to new defended localities, on 7 June 3/12th Frontier Force Rifles (3/12th FFR) was sent to B.650 on the escarpment overlooking the bypass

---

49 IWM: AL833: DAK War Diary, 14 June 1942.
50 TNA WO 291/405: Operations, 1942, 04477, 16 June 1942, CS.1270, Prime Minister from General Auchinleck.
51 TNA WO 291/405: Operations, 1942 , CS.1265, 16 June 1942, Mideast to Troopers.p.2.
52 TNA WO 291/405: Operations, 1942 June, CS.1259, 15 June 1942, Mideast to Troopers.
53 War Office, *Infantry Training and War, Manual 1937* (London: War Office, 1937), pp.151–152.

road, and on 8 June 1st Worcesters moved to Pt.187.[54] There was some coordination with jock columns from 7th Motor Brigade strengthening El Adem, as they cleared the area south of El Adem on 14 June.[55]

Axis artillery began shelling from all sides and Stuka dive bombers made the first direct attacks on El Adem, on 14 June. Axis tanks and lorry borne infantry appeared by late afternoon, and the box was cut off for two days. The 90th Light Division made their main approach on the next morning, moving in short rushes to avoid the defensive artillery shelling. They captured 32 prisoners but suffered heavy casualties in troops and vehicles. They were forced to narrow their attack on the main defences because of a weakness in their own infantry numbers and the, 'minefields and wire entanglements protecting the strong point.'[56]

The 90th Light was given three batteries of heavy artillery which shelled El Adem until nightfall, when the attack was halted. The attack was resumed again on 16 June, over open terrain without, '…the slightest bit of cover,' so they managed to advance a few hundred metres. The battlegroup commander, Colonel Loeven, said they needed armoured support to, 'penetrate the well-fortified S.P.' because they were so weak in infantry. The answer came back from Rommel to get on and capture El Adem.[57] There was further discussion and Colonel Marcks convinced Panzerarmee HQ that it was a tough defensive position, so they decided to encircle it and starve it out.

In the evening, while a new fire plan was being worked out, Rommel ordered that 120 Indian POWs be brought (probably from B.650) and marched up to the El Adem perimeter, to urge their fellow Indian troops to lay down their arms. However, nightfall delayed this move and after 2000 hours they received messages that the defenders were evacuating, one POW later said there was no more water. At midnight, groups of defenders began to evacuate the position, to the south and north-east. The next day, 90th Light reported they had entered the box and captured 210 British and Indian troops, from 1st Worcesters, 1/5th Mahratta and 3/2nd Punjab battalions, but they could not find any artillery.[58] The box was finally evacuated 17 June because of command indecision. Messervy blamed the indecision by Ritchie, so Brigadier Reid withdrew his remaining two battalions, largely intact, south towards Bir el Gubi. This left fewer complete units able to keep open the 'back door' to Tobruk by 17 June. Messervy observed:

> … on no account was El Adem to be evacuated – they were to fight it out to the last. They were already surrounded … these were the Army commander's personal orders. Then I had a message, It might be evacuated if I thought it

---

54 HMSO, *The Tiger Kills: The Story of the Indian Divisions in the North African Campaign* (London: HMSO 1944), pp.127–129.
55 TNA WO291/405: Operations, 1942, Cositrep 405, 15 June 1942, Mideast to Troopers.
56 IWM: E127, 90th Light Division War Diary, 15 June 1942.
57 IWM: E127, 90th Light Division War Diary, 16 June 1942.
58 IWM: E127, 90th Light Division War Diary, 16 June 1942.

couldn't be held... Then it must be held; then...that it was to be evacuated if the brigade could get out. I passed this onto Denis Reid ... and they got out. This was an example of what was happening all the time.[59]

The 5th Indian Division said the evacuation was a success because they did get the infantry out, but the guns, equipment and vehicles were left behind. The 3/2nd Punjab and 1/5th Mahrattas walked out of El Adem in small parties, most escaped back to the frontier. The Axis were clearly pleased by the capture of El Adem, 90th Light said they had, 'dislodged from the fortress of TOBRUK, the S[outh] cornerstone of the advance line of defence, and the way has been opened to the N[orth]...and the E[ast] along the Trigh Capuzzo.'[60]

B.650, 15 June

The 3/12th Frontier Force Rifles had arrived on the ridge at B.650, and in just a few days, they had dug in their guns, some crawl trenches which enabled covered movement, and their anti-tank 2pdrs were well camouflaged. By 15 June, Axis columns had arrived and the Frontier Rifles were pinned by 90th Light Division. They occupied the ridge which overlooked B.650 and were able to bring down a heavy barrage from eight batteries, along with direct fire which knocked out the battalion 2pdrs one by one.

The Indians had made a determined defence, when engaging armour they returned fire only at point-blank range, but by late evening, only one 25pdr gun was still firing. Each fresh crew lasted just long enough to fire one or two rounds before being killed or wounded and replaced by more gunners, who in their turn fired until the same end. The C.O. had lost communication with Brigade, every cable had been cut and the wireless aerial taken down because it was an obvious landmark for enemy guns.[61] Two companies made counter-attacks and all fought on until they were surrounded, so that only a few escaped. As night fell, tanks from 21st Panzer drove in to dominate the infantry positions and force them to surrender. The tanks moved along the ridge from the west and closed in on the defenders by the evening. They captured over 700 prisoners.[62]

There was some hope for an evacuation, but the Axis capture on the evening of 15 June is confirmed by Brett-James. Auchinleck sent an optimistic report on 16 June, which stated that the B.650 defenders had beaten off the attacks and still held.[63] Also that El Adem had beaten off some determined attacks, with the help of jock columns from both 7th Motor Brigade and 11th Indian Brigade. Additionally the RAF had

---

59   Corelli Barnett, *The Desert Generals* (Edison, New Jersey: Castle Books, 2004) p.163.
60   IWM: E127: 90th Light Division War Diary, 17 June 1942.
61   Brett-James, *Ball of Fire*, pp.206–207.
62   IWM E127: 90th Light Division War Diary, 15 June 1942.
63   TNA WO 291/405: Operations, 1942, Cositrep 407, 16 June 1942, Mideast to Troopers.

made numerous sorties against ground troops in the El Adem area.[64] It was clear that this was an over-optimistic view of the situation.

Sidi Rezegh

This rear sector box was defended by 1st/6th Rajputana Rifles, from 20th Indian Brigade, along with sixteen 25pdr guns and a battery of 2pdrs. They had a new commander, Brigadier L. E. MacGregor, and like other units, had just arrived from Iraq. The box was poorly situated along the narrow Sidi Rezegh Ridge, which had been a feature in the Crusader battles. Its defensive strength was limited by the nature of the ground, which meant the battalion was dug in, with a line of rifle companies, rather than deployed in depth like other localities. The infantry had just a few days to dig the main positions and add linking trenches, to create a more developed defensive site.

The 90th Light Division had moved east again along the Trigh Capuzzo from El Adem and their artillery began to register targets in the morning of 16 June. The defenders noted elements from 90th Light and 15th Panzer Divisions as taking part in the attacks, though it was 21st Panzer in this sector.[65] The defenders were supported by RAF Maryland bombers which attacked targets where they could. The Afrika Korps attacked again at 7.30pm, along the western side of the box, with the setting sun behind them. As before, the defenders were pinned down by artillery, mortars and machine gun fire. This was followed up by engineers, who moved in to lift a path through the mines using the smoke screen and dust as cover.

The attackers also shelled the nearby trigh, which added more thick dust blowing across the defenders. Once the cleared paths had been created, 1,000 infantry plus numerous tanks attacked at dusk. The defenders could do little to stop such numbers, A company was overrun, but D company swung out and fired on the attackers, the fighting continued for a two further hours. The rest of the battalion was able to disengage and escape that night.[66] The Axis halted and waited for dawn to consolidate.

Belhamed and Ed Duda

The problem of deploying a newly arrived unit with limited desert experience was again combined with a lack of time for preparation for 20th Indian Brigade. The South Wales Borderers (1st SWB) were sent to garrison Belhamed Box. This sector

---

64   TNA WO 291/405: Operations, 1942, CS.1265, 16 June 1942, Mideast to Troopers.
65   IWM: E127: 90th Light Division War Diary, 17 June 1942.
66   Indian War Department, *Teheran to Trieste: The Story of 10th Indian Division* (Bombay: Times of India, 1947), p.7.

had been held by 21st Indian Brigade but handed over to 20th Indian Brigade. At Belhamed, the Borderers arrived on 16 June, and were determined to hold the position, so it sent its transport away and built up supplies to 'hold to the last man.' Ed Duda, a few miles to the west, was first taken over by 3/18th Garhwalis, but they also moved to Belhamed from 10 June. The defences here were also badly sited on the crest of the escarpment.

By 18 June, 90th Light was sending out detachments to take over the various defended localities in this rear area. The Kaiser Battalion from 90th Light was ordered to occupy Belhamed. Ed Duda was a few miles to the west, on the bypass, and this was occupied by one company from Battlegroup Kost, while Special Detachment 288 would go to Sidi Rezegh. They noted that the defenders here had destroyed their guns and retreated north-east overnight.[67]

Before dawn on 18 June, both battalions were moving eastwards partly in trucks and some on foot towards Gambut. The valley was wide but with a steep escarpment at Zaafran, on their left or northern side. As they attempted to escape they were trapped by German units, some of whom had gone north, but this group had swung up from the south.[68] Battlegroup Menton was despatched to Zaafran and ordered to remain mobile.[69] Many trucks were shot-up or lost. Some got back to Sollum, but the brigade lost 1,000 men of whom some 500 were from the Borderers, which were later disbanded in Cyprus – much to the men's' dismay. 20th Indian Brigade became part of the force trying to hold the escarpment at Sollum, but that force was outflanked and they ended up as part of Eighth Army's retreat into Egypt.

The defended localities had been a slender hope for the army to continue the battle west and south of Tobruk. Those positions in the rear areas had been overcome by a combination of factors; the loss of 4th Armoured, tactical problems within each position and the ongoing problems of a disjointed command. Ritchie later argued that the defeat of 4th Armoured Brigade near Sidi Rezegh (reduced from approximately 100 cruiser tanks down to just 35) forced them to abandon El Adem and Belhamed.[70] While El Adem had been holding on with a grim determination, 21st Panzer had been attacking the Sidi Rezegh Box and were then holding off 4th Armoured Brigade with an anti-tank screen. They halted further attacks because they intercepted a British R/T conversation about breakout from the box. The loss of Sidi Rezegh left El Adem isolated so they evacuated and broke through the Axis forces nearby. The Axis view was that with these defensive boxes gone, the defence of Tobruk was no longer a 'serious problem' to them.[71]

---

67 IWM: E127: 90th Light Division War Diary, 18 June 1942.
68 Indian War Department, *Teheran to Trieste*, p.7.
69 IWM: E127: 90th Light Division War Diary, 18 June 1942.
70 TNA WO201/379: Notes on Operations in North Africa, May–June 1942, Ritchie, p.15.
71 Mellenthin, *Panzer*, p.89.

8

Bir Hacheim, Breakout and Final Battles

The hungry crash of guns, the charge of lean
Unconquered men, the rock-strewn sand,
The shivering in a dawn wind keen;
Facing the menace of a mine-pocked land…

'But not Forgotten'
Gunner P. J. Flaherty[1]

The fighting to capture the southernmost position of the line at Bir Hacheim began on the first day and continued until the position was evacuated during the night of 10–11 June. In between it was a siege, before a final wave of heavy attacks, which precipitated the withdrawal of 1st Free French Brigade. The troops were exhausted but General Ritchie confirmed he could no longer guarantee further supply columns getting through. Ritchie stated that it was the French commander, Brigadier Koenig, who had a change of heart by 7 June, and that French liaison officers delayed resupply columns from 7th Motor Brigade, which led him to the decision to pull out.[2] While they were there, Bir Hacheim became a hallmark of an intrepid defence by the French troops and contributed to a huge morale boost for their cause against the Axis. The memory of their battle is preserved in a bridge in Paris named after the action along with a significant display of artefacts at the Musée de l'Armée.

Brigadier Koenig's force broadly consisted of four weak motor battalions along with artillery, engineers and anti-tank gunners, totalling around 3,000 men.[3] They arrived from the Delta in February and took over from 150th Brigade who transferred further north. Bir Hacheim looked, and felt, isolated; it was the last desert outpost for Eighth

---

1 Anon., *Poems from the Desert*, p.31.
2 TNA WO 201/379: Operations in North Africa: General Ritchie's report, May–June 1942.
3 Mordal, *Bir Hacheim*, p.39.

Army. Panzerarmee could still swing this far south around the position and cut it off from further support.

The Free French forces assumed control of the widely spread defence. They extended trenches and dugouts, added new gun posts and vehicle pits, so that nothing was visible above ground. They increased the scale of the minefields and sent out patrols to observe for enemy activity. Eighth Army made its final appreciations in May and orders were issued to divisions as to how and where they would fight. The 1st Free French Brigade was ordered to, 'defend BIR HACHEIM to last man and round.'[4]

The brigade was allocated two roles; first to defend for seven days, using small detachments to protect gaps in the minefield. Secondly, to send out Tomcol, a jock column to operate a delaying action to the west. They needed an active defence but here, Tomcol was ordered a good distance away from Hacheim itself.

In detail, Koenig's brigade consisted of four motor battalions each with three companies, a regiment of artillery with twenty-four 75mm guns, plus one company each of anti-tank guns, Bofors AA guns and some captured Italian 47mm guns. These additional guns were used in the anti-tank role, along with enough provisions for 10 days along with 20,000 rounds of ammunition.[5] Details from the battle are given in Koenig's report which he made on his return because when he evacuated Hacheim he burnt all of the unit documents. Susan Travers was a driver with the brigade, and with other accounts, she adds further particulars of what happened there.[6]

Bir Hacheim was situated on an isolated sector of higher ground, with a surface of sand, loose stones with an underlying rock. On the higher ground there were the crumbling remnants of an old Italian fort in the south and across the flat centre. In the north-west corner was a small hill called the Observatoire at Pt.186, which covered exit points to the west and north. Just south of Pt.186 were two low mounds over broken water birs, which the legionnaires happily christened *les mamelles* (the breasts). Covering the east exit was another redoubt position with extra mines laid to front and rear with both 75mm and anti-tank guns. Driver Travers noted that the General placed his small caravan at the centre of the box, with adjacent tents for other officers and the liaison officers. The men, 'set to, creating even more slit trenches, circular holes for equipment and gun pits,' larger tents were set up for the hospital, HQ and messes.[7]

The main advantage was that the position was approximately 20 feet higher than the surrounding desert, which provided an excellent view across the Libyan Sand Sea

---

4   TNA WO 169/4053: 1st Armoured Division War Diary, Operational Order No.12, 20 May 1942, (NB the number sequence is unclear in the file).
5   TNA WO 201/380: Operations of First Free French Brigade Eighth Army, May–June 1942.
6   See Susan Travers, *Tomorrow Be Brave* (London: Bantam Press, 2000), passim; Jacques Mordal, *Bir Hakeim* (Paris: Amiot-Dumont, 1951), passim and Richard Holmes, *Bir Hacheim Desert Citadel* (London: Pan-Ballantine, 1971), passim.
7   Travers, *Tomorrow Be Brave*, pp.143–145.

to the south and west. The central 'keep' of the old fort was slightly higher again.[8] The remainder was largely open and flat which allowed posts and gun positions to be more dispersed. The perimeter was said to be 10.5 miles or 17km in total. They set up observation posts at key points and laid another 50,000 mines in the immediate minefields. There were larger triangular minefields on the southern side, to divide attacking forces. There were two northern exits, one into the central area, covered by Pt.186, and a second which exited north, directly through the inner mine belt. The northern flank was said to be the weakest, because it was hidden from French OPs, and this was where the 90th Light was able to make the most progress in their attacks.

The Free French determinedly held the position beyond the expected 10 days and the post remained one of the main pivots of the line. They maintained a tough fighting spirit and retained high morale. They were fortunate to have collected more anti-tank guns than most of the brigades further north. The accounts disagree on the number of guns, but Mordal said they deployed 101 anti-tank guns and twenty-four 75mm guns.[9] The preserved gun at the Musée de l'Armée shows that they cut away the upper gun-shield, which gave them a much lower profile, once dug into their gun pits. Two battalions of 2nd Demi-Brigade covered both the north-west and south-western sectors, and 2nd/13th Demi-Brigade de Legion Étrangère (13th DBLE) covered the eastern side. The Fusiliers Marins manned some guns and along with 1st Regiment Artillery were deployed around the box with most facing south and west. If surrounded they had 10 days of supplies and 20,000 rounds of ammunition.

First Attack, 27 May

Tomcol had been divided into two half columns so could only watch and report on two large Axis columns which moved south from 1500 hours on 26 May. By the mid-evening they retired back to Bir Hacheim and leaguered just outside the southern gap. More large-scale vehicle movement continued into the night and Tomcol was ordered to return to its patrol routes, while another jock column was ordered east of the minefield. In the night there were bright flashes of gunfire in the north and again at dawn.[10]

Early on 27 May, they heard firing from the Indian Brigade position and were later informed by division that the attack by Panzerarmee had begun. At 0800 hours tanks were seen forming three miles to the south-east. Due to some morning mist, they might have been 4th Armoured reaching their battle positions, so the French artillery did not engage them, despite large-scale enemy movements to their rear. A column of at least 70 tanks approached them an hour later, followed by an equal number of vehicles with infantry; the French were shelled and the tanks fired on any visible targets,

8   *Musée de l'Armée, Les Invalides* <www.musee-armee.fr> (accessed 20 Aug 2021).
9   Mordal, *Bir Hacheim*, p.86.
10 Travers, *Tomorrow Be Brave*, p.152.

so the French guns opened fire.[11] The attack was made by 9th battalion from Ariete Division. They attacked using 50 M14 tanks, under Colonel Prestisimone.

This first armoured assault suffered heavy losses as they crossed the minefield and from being hit by anti-tank guns. The unlucky Italian Colonel lost his second tank of the day and bravely led a second attack of 30 remaining tanks, which was also defeated by the intrepid legionnaires.[12] The French troops vigorously engaged the Italians, climbing onto the AFVs to shoot the helpless crews inside. They knocked out 35 tanks and captured some 70 prisoners. Further harassing patrols were sent out during the rest of the day and another 100 prisoners were taken.[13] The French lost two casualties and one gun knocked out. Having suffered such heavy losses, the Italians withdrew to reconsider how to capture such a difficult and determinedly defended position.

Bir Hacheim was contained by Panzerarmee to the end of May, as other battles continued further north. Probes were made against the northern gap, where D detachment engaged some armoured cars and exchanged fire with enemy 105mm artillery. A few tanks advanced again on 29 May and D detachment withdrew into the main position. The Germans also handed over some 620 Indian POWs captured from 3rd Indian Brigade, because the Axis could not spare any food or water. These troops later left with a Rifle Brigade convoy by night. The supply convoys successfully delivered another 6,000 rounds of 75mm ammunition and more water to keep the defenders going. During these skirmishes, the French were also assisted by strong RAF support, which flew 250 sorties attacking Axis supply columns around Bir Hacheim. They also forced two waves of Stukas to turn about and jettison their bombs.[14] Sandstorms prevented effective sorties for the next two days.

The Brigade received orders to send a jock column to the Rotunda Segnali, to harass enemy columns, but there was a shortage of vehicles to go out as they needed their own supply trucks back, so only one battalion was ready by 1 June. After this first phase, General Koenig confirmed that they had knocked out 41 tanks, seven armoured cars and numerous MET, along with the capture of 250 prisoners, all for the loss of two men killed and four wounded.[15] They had given the Axis a bloody nose, and showed no sign of giving in, despite constant shelling and air attacks.

Over the next couple of days Hacheim was attacked by dive bombers throughout the day, which caused a trickle of casualties, but shot down four Stukas. The jock column left in the early morning and later destroyed one tank. That evening, 7th Armoured HQ cancelled the operation and the column returned in the midst of the

11 Travers, *Tomorrow Be Brave*, p.152.
12 Walker, *Iron Hulls Iron Hearts*, pp.116–117.
13 TNA WO 201/380: Operations of First Free French Brigade Eighth Army, May–June 1942.
14 Denis Richards & Hilary St G. Saunders, *Royal Air Force, Vol. II* (London: HMSO, 1954), p.199.
15 TNA WO 201/380: Operations of First Free French Brigade Eighth Army, May–June 1942, 28–31 May 1942.

heavy sandstorm. Brigadier Amilakvari led several 'daring hit and run attacks on the convoys, capturing men, vehicles and ammunition.'[16] At Panzerarmee HQ, Rommel informed General Nehring about operations for the next day when both 90th Light Division and Trieste Division were to assault Hacheim. The rest of DAK would make feint attacks further north to distract Eighth Army.[17]

By 3 June, General Koenig reported they were now properly invested, and the battle fell into two final phases from then on. A liaison officer informed them that enemy columns were heading south from Bir Harmat. Secondly, another resupply column was captured by armoured cars. Panzerarmee sent over two Italian officers under a flag of truce, who demanded Bir Hacheim be surrendered or be wiped out, like 150th Brigade to the north. French officers politely refused and soon after the position began to be shelled. Although they could see them, the 75mm guns did not have the range to engage enemy concentrations of troops to the east and north-east. Hacheim then came under very heavy bombardment with five waves of Stuka attacks over the rest of the day.[18]

The Air Force continued to provide air cover for them, Coningham redirected part of the WDAF to specifically support the defences. They intercepted one of the Stuka attacks and the French saw them shoot four enemy aircraft down, while the WDAF official history claimed seven by No.5 South African Squadron. The detailed research by Chris Shores et al confirmed four were lost and a fifth Stuka damaged. Kitty bombers destroyed some 60 MET to the south while fighters disrupted the Stuka attacks.[19] Similar attacks continued the next day, with more MET knocked out and further Stuka attacks broken up. The Air Force sent their famous message of congratulations to the Free French, *Merci pour le sport*.[20] RAF squadrons made three or four sorties each day to protect Bir Hacheim from Luftwaffe air attacks. Kittyhawks from 2nd SAAF Squadron shot down five Stukas, before their escorts dived in to protect the dive-bombers, the fighter squadron II/JG 27 claimed two WDAF planes in return. The air battle intensified with pilots on both sides being shot down, made prisoner, or crash-landing and returning to their squadrons the next day.[21]

The stubborn defence of Bir Hacheim continued over the next few days. An attack was made by 90th Light which closed to 700 metres from the defences but was again stopped by strong defensive fire from positions that were excellently camouflaged. The German infantry were left stuck in the open.[22] Such a strong defence was affecting the plans being made by Panzerarmee. French patrols harassed supply columns, and

16 Travers, *Tomorrow Be Brave*, p.153.
17 IWM: AL833: DAK War Diary 1942 14 May–1 August, 1 June 1942.
18 TNA WO 201/380: Operations of First Free French Brigade Eighth Army, May–June 1942.
19 Shores et al, *Mediterranean Air War 1940–1945. Vol. Two*, p.123.
20 Richards & St G. Saunders, *Royal Air Force, Vol. II*, pp.200–201.
21 Shores et al, *Mediterranean Air War 1940–1945. Vol. II*, p.125.
22 IWM: E127: 90th Light Division War Diary, 6 June 42.

minefields added further casualties to tanks and vehicles so the advance by 21st Panzer Division to the north was delayed again. The build-up near Bir Harmat for Operation Aberdeen also made DAK wary of advancing north again. Gause, the Chief of Staff, ordered there to be no advance north until Bir Hacheim had been destroyed. DAK was hedge-hogging its defences and covering the new gaps in the mine-marsh. It had extended south to enable supply columns to move more freely. By the evening of 3 June, Rommel still believed that Hacheim would surrender the next day.[23]

Following the decisive defeat of Aberdeen on 6 June, Rommel visited 15th Panzer HQ and informed Colonel Craseman that Bir Hacheim was expected to fall by 8 June. Ariete Division would relieve them overnight on 7 June, which would enable them to regroup on the Bir Aslagh ridge.[24] Further plans were made with Ariete, while 15th Panzer Division suffered the usual harassing fire and observed enemy tanks to the north-east. Rommel ordered the 90th Light to make a new attack on Hacheim at 1100 hours, directed at a point 800 metres from the 'redoubt.' If the defences were too strong the investment would be tightened overnight.[25] An armoured column of 20 tanks made a demonstration to keep the defenders on the alert. During the evening, more tanks pushed back the forward troops into the main defences.[26]

After a day of heavy artillery bombardment, further major attacks by elements of 90th Light Division took place on 8 June. Overnight they surrounded Hacheim with guns of all calibres to support them. French batteries had been pinpointed and the best approach would be on the north-west face, using the hidden approach.[27] The first attack was begun by 25 Stukas dive bombing the French.[28] The engineers from 90th Light cleared new gaps in the minefield and took advantage of the poor early morning visibility, while the assault troops gathered ready. A major bombardment of the northern side followed which spread across the entire area. At 1000 hours the infantry advanced but were again halted by the intense defensive fire.[29]

After a pause, in the early afternoon, another 60 aircraft bombarded the sector and another attack was made supported by 20 tanks, of which two were knocked out. Infantry from 90th Light made pathways through the mines on three sides, to lodge between the Battalion Pacifique and the Legionnaires, but they were stopped again by further concentrated fire. Later on, more attacks were made on the west face, supported by fresh batteries that rained shells down on the French gun positions. This attack was also stopped with further help from the RAF. A third attack was made

---

23 IWM: AL833: DAK War Diary, 14 May–1 August 1942, 3 June 1942.
24 IWM: AL833: DAK War Diary, 14 May–1 August 1942, 6 June 1942
25 Mordal, *Bir Hacheim*, p.151.
26 TNA WO 201/380: Operations of First Free French Brigade Eighth Army, May–June 1942.
27 TNA WO 201/380: Operations of First Free French Brigade Eighth Army, May–June 1942.
28 IWM: E127: 90th Light Division War Diary, 8 June 1942.
29 Mordal, *Bir Hacheim*, p.152.

after 1800 hours and again failed. The French suffered as they tried to move up a reserve company in the open but sustained heavy casualties.[30]

The support given by the WDAF had been vital, so much so that Rommel turned his forces south again to concentrate on the beleaguered garrison. The 90th Light attacks succeeded in capturing a vital OP position in the north-west sector, along with a 75mm gun. That night, the French repositioned three guns from 1st Artillery behind the first line in readiness for further tank attacks the next day. The Axis increased the tempo of their attacks and followed this with another extremely heavy artillery and air bombardment made the next day.[31]

The 90th Light spent all morning directing heavy shelling and air attacks by waves of 60 Stukas, until the first ground attack at 1330 hours. 20 panzers advanced towards the defences with 10 more making progress in the north, but they halted again as both sides exchanged heavy fire. Another heavy bombardment was made, but soon the infantry were seen falling back. In the evening more bombers came overhead, and this attack hit the dressing station which killed 20 wounded men.[32] Travers had managed to return to Bir Hacheim, said that the hospital tent was the only one showing above ground with its red cross prominently displayed, mainly for the German pilots.[33] Another assault was made by the Light Battalion of I.R.155. They broke the mini-gap and reached within 200 metres of the French lines, the attack was halted as they were reduced to less than 200 men.[34] Koenig said that the 75mm guns had used up all of their ammunition, halting these attacks and that many lorries had been burnt out.[35]

In the early evening of 9 June, 7th Armoured HQ informed Koenig that Hacheim no longer needed to be held, and asked what resources were needed to evacuate. He told them that the night of 9/10 June was best and 60 trucks would be needed to rendezvous at B.837. This position was six miles to the south-west of Hacheim and would involve breaking through covering Axis forces. HQ replied they could not gather enough lorries so the evacuation was delayed until the next night, 10–11 June. German intercepts reported that conversations between British and French commanders, were about the failure to get supplies through that were urgently needed. The German commanders deduced that a breakout overnight was now likely.[36] Ritchie later argued that 7th Motor Brigade was just re-supplying/keeping open the link to Hacheim. He

30   TNA WO 201/380: Operations of First Free French Brigade Eighth Army, May–June 1942.
31   TNA WO 201/380: Operations of First Free French Brigade Eighth Army, May–June 1942, p.7.
32   TNA WO 201/380: Operations of First Free French Brigade Eighth Army, May–June 1942, p.7.
33   Travers, *Tomorrow Be Brave*, p.159.
34   IWM: E127: 90th Light Division War Diary, 9 June 1942.
35   TNA WO 201/380: Operations of First Free French Brigade Eighth Army, May–June 1942, p.8.
36   IWM: E127: 90th Light Division War Diary, 8 June 1942.

wanted them to be much more offensive and not just tied down as a supply column. Hacheim had served its purpose and the French had drawn off Axis units from the Cauldron sector, but this period of the battle was over. He issued a warning order to evacuate, although Auchinleck was against this move.[37]

He was also critical that a supply column had arrived the previous night, but the French liaison officer apparently stopped the vehicles going in. The next night, 9/10 June, a column of 50 vehicles waited to pass through the lines, but this was stopped by General Koenig. Ritchie said that Koenig's personal view of the defence had changed. Jock columns and an armoured regimental group carried out diverting operations on 9 June (4th Armoured) to relieve the pressure on Hacheim, but Ritchie said he was convinced that an evacuation should take place the night of 10/11 June.[38] The Germans reported two approaches, one by 20 to 30 tanks from the east and one from the south-east, which was probably a jock column. However, their approach was tentative and broken up by the defensive fire from the heavy 10cm batteries, which forced them to turn away.[39]

The last day saw 90th Light carry out more determined attacks on the main defences, preceded again by waves of Stuka attacks and a heavy bombardment. They made two break-ins and captured 30 prisoners and believed that one more assault the next day would win the position. German intercepts heard the orders to evacuate to the west and south-west to meet the 7th Motor Brigade vehicles waiting for them. The division said they inflicted many casualties on the retreating French but could not stop the majority from escaping.[40] The WDAF made another supportive attack by the first squadron of Spitfires to be deployed in Libya to break up the heavy Axis air attacks being made by more than 50 bombers.[41]

The evacuation was largely successful with some 3,600 men evacuated but the majority of their guns were lost. Koenig said the gap in the minefield was not properly made as the engineer C.O. had disappeared. They left in five columns and it was a firefight most of the way. He listed 1,200 casualties and another 200 wounded but who reached army hospitals. Ritchie noted, 'The power to resist cracked in an alarmingly short time (see U.1339 of 10 June).'[42] He clearly laid the blame on the Free French for a collapse in spirit, though we also see Koenig's account of being ordered to leave, and about the lack of trucks. Travers said the Stuka attacks were the worst and the Luftwaffe flew 1,400 sorties and dropped 1,500 tons of bombs,

---

37 TNA WO 201/379: Operations in North Africa: General Ritchie's report, May–June 1942.
38 TNA WO 201/379: Operations in North Africa: General Ritchie's report, May–June 1942.
39 IWM: E127: 90th Light Division War Diary, 9 June 1942.
40 IWM: E127: 90th Light Division War Diary, 10 June 1942.
41 Richards & St G. Saunders, *Royal Air Force, Vol. II*, p.201.
42 TNA WO 201/379: Operations in North Africa: General Ritchie's report, May–June 1942.

alongside many artillery bombardments, which was more anyone than could stand for so many days.[43]

It had been an intrepid defence, General Brooke sent Koenig his sincere admiration on 15 June.[44] If the French had achieved anything, it had been delaying the Axis timetable for the campaign. Later commentators said that the additional nine days of defence by the Free French, to 10 June, had seriously upset the Axis plans to be on the Egyptian frontier by 20 June, which would then allow the attack on Malta, Operation *Herkules*, to begin. The Luftwaffe reported that, 'those nine days were irrecoverable.'[45] The 1st Free French Brigade had more than achieved its objectives.

Final Battles and the Northern Breakout

… and now, Tobruk is now a name
And sacked and burned like Troy.
… Its white walls are crumbled, and its flowers
Buried by rubble of bombs; its sloping streets,
Littered with dust and debris and decay,
Are peopled by a band of alien ghosts.

'Tobruk'
Captain John Jarmain[46]

The withdrawals from Bir Hacheim and Knightsbridge effectively undermined the minefield as a line of defence. This left Tobruk under direct threat of being cut off and attacked, despite a sizeable garrison and a defensive perimeter. The two divisions in the northern boxes had to be withdrawn or face being cut off by Panzerarmee. Even if Tobruk held out, there was no guarantee of being able to supply these two divisions. Most remaining units were operating as jock columns south-east of Tobruk or were in the process of retiring to the frontier, which was the next line of defence. Also south-east of Tobruk was the remaining armour, with regiments being allocated to 4th Armoured Brigade. They engaged the Axis columns in one further day of battle but were outmanoeuvred themselves and forced to retire. These were the final battles of Gazala, before the attack on Tobruk.

---

43 Travers, *Tomorrow be Brave*, p.164.
44 Anon., *Bir Hakeim* (London: French Combat Publications, 1942), p.26, General Sir A. F. Brooke correspondence.
45 Richards, & St George Saunders *Royal Air Force, Vol. II*, p.202.
46 John Jarmain correspondences, University of Exeter Digital Collection, EUL MS 413, 1942–1943. Aerogramme dated 16 December 1942; 'Tobruk' poem draft and revisions of 'Sandbags' and 'For Alamein respectively.

1st South African Division

This division had held and developed the three northern boxes for most of the spring and throughout the battle. They engaged in a defensive battle against the diversionary attacks made by Panzerarmee to distract and pin these five northern brigades and maybe even draw off some armour towards the coast, in order to make the flank march around Bir Hacheim. These early attacks included Stuka air attacks during the approach marsh to the south. In the afternoon and evening Italian infantry and their supporting German battlegroup (15th Rifle Regiment) advanced to close the gap in no man's land, closing up to the minefield.[47]

When the main attack began in the south, small parties of Italians approached the South African wire, and were engaged by the watching infantry. Some early attacks were made against 1st S.A. Brigade positions at Alem Hamza, and were observed by the neighbouring 6th DLI, in the adjacent box. There was further shelling in the early afternoon directed by a spotter plane and later they were dive-bombed by six Stukas. Still operating on the Axis side of the wire, South African armoured cars reported to HQ on groups of enemy tanks advancing across the 151st Brigade front, and by 1500 hours these were heading towards the South Africans. Then their infantry debussed and began to dig in. The South Africans engaged the column and knocked out three tanks, identified later as Italian. The adjacent 151st Brigade artillery engaged smaller columns of MET as they moved past the brigade front. In the evening they shelled suspected enemy leaguers across the wire.[48]

A much larger scale attack was made the next day, against the South African lines, again with a few tanks in support. They made a 'lodgement' into the minefield but got no further. The defenders believed the attacks seemed half-hearted, as if they were diversions. Later copies of the Italian orders showed they had been ordered to make a specific assault.

If the Italians had made a breakthrough, they would have captured Gazala pass, on the escarpment, which was a vital objective. As Panzerarmee advanced north on the first day, 21st Panzer columns had ranged towards the pass and given the few troops at the Eluet et Tamar box, a rough time, because it blocked the approach to the pass. The frustrated panzers later overran a small infantry force at the nearby Commonwealth Keep. One exposed outpost at Bir en Naghia was attacked again in the evening, and this position dominated the Transvaal Scottish lines, and those of the adjacent battalions. Lieutenant M. H. Hinton Webb led two sections to reoccupy the post, despite coming under 'terrific shell and MG fire.' He held the Naghia post for two days and

---

47 L. C. F. Agar-Hamilton & J. A. I. Turner (eds.), *Crisis in the Desert May–July 1942* (Cape Town: OUP 1952), pp.32–33.
48 TNA WO 169/5007: 6th Durham Light Infantry War Diary, 26 May 1942.

ejected some Italians who tried to dig in nearby. His leadership contributed to the capture of 100 Italians and for this he was awarded the MC.[49]

The desperate supply problems for Panzerarmee by the second day, made Lieutenant Colonel Westphal at the forward HQ demand that Group Crüwell again attempt to break through the South African defences.[50] They could only shell the coast road from the nearby escarpment above, so the South African and 50th Divisions remained relatively safe from these overstretched Axis columns in their rear.[51] The most serious attack was made by Sabratha Division on 29 May. It failed because they gave away their preparation the night before, by making so much noise digging in and moving vehicles. In daylight they attacked across a depression which lay between the Cape Town Highlanders and the Transvaal Scottish positions, some 400 yards opposite. These were from 1st and 2nd Brigades respectively, so that attack was directed at ground between the two brigades. The Italian 'PBI' were machined gunned and shelled in their dozens. They attempted to change direction uphill towards the Highlanders, but then broke and ran, under the weight of defensive fire. Over 400 infantry were trapped by the supporting shellfire and forced to surrender. One officer said they had been totally unprepared for the strength of the South African defences and the weight of their defensive fire.[52] The attacks were a complete failure for Panzerarmee and the real success for Group Crüwell was the opening up of two gaps either side of 150th Brigade which greatly eased the supply routes, through the mine-marsh.[53] From then on Panzerarmee was resupplied much more effectively. Group Crüwell also continued to pin the two divisions, but apart from sending more supplies, they were also pinned themselves.

Minor skirmishes continued against the South Africans until they withdrew on 14 June. They were ordered to leave a jock column within each brigade box and start pulling back from mid-morning. Each brigade would retire either side of the coast road towards Tobruk.[54] As the withdrawal got underway, German forces made determined attacks to break in and overcome the defences at Eluet et Tamar. A tank attack developed in the evening by 15 tanks from the south and 32 tanks from the west faces. Enemy infantry penetrated to within 300 yards of the HQ. Sergeant J. R. Wallace from the Cape Town Highlanders led a platoon counterattack, despite heavy MG fire and sniping across the position. This attack enabled the battalion to withdraw during the night.[55] Another group of Germans penetrated the minefield and pinned a nearby anti-tank gun. Corporal E. P. Hardy led a section-attack which protected the gun

49 TNA WO 373/21/133: Recommendation for Award, Lieutenant M. H. Hinton-Webb, 28–29 May 1942.
50 Hamilton & Turner, *Crisis in the Desert May–July 1942*, p.33.
51 Hamilton & Turner, pp.29–30.
52 Hamilton & Turner, pp.33–34.
53 Hamilton & Turner, p.35.
54 TNA WO 201/392: 1st South Africa Division: Gazala defensive battle, operational reports, 14 June 1942.
55 TNA WO 373/21/325: Recommendation for Award, Sgt J.W. Wallace, 14 June 1942.

crew, so they could open fire again to knock out a pernicious twin Breda MG. Hardy's section went on to capture nine German prisoners and repel the break in. Both NCOs were awarded the Military Medal for their leadership and gallantry.[56] The South African columns were delayed by the long queues of vehicles making their way across the Tobruk defences. Two rearguard groups suffered heavy casualties crossing the Tobruk west perimeter due to an enemy group having established itself near the Wadi es Sueniat. Engineers were able to demolish all three passes west of Tobruk, onto the coastal plain, once 50th Division columns had gone through. The division regrouped on the frontier to protect two gaps in the wire near Sherfezen, by 19 June. However the next day the Army BGS informed them of a 'serious situation' in Tobruk and the likely loss of 2nd S.A. Division. Almost immediately they were ordered back to Alamein, arriving on 26 June, apart from rearguard demolition units.[57]

50th Division in the Line and Breakout

69th Brigade remained static during May, while 150th Brigade continued its battle, although they maintained patrols and watches to the front and rear of the minefields. On 27 May, 7th Green Howards covered the front of the box. The regimental history noted an attack by a large group of unsupported Italian infantry.[58] The defending Yorkshiremen opened fire and caused numerous casualties, which made the Italians go prone near the dummy minefield. The Green Howards won the subsequent firefight. They had prepared trenches and supporting artillery fire on call, the remaining enemy withdrew after heavy losses.[59] Their fellow 6th Green Howards were commanded by Lieutenant Colonel E. C. Cooke-Collis. They had a more static battle in their sector, but the Italians opposite kept them under constant artillery and MG fire. Lieutenant Colonel Cooke-Collis stayed up with his forward companies throughout the battle and provided calm leadership. His constant guidance inspired his men and ensured that overall casualties remained low. For his actions he was awarded an immediate DSO for his 'outstanding gallantry'. He continued to lead the battalion during the breakout and retreat to the wire and from Mersa Matruh, at the end of June.[60]

---

56 TNA WO 373/21/331: Recommendation for Award, Corporal E. P. Hardy, 14 June 1942.
57 TNA WO 201/392: 1st South Africa Division: Gazala defensive battle, operational reports, 19 26 June 1942.
58 Oddly the 7th Green Howards War Diary is missing the page for 27 May, so this action is not shown. The days either side are completed hour by hour. Also missing are the pages for 1–10 June. The 9th DLI has key dates missing as well.
59 W. J. Tovey & A. J. Podmore, *Once a Howard Twice a Citizen* (Middlesbrough: Volunteers Press, 1995), p.79.
60 TNA WO 373/21/9: Award to Lieutenant Colonel E. C. Cooke-Collis, 3 Aug 1942. Distinguished Service Order.

The 5th East Yorks operated a jock column east of the minefield, as Panzerarmee struck north towards Eluet et Tamar. They had some good results and helped to stop 21st Panzer from overrunning this rear area on 27 May. They spent the rest of the battle inside the perimeter, exchanging shell fire with Axis artillery. Captain D. J. Penwill led two platoons of A company in an evening attack to close a gap in the minefield. They captured a ridge and covered an engineer section, as it relayed the mines. The determined group took on 300 Italians in a brisk two-hour firefight and suffered only 10 casualties. The mines were re-laid but the Italian made gap was never found.[61]

There was a good deal of air activity that day, 29 May, watched by 7th Green Howards as they waited to exchange with their fellow 6th Battalion who had returned from the mobile reserve. The next day there was a mass of Axis movement around them. A column of 50 enemy tanks moving up from the cauldron, with another moving down west of the minefield. They observed over 500 MET moving east–west, with another 500 MET along Tamar Ridge. By mid-afternoon there was a column four miles in length moving west, just below them, from Sidra Ridge towards the wire.[62] They could do little against such numbers and were forced to sit tight in their positions.

They received no orders to move south and perhaps attempt a breakthrough to 150th Brigade. The last day of May was a quiet day for them, with just a Stuka attack in the evening while they awaited the arrival of Robcol. The 5th East Yorks reported repeated shelling of the perimeter until the breakout.[63] By 11–12 June Col Column was operating north of the cauldron but were forced to withdraw by heavy shelling. When Panzerarmee attacked the Scots Guards on Rigel Ridge, the column artillery shot a series of harassing fire against MET between the Sidra and Rigel ridges on 13 June.[64] We only get a sense of 69th Brigade movements because of numerous missing pages in the War Diary. For the Green Howards, the next day was given over to preparing for Operation Freeborne – the escape to the west that night.

By 13 June, the defeat of the armoured brigades ended their need to hold the line any longer. Ritchie informed GHQ of the situation regarding the remaining armour near Acroma, holding the coast road open. With enemy armour now likely to cut the coast road west of Acroma, there was no alternative but to draw out 1 S.A. and 50 Divisions from the Gazala line. British armour had been reduced to 50 Cruisers and 20 'I' tanks with some Stuarts and they were outnumbered two to one.[65] The battle was effectively over but would play out in four more days of fighting.

Both 69th and 151st Brigades had remained largely static alongside the South Africans and now they planned the breakout. Panzerarmee again crossed the Trigh

---

61   TNA WO 169/5076: 5th East Yorks War Diary, 27–29 May 1942.
62   TNA WO 169/5023: 7th Green Howards War Diary, 29–30 May 1942.
63   TNA WO 169/5076: 5th East Yorks War Diary, 1–13 June 1942.
64   TNA WO 169/5023: 7th Green Howards War Diary, 11–13 June 1942.
65   TNA WO 201/405: Telegrams 12–16 June 1942, U1388 Eighth Army to Mideast 14 June 1942.

Capuzzo and headed north to the escarpment overlooking the coast road, the only viable escape route for 50th Division was to head west, through the minefield, and then south and east to the frontier, about a day's drive away. While 1st S.A. Division evacuated eastwards, through Tobruk, Major General Ramsden planned an aggressive, fighting withdrawal, and company commanders were briefed at 1100 hours that morning.[66] The leading battalion columns would establish a temporary bridgehead on the Gabr el Fachri Ridge for the rest to gather before heading south to Hacheim. Having secured the two bridgeheads the remaining brigade columns began to pass between them. They would then break through the Italian positions opposite in numerous small columns, and head south and then east to the frontier wire. The division only had about 90 trucks to move everyone, so most of the guns and stores had to be left behind. Fortunately, a major dust storm blew up on the afternoon and evening of the 14th, which covered most of the preparations.[67]

Within 69th Brigade, Operation Freeborne was put into action, to evacuate the brigade. They destroyed 16 days' worth of supplies – food, water, ammunition and petrol – and the men had to wear cardigans and light equipment only. The 7th Green Howards formed two columns of companies with supporting units, and two separate artillery columns.[68] The move west began but the leading columns were late reaching the divisional gap and so the C.O. ordered them to move through together. Delays occurred as the columns merged into one through the narrow gap in the minefield. Marker lights went out, and some trucks ran into slit trenches. One company became detached, and a support unit ran into the minefield and lost some trucks. By 0100 hours only the leading units were ready to turn west to Pt.167, heading for the Gabr el Fachri Ridge. They made one last effort to bring in the lost groups. The C.O. and another party returned to flash signal lamps along the route to guide in the others, but they heard carriers and vehicles moving north-east, so at 0300 hours they headed south.

Some enemy positions fired on them with mortars and MGs as they passed by, but others offered no resistance. The C.O.'s column passed through three enemy HQ positions and only received one challenge, which they ignored. By 0430 hours the columns were about midway and crossed over 'many tracks' and the Trigh Capuzzo, west of the old 150th Brigade position. At daylight they paused to allow straggler vehicles to catch up and proceeded without further problems east to the frontier, reaching the wire by 1600 hours.[69]

The escape for 151st Brigade was more dramatic for some columns. The 6th DLI moved south-west in three columns heading for the 8th DLI bridgehead on the ridge

---

66 P. J. Lewis, *8th Battalion The Durham Light Infantry 1939–1945* (Uckfield: Naval & Military Press, 2004), p.98.
67 Clay, *Path of the 50th*, p.65.
68 TNA WO 169/5023: 7th Green Howards War Diary 1942. Operation Freeborne.
69 TNA WO 169/5023: 7th Green Howards War Diary 1942, Operation Freeborne.

at Pt.168.[70] This was a useful ridge just west of the Rotunda Mteifel, but also crossed one of the main Axis supply routes. Each group was set up like a mini jock column, with two platoons of infantry, one section of AT guns, one troop of 25pdrs from 74th Regiment RA, plus RE and field ambulance detachments. The third column under Major M. R. Ferens, acted as a rearguard until 9th DLI had passed through. They had the option of retiring north, and then east, with the South Africans if this was more practicable. At about 0200 hours the third column reached Strickland Post and found Lieutenant Colonel Percy and his column from 9th DLI, who had also decided to return and go through Tobruk instead.

For Colonel Percy's column there were more delays when three vehicles ran onto mines, moving back through the Stanley Gap. By early morning the mixed column of 6th and 9th DLI reached the Gazala pass. Unfortunately, South African engineers had just mined this gap, so they moved east to the Agheila pass, which was also mined. Fortunately, engineers soon cleared a path for them to continue down to the base of the escarpment, before reaching the coast road west of Mrassas.

They continued east but were soon mixed up with numerous South African vehicles. Such a target was rapidly dive-bombed and strafed by enemy aircraft and later shelled (inaccurately). The column rearguard halted in cover when they were engaged by an enemy mixed column. The attached 25pdr guns quickly deployed and knocked out some of the Axis tanks, driving off the German attack, leaving 27 prisoners behind. The Durham's column resumed, passed through Tobruk that evening and leaguered five miles beyond the port. They reached the frontier wire by the following midday and rejoined the division. The 6th DLI managed to retain a good strength of 21 officers and 628 ORs.[71]

The 9th DLI also had additional delays and problems for their groups as they headed east. They vacated the Percy Box (named after the 9th's commanding officer, Lieutenant Colonel J. S. Percy), and had attempted to exit the minefield to the west that night. They came under very heavy anti-tank and MG fire and so turned back to retreat through Tobruk, as ordered. They were joined by the 6th DLI column and headed north to Gazala pass with Lieutenant Colonel Percy's columns being guided by 2nd S.A. armoured cars. At the top of the Agheila pass they were shelled by some South African artillery but were allowed to continue once they had given the recognition signal. Later, several guns were lost from Stuka attacks.[72]

Meantime, Major J. C. Slight's column reached the Gazala pass just as South African engineers were about to mine it, but the column was able to pass through to the coast road below. His group moved east, but soon came under heavy artillery fire from the top of the escarpment from artillery which now overlooked the road. They

---

70 TNA WO 169/5007: 6th Durham Light Infantry War Diary 1942, Third Column Report 14–15 June 1942.
71 TNA WO 169/5007: 6th Durham Light Infantry War Diary 1942. Third Column Report 14–15 June 1942.
72 TNA WO 169/5009: 9th Durham Light Infantry War Diary 1942. 14–15 June 1942.

were held up at Mrassas, 16 miles west of Tobruk, by a German mixed column which was already dug in and was supported by artillery and tanks. The column put in an immediate attack, supported by the battery from 74th Field Regiment RA and the armoured cars. The German infantry were routed, seven Mk IIIs were knocked out and some 60 prisoners were captured, for the cost of 50 DLI who became casualties. In the attack, Lieutenant R. Braithwaite was seriously wounded leading his platoon and he died later in hospital at Tobruk. The 9th DLI's Adjutant and MO were unlucky enough to be captured in the breakout. The group divided into two columns again and leaguered on the far side of Tobruk that evening. Next day they were diverted south onto the Trigh Capuzzo and reached the Sherferzan gap, before rejoining 50th Division in the assembly area near Bir Thalata.[73]

The 8th DLI spent the day making preparations to breakout, using a heavy sandstorm as cover. Water barrels were divided amongst each truck, and the floors were reinforced by sandbags against mines. That evening two columns moved out west and reached the Stricklands post by 2015 hours, when the skies cleared as the sandstorm blew itself out. The clear evening allowed the Italian artillery to range in on the column, but shelling eased as night fell. The Battalion progressed another five miles south-west to Pt.168. Both columns moved steadily forward in the clear night despite further heavy shelling. The vehicles' unprotected sides were hit by shrapnel and the guiding officers and NCOs perched high up on the cabs were particularly exposed.

Different columns had different outcomes; Clarkecol passed through largely unscathed and leaguered near Patrol grove and Pt.168, west of the Rotunda Mteifel. Most of the enemy fire was inaccurate and whistled over them, and they suffered only from being split up or from running into further minefields. Private Swallow was awarded the Military Medal for leading the column through one minefield, despite his own vehicle having just hit a mine.[74] In contrast, Sellcol headed for their bridgehead objective, which turned out to be a strong defensive position held by three Italian companies, who opened up on the column with heavy MG fire. Lines of tracer whipped through the column and Major Sell's truck was hit by an anti-tank shell and exploded. Despite this, he and his batman Private Etherington, joined in the close attack to clear the position, the Durhams used grenade and bayonet to overrun each strongpoint.

Away to the south-east one 69th Brigade column came under fire which set alight numerous trucks which drew more artillery fire onto the other vehicles. Other Italian companies simply moved out of the way of the advancing columns, one group of Italian prisoners even asked for a lift to Alexandria.[75] Sellcol was forced to breakthrough a German company, and led by some South African armoured cars they charged it head-on with all guns blazing. The Germans fought back tenaciously firing their MGs until they were overrun. Many men were wounded or killed as the trucks

---

73 TNA WO 169/5009: 9th Durham Light Infantry War Diary 1942. 14–15 June 1942.
74 Lewis, *8th Battalion*, p.102.
75 Lewis, pp.100–101.

were raked by fire. After this the column pushed on south, and then east to the wire.[76] D company was still largely intact and Major Sell received the Military Cross for his leadership. These unlucky brigades would have to survive another beleaguered defence and breakout from Mersa Matruh within 10 days of leaving Gazala.

Fourth Armoured Brigade's Final Battle, 17 June

Overnight from 14 June and for most of the next day, the remaining tanks and vehicles in 4th Armoured weaved their way eastwards among a huge congestion of vehicles on or near the Axis bypass road. The Brigade noted that, 'The road to CAPUZZO was crammed with transport and organised movement was impossible.'[77] They finally halted west of Gambut on the coast road, gathering with the rest of 2nd and 22nd Armoured and adjacent to XXX Corps HQ. They were told to move south but said it was impossible as they needed time to reorganise themselves.

They moved south next day, though this proved a difficult move across the railhead and the steep-sided escarpment at Bir Chleta. Forty enemy tanks had been reported near Sidi Rezegh gap, so 4th Brigade moved out again to do battle. They advanced west again, with 6th RTR in the lead, 3rd CLY on the left and 3/5th RTR on the right. The Brigade reached the gap but were uncertain about moving further west and took up a defensive position facing north in the valley between two escarpments. Two jock columns pushed onwards to give the tanks time for some maintenance, each column had one battery from 1st RHA and one company from 1st KRRC. One column headed for the right flank slopes of Pt.175, and the other to the left flank escarpment at Pt.178, both were to harass the enemy.[78] They were also joined by 9th Lancers. The 9th had been asked in the morning, to watch over the sixteen 6pdr and two 25pdr guns on the ridge, in case they were overwhelmed.[79] 7th Armoured HQ requested help for the Belhamed Box to their northwest, but selected an unsuitable position in the next valley, which 4th Armoured protested. This command 'discussion' continued into the afternoon, when Brigadier Richards returned to XXX Corps HQ. In the meantime enemy tanks were spotted approaching 9th Lancers after 1700 hours and soon 3/5th RTR said they had another column of 35 tanks advancing on their positions, and both units were soon under attack.

Brigadier Richards summoned the C.O. of 9th Lancers, and said he was going to advance against a concentration of panzers west of Sidi Rezegh Airfield, to their north-west, just then the latter were bombed by some RAF Bostons. The Germans decided to attack first and between 30 and 40 tanks advanced towards them. The

---

76 Lewis, pp.102–103.
77 TNA WO 169/4216: 4th Armoured Brigade War Diary, 14–15 June 1942.
78 TNA WO 169/4216: 4th Armoured Brigade War Diary, 17 June 1942.
79 Bovington: 9th Lancers War Diary, 17 June 1942.

Grants opened fire at 1,500 yards and the two sides closed to 600 yards. The Lancers were surprised to see the 6pdr guns being pulled out and there was no supporting fire from the 25pdr batteries.[80] The Lancers found themselves heavily shelled and outflanked on both sides and their Grants outnumbered by three or four to one. Soon these were knocked out, and the cruisers reported they would be wiped out if not pulled back. The C.O. ordered a smoke screen, behind which they retired firing as they went and being chased in a running fight with about 30 Mk IIIs. They increased speed to 15mph and were soon beyond the Mk IIIs but still sustaining shellfire They lost numerous crews, wounded and killed. They formed a single cruiser A squadron by 18 June, and the last Grant went to 3/5th RTR.[81] The rest of the regiment joined the long retreat towards Alamein.

The brigade complained they had little fire support because the two batteries were on the escarpments in the jock columns. By early evening both regiments were being outflanked and looking to retire. The move around 9th Lancers was stopped by Sergeant William Lloyd's troop, as they held off superior numbers of enemy tanks. For this and other actions he was awarded the DCM.[82] On 16 June, Major K. J. Price had already led the two remaining squadrons from 9th Lancers to overrun one Axis flank guard,[83] and in this battle he was also commended for his defence against the German outflanking move and covering the withdrawal by 4th Armoured.[84] The worse threat was on the 3/5th RTR left flank, so 6th RTR were ordered to move across. Unfortunately, they were less sure of their position and were not heavily engaged.

They were also informed that further Axis columns of guns and infantry were moving both south and north of them in a wide encircling movement. This forced the Brigade to withdraw 23 miles south-east to B.574. The southern enemy column of 400 MET and 22 tanks was west of them. The brigade continued south to another FMC and regrouped the next day, 18 June. They had 24 Grants, 18 Cruisers, 16 Stuarts and 22 guns remaining. They spent another day of maintenance, were visited by both Ritchie and Norrie and were ordered east to Sherfezen near the wire, starting the next day.[85] 4th Armoured had fought itself out now; it was too far south-east of Tobruk to make any difference there and the remaining tanks were needed for the defence of the frontier.

South-east of Tobruk, 2nd and 9th Rifle Brigades operated jock columns on the southern flank of Panzerarmee as it closed around El Adem and Tobruk. Again, units were often switched from the armoured brigades or were deployed separately to protect the artillery as it harassed MET. 9th Rifle Brigade went to Eluet et Tamar

---

80 Bovington: 9th Lancers War Diary, 17 June 1942.
81 Bovington: 9th Lancers War Diary, 18–21 June 1942.
82 TNA WO 373/21/404: Recommendation for Award, Sergeant W. Lloyd, 17 June 1942.
83 Bright, *Ninth Lancers,* p.81. It was considered 'as nice a bit of tank handling as was ever seen.'
84 TNA WO 373/21/40: Recommendation for Award, Major K. J. Price, 16–17 June 1942. For these actions he was awarded an immediate MC.
85 TNA WO 169/4216: 4th Armoured Brigade War Diary, 17 June 1942.

from 7 June and companies were used as escorts to various batteries, who engaged the enemy around Knightsbridge. Separation by task was still common, C Company was detached to support another battery and only rejoined the battalion on 17 June. 9th Rifle Brigade were finally ordered to join the Tobruk garrison, under 2nd South African Division, on 12 June, which involved a difficult night move negotiating minefields.[86] Many units complained about movement problems north of the Trigh Capuzzo, either due to narrow passes on the lateral escarpments or the various small minefields which crossed the area south of Tobruk.

The motor battalions were weakened by further division. A company was sent off to protect 339 Battery, leaving the battalion with only two companies. Next day they rejoined 7th Motor Brigade now operating south-east of Tobruk, and moved to B.497, some 15 miles south of Ed Duda on the Trigh Capuzzo. From here Brigade ordered them back to 'the wire' – the frontier.[87] Eighth Army was gradually reducing the number of units in the front line.

The extent to which the renewed jock columns were able to effectively support 4th Armoured Brigade on 17 June may have caused some diversion. The 9th RB column with 339 Battery, headed north from their leaguer to engage a large column of MET. In return the Germans sent a column of 14 tanks and 60 vehicles against them on the morning of 19 June, which forced the column to retire south again. Next day they were informed that Tobruk was now 'in danger' and all columns were again ordered north. They engaged some MET on the escarpment overlooking the Trigh Capuzzo near Sidi Rezegh.[88] As with previous attacks, mixed columns of Axis tanks and infantry were able to force them away from the main areas of operation; 9th RB later joined the 3rd Indian Motor Brigade and retreated to the frontier. By 22 June they found MET advancing towards the Sherferzan gap and were able to shell the column.

One of the problems on the frontier was that the Salum-Hamra 'fortresses' were just 60 percent and 30 percent complete respectively and required fresh armoured units to support them. Further back Mersa Matruh was considered to be strong, but with only a small port which could be put under observed fire. The aim was to prevent a new thrust by Panzerarmee which could cut off the rest of Eighth Army from retreat past Salum.[89] However, rapid advances by Panzerarmee had undermined the frontier position and next day most units were back at Matruh.

GHQ's new appreciation of the situation said that the main objective now was to, 'secure our base in Egypt.'[90] The frontier area had seven infantry brigades 'of sorts,' but only 5th Indian Brigade was complete with artillery but had no anti-tank

---

86 TNA WO 169/5057: 9th Rifle Brigade War Diary, 1942, 7–17 June 1942
87 TNA WO 169/5057: 9th Rifle Brigade War Diary, 1942, 7–17 June 1942.
88 TNA WO 169/5057: 9th Rifle Brigade War Diary, 1942. 7–17 June 1942.
89 TNA WO 201/404: Operations: telegrams & reports, June 1942, General Staff Appreciation 13 June 1942, p.2.
90 TNA WO 201/404: Operations: telegrams & reports, June 1942, General Staff Appreciation 13 June 42, p.1.

component. Many of the other brigades had enough infantry but were short on weapons and artillery. They called for all artillery to be sent forward and at least one fresh division. It was a perilous state to be in. They hoped that Eighth Army HQ would be relieved and GHQ would take control of the frontier forces. Any armoured units should be commanded by the HQ from 10th Armoured Division, which was available.

Conclusion

Tobruk way were the graves, not many,
As numbers go, as casualties in war,
Though in the isolating moon they seemed
Milestones over the world, and in the sunlight
Their identities oppressed …
Most were anonymous, the scattered ones,
With stones heaped over them to keep their bones …
Ein unbekannter englischer Soldat

'Portrait and Background'
James Walker[1]

Gazala had been another epic struggle of the North African campaign. In number of days it had lasted longer than either Crusader or Second Alamein. Soldiers from all sides had proved their mettle under fire and against the harsh conditions of the desert. For Eighth Army it was a major defeat, which gave them no option but to retreat and regroup for future rounds of battle further east with Panzerarmee. In the short term Eighth Army had suffered serious losses in men and equipment, and its morale had been battered again. They had lost their large forward supply bases and Tobruk, which for higher leaders remained a political football because it was synonymous with an embattled defence to be held come what may. Unfortunately, this time it was lost and the army was forced back onto the supply bases in the Delta.

The final days of the battle, from 15 to 20 June were a whirl of rapidly changing plans and confused orders, which also form part of the story of the ill-fated defence of Tobruk. Lord Carver details the confusion of telegrams/advice which crossed each other, combined with the inability of both Ritchie and Auchinleck to change their minds over decisions made.[2] Auchinleck over-promised London that the army was 'standing and fighting' but was advising Ritchie to protect Eighth Army and hold the frontier. Ritchie maintains he was taken by surprise over the sudden collapse of

---

1   Selwyn, *Poems of the Second World War*, p.131.
2   Carver, *Dilemmas*, pp.106–107 and Chapter 7.

Tobruk, as Klopper had sent a message on 18 June saying he was, 'all ready'.[3] As units retreated, either into the Tobruk perimeter or back to the frontier, Auchinleck and Ritchie engaged in a whirl of confused telegrams about how they should continue to protect Tobruk from the south, and yet somehow remain in touch with other units holding along the frontier near Sollum. In reality this distance was too great, as had been seen during Crusader, and would have divided Eighth Army far too much. The painful reality was that many remaining units were combined remnants of armoured regiments, or jock columns made from former infantry brigades and similar amalgamated units. As Corps and Army HQs moved to the rear, the whole command lost its grip on events and this became a mess which contributed heavily to the rapid collapse of the defence of the Tobruk garrison, which was the ultimate blow of the entire battle.

Suddenly the defence of the frontier at Sollum became the key to holding back Panzerarmee. As early as 13 June, GHQ gave a detailed assessment which focused on the defences at Sollum. It was a fall-back position, where Eighth Army could regroup while Tobruk also held out. The summary order of battle showed a weakened group of brigades still situated at many points along the Egyptian coast. They included 5th Indian Division, less 29th Brigade and with no artillery, reorganising at Buq Buq. The 10th Indian Division had 21st Brigade, and also with no artillery and without the 1st DCLI (overrun on 6 June), 25th Indian Brigade with no artillery, and the 1st Free French Brigade at Sidi Barrani with no weapons, (all lost at Hacheim). The 5th Indian Brigade and 2nd Free French Brigade were at least complete, while the 3rd Indian Motor Brigade also had no artillery.[4] The length of the frontier, like Gazala, was still too long for these few, ill-equipped brigades.

The army had many other problems besides a weak grip on command. Many units remained unready for the next phase of battle. Further back in Egypt there were very few units which could be sent forward to defend the frontier. Those available included the largely untrained 8th Armoured Brigade with only 33 tanks per regiment and the 161st Indian Motor Brigade which had no artillery. There were two artillery regiments, one just converted to 25pdrs and one which still needed 50 vehicles. The recommendation was that GHQ would take command of the frontier area from Eighth Army, using X Corps as the forward HQ, with 5th Indian Divisional HQ holding the command until Corps HQ could reach them. Units from the rear areas would be rushed forward included two motor brigades, the understrength 8th Armoured, and elements of the returning New Zealand Division. Units which had been overrun in the cauldron, included 365 men from 150th Brigade, and the 2/4th Gurkhas were withdrawn to the Delta to refit.[5]

---

3   TNA WO 201/379: Operations in North Africa: General Ritchie's report, May–June 1942.
4   TNA WO 201/405: Telegrams 12–16 June 1942, Appreciation by DDO 13 June 1942.
5   TNA WO 201/405: Telegrams 12–16 June 1942, Appreciation by DDO 13 June 1942.

While these new plans for the defence of the frontier were being considered, Auchinleck wanted to hold south of Tobruk, 'Even if you have to evacuate Gazala you should hold ACROMA, EL ADEM and to south, while I build up reinforcements on Frontier… Are you ready to do this.'[6] He wanted Ritchie to remain with the forward HQ, but that the HQ should be 'thinned out' of personnel.[7] At the same time he was informing London that although armoured battles had been fought southwest of Acroma, mobile columns were continuing to be effective against the enemy, which was surely putting a gloss on events. Churchill was as keen to fight on and Auchinleck used the Prime Minister's views to pressure Ritchie to hold the defences around Tobruk, despite the reality of the situation. On 14 June he passed on the message from the Prime Minister to Ritchie, 'Your decision to fight it out to the end most cordially endorsed. Retreat would be fatal. This is a business not only of armour but of will power. God bless you all.'[8]

Auchinleck informed the CIGS of XIII Corps' withdrawal, and that Ritchie had been ordered to hold the Acroma-El Adem – Bir el Gubi line. Eighth Army would not be invested in Tobruk itself.[9] Unfortunately, in the southern sector various units had withdrawn into the Tobruk perimeter. He reiterated these intentions to Ritchie the same day, emphasising the use of mobile groups and artillery to counterattack and harass the enemy.[10] After El Adem had been attacked three times, they agreed the next day that Tobruk could be temporarily isolated. It seemed likely that both El Adem and Belhamed might be overrun very soon so they would evacuate by 17 June, when 4th Armoured Brigade was 'severely handled' and forced to withdraw. The Corps and Army HQs were on the move. Ritchie visited 7th Armoured HQ by Lysander on 18 June and discussed future plans following 4th Armoured Brigade's battle the previous day. Orders that arrived from XXX Corps that evening to move towards the frontier[11] also pointed out the, 'conflicting issues arising out of offensive forward policy and needs for defence of the frontier position.'[12] Either way Eighth Army was becoming overstretched. Some units were still reasonably intact and heading for the frontier. Others headed into Tobruk but were exhausted and trying to sort themselves out as well as dig in on the perimeter but with no clear direction from the garrison HQ. In Tobruk, some experienced officers could see what was needed to keep Panzerarmee

6   TNA WO 201/405: Telegrams 12–16 June 1942, C/11580 Mideast to Eighth Army 14 June 1942.
7   TNA WO 201/405: Telegrams 12–16 June 1942, C/1264 Mideast to Eighth Army 14 June 1942.
8   TNA WO 201/405: Telegrams 12–16 June 1942, CS/1249 Mideast to Eighth Army 14 June 1942.
9   TNA WO 201/405: Telegrams 12–16 June 1942, CS/1256 Mideast to Troopers 14 June 1942.
10 TNA WO 201/405: Telegrams 12–16 June 1942, CS/1257 Mideast to Eighth Army 14 June 1942.
11 TNA WO 169/4216: 4th Armoured Brigade War Diary, 18 June 1942.
12 TNA WO 201/379: Operations in North Africa: General Ritchie's report, May–June 1942.

beyond the wire. The 1st Worcesters were allocated a counter-attacking role having regrouped about 500 men from the battle at Pt.187, but they had no transport and just a few spigot mortars.[13] Even if Tobruk had been held there were still tons of stores and vehicles, out in the FMCs, which the Axis could use. Panzerarmee rapidly invested the port, and directed by Rommel, made a successful assault on 20–21 June, with a rapid advance cutting through the defences and an equally confused and rapid surrender by the unfortunate garrison commander, General Klopper.

The loss of Tobruk on 21 June was seen at the time as a major blow to British political and military prestige, especially as it followed the defeats in the Far East in the spring. Churchill was informed while he was sitting with President Roosevelt, in the Oval Office, when the news came through from London. He called it, '…one of the heaviest blows I can recall during the war',[14] but one from which, politically, he was able to recover quite quickly once back in the House of Commons. Despite the defeats at Gazala and Tobruk, the British war effort in North Africa continued, with fresh resources of men and material arriving to rebuild and reequip Eighth Army. Panzerarmee would be fought to a stalemate in July, during First Alamein, and later decisively defeated at Alam Halfa and Second Alamein that November 1942.

There were many turning points for Eighth Army during Gazala, besides the failures in command. In the build-up, units being reequipped with fresh men and equipment, increased the time taken to get used to their new tanks and guns. Other units were drawn in from Cyprus and Iraq, and were rushed over to Libya, with little chance of becoming acquainted with daily procedures, navigation, let alone practising battle drills. Some units were thrown into battle as they arrived, such as the unlucky 1st DCLI, but most of these new arrivals were then allocated administrative tasks, anti-invasion patrols, or as garrisons for supply dumps. All of these were important to the army and perhaps helped them settle in to life in the blue, but they had little chance to develop proper training. Ritchie later argued that, 'our standard of training in mobile operations is far below what it should be,' he said that there was a general shortage of equipment. His final point was that, 'We are still too "static-defence" minded…much valuable time is taken up in the construction of field fortifications to the detriment of training.' He also suggested that Corps HQs become more administrative, with Army Command dealing directly with Division HQs in operations.[15]

Another weakness for Eighth Army was the overreliance on jock column activity. Being part of a column and going on patrol for 10 days or 2 weeks gave units valuable practice in night patrols, navigation, small actions and harassing fire. They provided valuable intelligence on the smallest changes in enemy movements or about new positions, but how effective really were they against the main concentrations of enemy units remains questionable. A good deal of time was taken up preparing for a column,

---

13 TNA WO 169/5074: 1st Worcesters War Diary, Report on Tobruk 20–21 June 1942.
14 Churchill, *The Hinge of Fate, Vol. IV*, p.343.
15 TNA WO 201/379: Operations in North Africa: General Ritchie's report, May–June 1942.

and the maintenance of worn-out vehicles that was needed after they returned left many tired. So how useful was this in bringing units together to effectively engage the more concentrated panzer columns?

The generals who were criticised so much during and after Gazala, would be gradually moved on or become casualties of later battles. A few days after the fall of Tobruk, Ritchie was sacked, with Auchinleck taking direct command of Eighth Army and remaining as C-in-C Middle East, until his own dismissal in August. Neil Ritchie later became a corps commander under General Montgomery in the North-West Europe campaign. 'Strafer' Gott, of course, was tragically killed in August, heroically trying to save others from the burning aircraft in which he had just crashed. He was viewed with great affection by many in Eighth Army, but like Norrie, had been too exhausted or felt he had run out of ideas to outmanoeuvre Rommel. Messervy was sacked on 19 June while Renton briefly commanded 7th Armoured Division before he was also sacked.[16] Pyman believed he had never been given a proper chance to develop as a divisional commander.[17] Herbert Lumsden was famously sacked by Montgomery after Second Alamein and was later killed in January 1945 in the Pacific.[18]

Eighth Army's defeat was not a fatal blow but it meant that the campaign dragged on, and it would take further heavy fighting in Egypt before Panzerarmee was finally pushed back into Tripolitania at the end of 1942. The army had fought hard at Gazala and sacrificed a good many men and units, typified by the battles of the Indian troops at Pt.171 and the Scots Guards at Rigel Ridge, but their commanders had failed to gain a decisive victory, and this failure extended the campaign by another six months.

16   TNA WO 169/4216: 4th Armoured Brigade War Diary, 19 June 1942.
17   Pyman, *Call to Arms*, p.44.
18   Nick Smart, *Biography of British Generals of the Second World War* (Barnsley: Pen & Sword, 2005), p.197.

Note on Sources

Regimental/battalion diaries and related reports offer the best information about life within Eighth Army and provide excellent detail on the battle. Understandably, many of the units which were overrun or destroyed have key days or months missing or were rewritten later from memory. General Koenig's 12 June report on Bir Hacheim noted that all brigade records were destroyed prior to the evacuation.[1] Other diaries have just a few months, often up to April, leaving us to pierce together a jigsaw of how the unit operated later on. In the 150th Brigade Group, overrun on 1 June, only 5th Green Howards leave a key account, while the other battalion diaries stop in February and April and the attached 7th Medium Regiment RA leaves only a file from the signals section.[2] Fortunately, captured senior officers made a record of the battle during their time as POWs, and published this in 1944, and so this account combines well with the others from the battle.[3]

The diaries also give useful weekly and monthly details such as unit strengths, movements et cetera, but most importantly some post-action reports and diagrams, which give a much better insight into what happened. Brigadier Filose from 3rd Indian Motor Brigade wrote two accounts of the first morning of the battle for the brigade, which shows both how they did what they could to prepare in the time available and the events of those first hours.[4] Equally the diaries of the 2/4th Gurkhas and the 3/9th Jats, give more detailed information and diagrams of their defence on 5–6 June, during Operation Aberdeen.[5] The concise after-action reports give us much greater detail on the sequence of events and why decisions were made in the heat of battle. For example, we see the confusion of the 3/9th Jats during

---

1   TNA WO 201/380: Operations of First Free French Brigade Eighth Army, May–June 1942.
2   TNA WO 169/5021: 5th Green Howards; WO 169/5020: 4th Green Howards, January–February 1942; WO169/5075: 4th East Yorks, January-April 1942; WO 169/5506 7th Medium Regiment Signal Section.
3   W. E. Bush, (ed.), *150th Infantry Brigade (50th Northumbrian Division) in the Middle East, June 1941–June 1942* (London: Green Howards Regimental Journal, 1944),
4   TNA WO 169/2698: 2nd Armoured Brigade War Diary, action of 3rd Indian Motor Brigade 27 May 1942.
5   TNA WO 169/7791: 2/4th Gurkhas War Diary and WO 169/7677 3/9th Jats war diaries 1942,

Operation Aberdeen, whose C.O. went forward to clarify the forward situation, but this left battalion HQ frustrated when new orders and intelligence arrived.[6] Other reports were also given by officers and men captured during early actions, but who escaped within a few days.

Regiments also updated intelligence details about the enemy, which enabled commanders to improve their tactics, which showed that the higher level HQs were not always so in the dark. Rifle Brigade personnel were most indignant because they noted how they had constantly reported the southern flanking move made by Panzerarmee on 26 May, sending 53 messages to 7th Armoured HQ that afternoon and throughout the night.[7] Though whether they believed or acted on the information received is another matter often discussed. These unit files are ably supported by the various operations and planning files (TNA series WO 201) for 1942.

The diaries often give map references along with unit moves which helped to pin down various actions. These also provide a stronger argument for the importance of certain areas of the battlefield, such as the northern ridgeline of the cauldron sector and the Naduret el Ghesceuasc Ridge, south of Knightsbridge. Some units also made large-scale diagrams of the grid-squares they occupied, such as 2/4th Gurkhas before they were overrun. This gave invaluable detail about the deployment of platoons, guns and distances between ridges.[8] The award citations from TNA WO373 series provide many examples of individual actions.

Panzerarmee and Afrika Korps diaries from the Bundesarchiv and some divisional diaries from the Imperial War Museum, have added detail on the Axis view of events. These documents augment on-line diaries and orders of battle and have been helpfully digitised by campaign enthusiasts. While these web sources lack the related papers of the complete files, they do at least give us the movements and battles for these regiments, e.g. 3rd County London Sharpshooters, from 22nd Armoured Brigade.[9]

Various published wartime memoirs by journalist Alan Moorehead and others provide excellent accounts which can add life to the administrative tone of regimental papers. Other early post-war works include the young cavalry officer Roy Farran's *Winged Dagger* in 1948, and Cyril Joly's epic tale *Take These Men*. More recently published memoirs include Mike Peyton's *An Average War*, John Cowtan, *Gazala Line to Behind the Lines* and *My Wartime Wanderings* by Rifleman Kenneth Phillips.[10] German material included Rommel's edited papers and the often-used works by von

---

6   TNA WO 169/7677: War Diary 3/9th Jats, 5 June 1942.
7   J.M.L.R., 7th Motor Brigade, During Summer 1942 cited in H. G. Parkyn, *The Rifle Brigade Chronicle for 1942* (London: Rifle Brigade Association, 1943), p.95.
8   TNA WO 169/7791: War Diary 2/4th Gurkha Rifles, January-August 1942 & October-December 1942.
9   *3rd CLY Sharpshooters War Diary* <www.warlinks.com> (accessed 17 Aug. 2020).
10 Mike Payton, *An Average War* (Chelmsford: Maypole Press, 2014), John Cowtan, *Gazala Line to Behind the Lines* (Milton Keynes: Author House, 2011) and Kenneth L. Phillips, *My Wartime Wanderings* (Gloucester: Choir Press, 2021).

Mellenthin, Hans von Luck and H. W. Schmidt. A few nuggets were gleaned from Corporal Gunther Bahnemann's *I Deserted Rommel*.

Past anniversaries have brought out some valuable studies of this period of the campaign. Gazala itself has been covered from different perspectives and detail, one of the best works being Michael Carver's *Dilemmas of the Desert War*.[11] David French also made a detailed summary of the key reasons for Eighth Army's failures in mid–1942.[12] Many others tell the story of Gazala in less detail, often as part of a longer narrative of the campaign, taking in the fall of Tobruk, and/or First Alamein. Carver's various works saw Gazala as part of the battle for Libya-Tobruk, linking it with Crusader. I have chosen to focus on the build-up to and the main battle itself prior to 20 June 1942.

For simplicity, I have mainly referred to units as 'British', but the term covers all units within Eighth Army, which at this time included Indian and South African units as well as a Free French Brigade. Other veteran divisions were being rested and trained in Syria, such as 2nd New Zealand, which would be recalled for the Alamein battles. This was one period of the campaign when Eighth Army contained a majority of British regiments. I also mostly refer to Axis or Panzerarmee units, covering both Italian and German formations.

To supplement these primary accounts are the mostly excellent post-war regimental and divisional histories, often written soon after the war, with many details given by those who fought there, and taken while memories were still relatively fresh. Examples include the Northumberland Fusiliers, the Kings Royal Rifle Corps, and the Scots Guards histories, all of which provide much greater detail on those infantry battles than can be obtained from the war diaries. The useful divisional works include *Ball of Fire* for the 5th Indian Division and *Path of the 50th*.[13] Many regimental histories have been updated by more recent prolific writers such as Patrick Delaforce and Richard Doherty, who combine primary material with interviews with veterans.[14] The training across various units and the plans for the defensive battle along with the successful German tactics ranged against them is seen in *Middle East Training Pamphlets* and *German Methods of Warfare in the Libyan Desert* from 1941–1942 and so give us helpful insights into doctrine and tactics for both sides from the period.[15]

---

11   Michael Carver, *Dilemmas of the Desert War: The Libyan Campaign 1940–1942* (Staplehurst: Spellmount, 2002), passim. See also his earlier work *Tobruk* and later memoir, *Out of Step* for further perspectives on these controversies.
12   David French, *Raising Churchill's Army* (Oxford: Oxford University Press, 2001), pp.212–239.
13   E. W. Clay, *The Path of the 50th* (Uckfield: Naval & Military Press 2020 reprint of 1950 edition). It is interesting to note that the 2nd Rifle Brigade Diary noted that a patrol including Lieutenant E. W. Clay was recovered successfully from west of the Gazala mine belt during the battle.
14   Patrick Delaforce, *Monty's Marauders* (London: Chancellor, 2000), and Richard Doherty, *Ubique: The Royal Artillery in the Second World War* (Stroud: History Press, 2008).
15   *Middle East Training Pamphlets* Parts 1 & 2, (Buxton: MLRS, 2011) and United States War Department, *German Methods of Warfare in the Libyan Desert, U.S. War Dept 1942* (Buxton: MLRS, 2004).

There are a number of very good accounts about the battle which also provide useful analysis of the reasons for defeat. The much discussed and often overriding factor being the poor leadership and decision-making within Eighth Army through this period of the campaign. The official history, *Mediterranean & Middle East* volume III, is mostly neutral on this, but is unusually critical of the complicated 'system' of British command in this period.[16] These can be combined with other official histories and Professor Bennett's *Ultra and Mediterranean Strategy*, to provide the overview of what intelligence was available at the time. Adrian Stewart is scathing with regard to Auchinleck's command style and decisions back at GHQ Middle East. He and others are also critical of the commanders at the front, a 'weakness in command at Army, Corps and Divisional levels.'[17] James Holland and others have also written very effective 'soldier narratives' which aim to move the campaign forward, largely through the eyes of the many brave individuals, in *Together We Stand* Peter Hart interviewed many veterans to tell the story of the ill-fated South Notts Hussars.[18] Barrie Pitt's *Crucible* series, volume II, is critical of command, along with other factors such as lack of Grant tanks and the newly arrived 6pdr guns. This study has aimed to give a more nuanced story, as brigades and regiments attempted to complete tasks without adequate resources, over difficult terrain, and were subsequently defeated in detail. The abdication of command decisions throughout the battle exacerbated these local defeats, and left units exhausted and reduced in numbers, so that retreat was the only option.

---

16 I.S.O. Playfair, *The Mediterranean and Middle East. Vol. III* (Uckfield: Naval & Military Press, 2004), p.235.
17 Adrian Stewart, *The Early Battles of Eighth Army: Crusader to the Alamein Line 1941–1942* (Barnsley: Leo Cooper, 2002) p.64 and D. W. Braddock, *Britain's Desert War in Egypt and Libya 1940–1942: The End of the Beginning* (Barnsley: Pen & Sword, 2019), p.132.
18 James Holland, *Together We Stand. North Africa 1942–1943: Turning the Tide in the West* (London: Harper Collins, 2006) and Peter Hart, *The South Notts Hussars: The Western Desert 1940–1942* (Barnsley: Pen & Sword, 2010).

Bibliography

Primary Sources

The National Archives of the United Kingdom (Kew)

Cabinet Papers (CAB)
CAB 66/24/26: Telegram from Middle East Defence Committee, No. CC/42, dated 9th May, 1942, Extract from Telegram CS849 22 March
CAB 66/24/45: War Cabinet Weekly Résumé 142 to 21st May 1942, Mediterranean situation
CAB 79/20/10: COS Committee Minutes, 6 April 1942, Conclusions JISC Report Enemy Intentions
CAB 79/56/3: COS Committee Meeting, 13 January 1942, Minutes, Operation ACROBAT
CAB 79/19/12: COS Committee Minutes, Friday 13 March 1942, 13. Combined British and American Strategy
CAB 79/19/24: COS Committee Meeting, 24 March 1942, Mediterranean
CAB 80/34/4: War Cabinet Weekly Résumé no.129, 19 February 1942
CAB 80/36/1: COS Committee Memorandum: Relation of Strategy In Middle East and India, 10 April 1942
CAB 80/36/1: War Cabinet Weekly Résumé 136, to 9th April 1942, military situation
CAB 80/61/3: COS Committee Memorandum, Shipping Situation 9 February 1942
CAB 80/61/3: COS Committee. Situation in Libya, 1 March 1942
CAB 101/248/3: Telegrams, March 1942.
HW series
HW 1/513: Southern Russian Front: GAF bomber fighter reinforcements, April, 1942

Regimental War Diaries
WO 169/3910: 2/4th Gurkhas, 1942
WO 169/4520 44th Royal Tanks, January-October 1942
WO169/4053: 1st Armoured Division HQ, 194
WO 169/4065 1st Armoured Brigade Support Group 1942
WO169/4199: 1st Army Tank Brigade HQ, 1942

WO169/4251: 22nd Armoured Brigade HQ, 1942
WO 169/4486: 8th Hussars, 1942
WO 169/4489: 10th Royal Hussars, 1942
WO 169/4494: 2nd Royal Gloucestershire Hussars, 1942
WO 169/4495: 3rd County London Yeomanry, 1942
WO 169/4496: 4th County London Yeomanry, 1942
WO 169/4509: 6th RTR, 1942
WO 169/4520: 42nd RTR, 1942
WO 169/4521: 44th RTR, 1942.
WO 169/4555: 1st Royal Horse Artillery, 1942
WO 169/4556: 2nd Royal Horse Artillery, 1942
WO169/4563: 107th Royal Horse Artillery, 1942
WO 169/4581: 28th Field Regt RA, 1942
WO 169/4982: 3rd Coldstream Guards, 1942.
WO 169/4983: 2nd Scots Guards, 1942
WO 169/5007: 6th Durham Light Infantry, 1942
WO 169/5009: 9th Durham Light Infantry, 1942
WO 169/5021: 5th Green Howards, 1942
WO 169/5023: 7th Green Howards, 1942
WO 169/5032: 1st KRRC, 1942
WO 169/5033 2nd KRRC, 1942
WO 169/5034: 9th KRRC, 1942
WO 169/5057: 9th Rifle Brigade, 1942
WO 169/5074: 1st Worcesters, 1942
WO 169/5077: 2nd West Yorks, 1942
WO 169/7718: 2nd Royal Lancers, 1942
WO 169/7723: 11th PAVO, 1942
WO 169/7741: 2nd Indian Field Regiment IA, 1942
WO 169/7619: 10th Indian Brigade, 1942
WO 169/7770: 4/10th Baluch Regiment, 1942

War Office Papers
WO 32/10387: Army Organisation: Tanks (Code 14(G)): Re-organisation of Armoured formations; Proposal from Middle East 1942
WO 201/379: Operations in North Africa: General Ritchie's report, May–June 1942
WO 201/380: Operations of First Free French Brigade Eighth Army, May–June 1942, Account of Operations of 3rd Motor Brigade in the area south of Bir Hacheim, 26–27 May 1942
WO 201/392: 1st South Africa Division: Gazala defensive battle, operational reports, 19–26 June 42
WO 201/397: Cipher telegrams: General Auchinleck & Prime Minister, May 1941-June 1942, 1718 cipher 2/2 dated 3/2/42

WO 201/398: Cipher telegrams: General Auchinleck and PM, December 1941–June 1942, Troopers from Mideast CS/747 20 February 1942
WO 201/401: Operations: telegrams and reports, 1942 January–March, Personal to General Ritchie from C-in-C 66997, 16 Feb 42
WO 201/404: Operations: telegrams and reports, June 1942, General Staff Appreciation 13 June 42
WO 201/419: Cyrenaica campaign: planning, 1942 March–October, 12 March 1942
WO 201/420: Cyrenaica campaign: planning, June 1942, Appreciation 10 June 42
WO 201/421: Cyrenaica campaign: planning, 1942 March–October Estimates, 24 March 1942
WO 201/450: Cyrenaica: lessons from operations November 1941–March 1942
WO 201/500: General Auchinleck's despatch on operation `Crusader', 1941 December–1943 November. Brief survey of Operations between 21 January–5 February 1942 by Lieutenant General Godwin Austen, p.2.
WO 201/522: 13 Corps: operations, January–November 1941. Notes on Lessons from recent operations
WO 201/532: Eighth Army: Commanders conferences, December 1941–May 1942
WO 201/537: 1 Armoured Division: report on operations in Western Desert, May–July 1942
WO 201/539: Eighth Army: intelligence matters, November 1941–August 1942
WO 201/2698: Operations of 2 Armoured Brigade Group, 1942 May–June, Notes on the action of 3rd Independent Motor Bde SW of Bir Hacheim 27 May 1942
WO 373/20/33: Recommendation for Award, Captain J. R. Barton, 4th RHA, 26 May 1942
WO 373/20/97: Recommendation for Award, Sergeant C. Cheney, 1st RHA, 30 May 42
WO 373/20/107: Recommendation for Award, Sergeant G. G. Griffiths 4th RHA, 27 May 42
WO 373/20/79: Recommendation for Award, Captain D. M. Reynolds, 2nd Royal Lancers, 27 May 1942
WO 373/20/166: Recommendation for Award, Dafadar G. Babbani, 2nd Royal Lancers, 27 May 1942
WO 373/20/167: Recommendation for Award, Dafadar R. Singh, 2nd Royal Lancers, 27 May 1942
WO 373/21/9: Recommendation for Award, Lieutenant Colonel E. C. Cooke-Collis, 3 Aug 1942
WO 373/21/40: Recommendation for Award, Major K. J. Price, 16–17 June 1942
WO 373/21/41: Recommendation for Award, 2nd Lieutenant Jones Williams, 29 May 1942.
WO 373/21/181: Recommendation for Award for Corporal Withers 10 Hussars, 25 June 1942
WO 373/21/331: Recommendation for Award, Corporal E. P. Hardy, 14 June 1942

WO 373/21/133: Recommendation for Award, Lieutenant M. H. Hinton-Webb, 28–29 May 1942
WO 373/21/404: Recommendation for Award, Sergeant W. Lloyd, 17 June 1942
WO 201/500: General Auchinleck's despatch on operation 'Crusader', 1 December 1941–30 November 1943

Bovington Tank Museum
3rd RTR War Diary and Papers.
4th RTR Papers.
7th RTR Papers.
9th Lancers War Diary.
44th RTR War Diary and Papers.

Churchill Archives Centre (Cambridge)
Papers of Lieutenant General Thomas Corbett
Papers of Lieutenant General Sir Alexander Galloway

Imperial War Museum (London)
IWM AL833: DAK War Diary, 14 May–1 Aug 1942
IWM E127: 90th Light Division War Diary, 15 May–5 July 42.
IWM Doc.8109. Box RB2/5: Private papers of Major General Raymond Briggs, 1942
IWM Doc.7004: Private Papers of Major J.M. McSwiney, 1942
IWM, Private Papers of Lieutenant Colonel M. E. Parker; Parker, Michael Edward, Catalogue number, Documents. 479.

Liddell-Hart Centre for Military Archives, Kings College London
Papers of G. P. B. Roberts, Pamphlet article by A. C. Edwards about Briggs, 'Raymond Briggs and the Western Desert.' Published post-war, 1950s

National Army Museum (NAM)
NAM Papers of Major General Dorman-Smith

University of Exeter Digital Collection
Letters of John Jarmain, EUL MS 413, 1942–1943

Bundesarchiv
Bund: RH24–200/107: DAK supply War Diary, 1 March to 15 August 1942, 1 & 7 March.
RH19/VIII/443: PzAOK, DAK War Diary, for Teil 5 docs,
RH26/90/90: 90th Lt Division War Diary 2, documents, 1 April 1942,
RH19/VIII/13: PzAOK War Diary, 7 Feb–25 May.
RH19/VIII/15: Order of 20 May 1942.
RH19/VIII/ 20: PzAOK Battle Report, 26 May–27 July 1942, xx docs

Published Primary Sources

Anon., *Poems from the Desert: Verses by Members of the Eighth Army* (London: Harrap & Co, 1944).
Anon., *Bir Hakeim* (London: French Combat Publications, 1942).
Billany, Dan, *The Trap* (London: Panther, 1964).
Bowlby, Alex, (ed.), *R. L. Crimp: The Diary of a Desert Rat* (London: Pan 1974).
Bowman, T, *The Military Papers of Field Marshal Sir Claude Auchinleck, Vol. I: 1940–42* (Woodbridge, Boydell Press, 2021).
Bush, W. E, (ed.)., *150th Infantry Brigade (50th Northumbrian Division). in the Middle East, June 194 –June 1942* (London: Green Howards Regimental Journal, 1944).
Ciano, G., *Diary 1937–1943* (London: Phoenix Press, 2002).
Danchev, Alex & Todman, Dan, (eds)., *Alanbrooke War Diaries 1939–1945: Field Marshal Lord Alanbrooke* (London: Phoenix Press, 2002).
Forty, G. (ed.)., *Tanks Across the Desert. The War Diary of Jake Wardrop* (London: William Kimber, 1981).
HMSO, *Middle East Training Pamphlets* (Buxton: MLRS, 2011).
Liddell-Hart, B. H., *The Rommel Papers* (Boston: Da Capo Press, 1982).
Moorehead, Alan, *African Trilogy* (London: Hamish Hamilton, 1946).
Parkyn, H. G., *The Rifle Brigade Chronicle for 1942* (London: The Rifle Brigade Club, 1943).
US War Department, *German Methods of Warfare in the Libyan Desert* (Buxton: MLRS, 2004).
War Office, *Infantry Training and War, Manual 1937* (London: War Office, 1937).

Secondary Sources

Official & Regimental Histories

Agar-Hamilton, J.A.I. & Turner L.C.F., *Crisis in the Desert May–July 1942* (Cape Town: Oxford University Press, 1952).
Barclay, C.N., *The History of the Royal Northumberland Fusiliers* (Uckfield: Naval & Military Press, 2009).
Bright, Joan, *The Ninth Queens Royal Lancers* (Uckfield: Naval & Military Press, 2020).
Butler, J. R. M, *Grand Strategy, Vol. III, Part II* (London: HMSO, 1964).
Churchill, W. S. C., *The Second World War, Vol. IV: The Hinge of Fate* (London: Cassell, 1951).
Clay, E. W., *The Path of the 50th* (Uckfield: Naval & Military Press, 2020).
Dawnay, D, et al, *The 10th Royal Hussars in the Second World War, 1939–1945* (Aldershot: Gale & Polden, 1948).
Erskine, D, *The Scots Guards 1919–1955* (Uckfield: Naval & Military Press, 2001).
Godfrey, E. G., *The Duke of Cornwall's Light Infantry 1939–1945* (Malvern: Images, 1994).

Howard, M & Sparrow, J, *The Coldstream Guards 1939–1946* (Oxford: Oxford University Press, 1951).
Indian War Department, *Teheran to Trieste. The Story of 10th Indian Division* (Bombay: Times of India, 1947).
Lewis, P. J. *8th Battalion The Durham Light Infantry 1939–1945* (Uckfield: Naval & Military Press, 2004).
Liddell-Hart, B.H., *The Tanks: The History of the Royal Tank Regiment, Vol. II* (London: Cassell, 1959).
Mills, G. & Nixon, R, *The Annals of the King's Royal Rifle Corps Vol.VI, 1921–1943* (London: Leo Cooper, 1971).
D. K. Palit, *History of the Regiment of Artillery. Indian Army* (London: Leo Cooper, 1972).
Pitman, Stuart, *Second Royal Gloucester Hussars, Libya-Egypt 1941–1942* (Uckfield: Naval & Military Press, 2014).
Playfair, I. S. O., *The Mediterranean & Middle East Vol. III* (Uckfield: Naval & Military Press, 2007).
Richards, D, & St George Saunders, H, *Royal Air Force 1939–1945, Vol. II The Fight Avails* (London: HMSO, 1954).
Scott-Daniell, D, *4th Hussars: The Story of a British Cavalry Regiment* (Aldershot: Gale & Polden, 1959).
Stewart, P. F., *The History of the XII Royal Lancers* (London: Oxford University Press, 1950).
Wilson, E., *Press on Regardless. The Story of the Fifth Royal Tank Regiment in World War Two* (Staplehurst: Spellmount, 2003).

Other Secondary Sources
Barnett, C., *The Desert Generals* (Edison: Castle Books, 2004).
Bennett, R, *Ultra and Mediterranean Strategy* (New York: William Morrow, 1989).
Bierman, J. & Smith, C., *Alamein: War without Hate* (London: Viking, 2002).
Bradford, E, *Siege: Malta 1940–1943* (Harmondsworth: Penguin, 1987).
Bowlby, A, (ed.)., *The Diary of a Desert Rat R. L. Crimp* (London: Pan Books, 1974).
Carver, M, *Tobruk* (London: B.T. Batsford, 1964).
Carver, M, *Dilemmas of the Desert War: The Libyan Campaign 1940–1942* (Staplehurst: Spellmount, 2002).
Carver, M, *Out of Step: Memoirs of a Field Marshal* (London: Hutchinson, 1989).
Colvin, J., *Eighth Army Versus Rommel: Tactics, Training and Operations in North Africa 1940–1942* (Warwick: Helion, 2020).
Connell, J, *Auchinleck* (London: Cassell, 1959).
Cowtan, J, *From the Gazala Line to Behind the Lines* (Milton Keynes: Author House, 2011).
Delaforce, P, *Monty's Marauders* (London: Chancellor, 2000).
Doherty, R, *Ubique: The Royal Artillery in the Second World War* (Stroud: History Press, 2008).

Farran, R, *Winged Dagger: Adventures on Special Service* (London: Cassell, 1998).
Fennell, J., *Combat and Morale in the North African Campaign: The Eighth Army and the Path to El Alamein* (Cambridge: Cambridge University Press, 2011).
French, D., *Raising Churchill's Army* (Oxford: Oxford University Press, 2001).
Gladman, B.W., *Intelligence and Anglo-American Air Support in World War Two: The Western Desert and Tunisia* (Basingstoke: Palgrave Macmillan, 2009).
Graecen, L., *Chink: A Biography* (London: Macmillan, 1989).
de Guingand, F., *Operation Victory* (London: Hodder & Stoughton, 1947).
Halstead, M., *Shots in the Sand: An Undergraduate goes to War* (East Wittering: Gooday, 1990).
Holmes, R., *Bir Hacheim: Desert Citadel* (London: Pan-Ballantine, 1971).
Hughes, E. (ed.)., *Keith Douglas: Poems selected by Ted Hughes* (London: Faber, 2006).
Hunt, D., *A Don at War* (London: Frank Cass, 1990).
Jolly, C., *Take These Men* (London: Constable, 1955).
Kennedy, J., *The Business of War* (London: Hutchinson, 1957).
Kippenberger, H., *Infantry Brigadier* (London: Oxford University Press, 1949).
Mander, D., *Mander's March on Rome* (Gloucester: Alan Sutton, 1987).
Merewood, J., *To War With the Bays. A Tank Gunner Remembers 1939–1945* (Cardiff: 1st, The Queen's Dragoon Guards, 1996).
Mordal, J., *Bir Hacheim* (Paris, Amiot-Dumont, 1951).
Nash, N.S., *Strafer: Desert General* (Barnsley: Pen & Sword, 2013).
Parkinson, R., *The Auk: Auchinleck, Victor at Alamein* (London: Granada, 1977).
Peyton, M., *An Average War* (Chelmsford: Maypole Press, 2014).
Phillips, K.L., *My Wartime Wanderings* (Gloucester: Choir Press, 2021).
Pyman, H., *Call to Arms* (London: Leo Cooper, 1971).
Roach, P., *The 8.15 to War: The Memoirs of a Desert Rat* (London: Leo Cooper, 1982).
Roberts, A., *Churchill: Walking with Destiny* (London: Allen Lane, 2018).
Shores, C. et al, *A History of the Mediterranean Air War 1940–1945. Vol. Two: North African Desert February 1942-March 1943* (London: Grub Street, 2012).
Smeeton, M., *A Change of Jungles* (London: Rupert Hart Davies, 1962).
Stewart, A., *The Early Battles of the Eighth Army: Crusader to the Alamein Line 1941–1942* (Barnsley: Leo Cooper, 2002).
Schmidt, H.W., *With Rommel in the Desert* (London: Constable, 1997).
Selwyn, V. (ed.)., *Poems of the Second World War. The Oasis Selection* (London: Everyman, 1987).
Smart, N., *Biography of British Generals of the Second World War* (Barnsley: Pen & Sword, 2005).
Tovey, W. J. & Podmore, A. J., *Once a Howard Twice a Citizen* (Middlesbrough: Volunteers Press, 1995).
Travers, S., *Tomorrow Be Brave* (London: Bantam Press, 2000).
Tuker, F., *Approach to Battle* (London: Cassell, 1963).
Urban, M., *The Tank War: The British 'Band of Brothers' – One Tank Regiment's World War II* (London: Abacus, 2014).

Ian Walker, *Iron Hulls Iron Hearts: Mussolini's Elite Armoured Divisions in North Africa* (Marlborough: Crowood Press, 2003).

Electronic Sources

3rd CLY Sharpshooters War Diary <http://www.warlinks.com>

Musée de l'Armée <http://www.Musee-Armee.fr, Les Invalides, Paris>

To War With the Bays, 27 May 1942 <https://www.bbc.co.uk/history/ww2peopleswar/categories/c55178/>

Tobruk 1942: Worcestershire Regiment <http://www.worcestershireregiment.com.>

WW2 BBC People's War <https://www.bbc.co.uk/history/ww2peopleswar/>

Index

GENERAL

Agheila, 34
Agheila pass, 158
Ain el-Gazala, 7, 11, 17, 37-38
Anti-tank gun, 39, 50–51, 54, 56–57, 59, 61–62, 66, 69–70, 73, 126, 134, 136, 145–47
Aslagh Ridge, 41, 83–84, 86–87, 92, 95, 97, 107, 112, 114, 116–17, 119–20
Auchinleck, General Sir Claude, 8–9, 11, 13–25, 28, 46–47, 49–50, 52, 123, 138–39, 141, 164–66, 168

Benghazi, 7–8, 13, 17, 26, 28, 34
Bir Aslagh, 86, 94, 96, 98, 101–2, 106, 113–15, 149
Bir Bellefaa, 77, 121, 131–32
Bir el Gubi, 31, 33, 41, 43–44, 51, 53, 58, 71, 73, 111, 140
Bir Geff, 84
Bir Hacheim, 10, 12, 29, 31–33, 36–38, 41–45, 64–72, 84, 110–11, 120–22, 124, 144–63
Bir Harmat, 41, 78, 80, 85, 94–96, 106, 112–15, 118, 131, 148
Bofors AA gun, 88, 145
Boucher, Brigadier Charles, 95–96, 99
Briggs, Brigadier Raymond, 51, 92–93, 110, 113
Brooke, General Sir Alan, 13, 17, 19–20, 49, 152

Cairo, 11, 16, 18, 20–22, 24, 26–27, 34, 54
Carr, Brigadier Matthew, 53, 101, 108
Carver, Lord Michael, 25, 48, 64, 164, 171
Churchill, Winston, 8, 13–18, 20–21, 34, 123, 166–67

Crusader tank, 27, 29–30, 36–37, 46–47, 51, 53–54, 60–62, 80, 92–93, 111, 113, 120–21, 164–65, 171–72
Cyrenaica, 7–8, 11, 13–17, 20, 22–26, 28–29, 34–35, 46, 51, 65, 97

Dafadar, 71

Egypt, 6–7, 10, 13, 28, 47, 106, 143, 165, 168, 172
El Adem, 40, 42–45, 49, 56, 58, 71–72, 75–76, 78, 100–101, 103, 125, 129–30, 132, 138–43, 166

Filose, Brigadier Anthony, 66–68, 70, 72, 169

Gabr el Fachri Ridge, 157
Gambut, 25, 42, 74, 122, 139, 143, 160
Gazala, 7–10, 12–17, 21–22, 27–29, 34–38, 40, 48, 50–51, 61, 84, 121, 154–56, 158, 164–65, 167–68, 170–71
Ghesceuasc Ridge, 45, 121
Gott, Lieutenant-General William 'Strafer', 36, 43, 48, 136, 166, 168
Grant tank, 49, 53–54, 56, 59–62, 73–75, 77, 79–80, 102, 108, 111, 113–14, 117–21, 123–26, 161, 172
Guingand, Major-General Frederick, 21, 123–24

Hagiag, 108, 125, 132–33
Haydon, Brigadier Cecil, 83, 85, 87, 89–90
Honey tank, 73

Iraq, 24, 94–96, 103, 142, 167

181

Jock columns, 30, 32, 47–48, 55–56, 58, 61, 64–65, 67, 72, 96, 139–41, 145–47, 151–52, 154, 160–61

Kippenberger, Brigadier Howard, 24, 36
Koening, General Pierre, 36, 44, 49, 144, 147–48, 151, 169
Kesselring, Field Marshal Albert, 23
Knightsbridge, 32–34, 36, 39–42, 44–45, 77–80, 82, 84, 86, 107–8, 111–12, 114–15, 117–28, 131–33, 135, 138
Knightsbridge Box, 33, 67, 102, 106, 121, 131, 135–36

Libya, 12–22, 24–25, 29, 32, 36, 106, 151, 167

Maabus, 115, 117, 134
Malta, 8, 12, 17, 20, 22–24, 28–29, 33–34, 45, 152
Matilda tank, 60, 62, 92
Mk IV tank, 90, 108

Naduret Ridge, 79, 124
Nye, General Archibald, 20–21

Operation Aberdeen, 2, 9, 49, 83, 91–92, 111, 117, 119, 123, 149, 169–70
Operation Acrobat, 13–16
Operation Crusader, 7, 13, 29, 63, 142
Operation Freeborne, 156–57
Operation Victory, 21, 95, 124

Panzer III tank, 61–62
Persia, 22, 24–25

Reid, Brigadier Denys, 140
Renton, Brigadier James, 49
Richards, Brigadier George, 108, 160
Ritchie, General Neil, 8–9, 17, 22, 25, 28–30, 91, 93, 111, 123–24, 126, 128–30, 138–40, 143–44, 150–51, 164–68
Rommel, General Irwin, 13-15, 17, 28–30, 32, 41, 82–84, 91, 115-16, 120, 122, 124–25, 130, 135, 140, 148, 150, 167-68, 171
Retma Box, 44, 56, 72
Rigel Ridge, 40, 124, 127, 131, 133–35, 138

Sidi Rezegh, 76, 129–30, 135, 142–43, 160, 162
Sidra Ridge, 52, 81, 91–92, 104, 117–18, 156
Sollum, 33, 96, 111, 113, 143, 165
Spitfire, 23, 151
Stuart tank, 52, 118
Stuka, 46, 89, 108, 114, 147–48, 150, 153
Syria, 24, 57, 171

Tamar Ridge, 41, 83–84, 87, 94, 97, 102, 113, 117, 156
Tobruk, 7–13, 17–18, 25–29, 34–37, 42–43, 45, 64–65, 81–82, 122–23, 129–31, 135–36, 138–41, 143, 152, 154–55, 157–59, 161–62, 164–68
Trigh Capuzzo, 32, 36–38, 40–43, 82, 84–85, 125, 129, 139, 141–42, 157, 159, 162

Valentine tank, 18, 58, 60, 62, 79, 86

Wadis, 40, 43, 75, 78–79, 133, 155
Western Desert, 27, 41, 91–92

FORMATIONS/UNITS

Armies
Eighth Army, 13, 16, 28-29, 32, 36, 40-41, 53, 63-64, 72, 77, 82, 84, 91, 109, 122-124, 130-131, 137, 139, 145, 164-167
Panzerarmee Afrika, 13, 28-29, 32, 36, 38, 43, 52, 63-65, 67, 69, 71, 76, 81-85, 88, 90-91, 103, 109, 111, 113, 115-116, 118, 120-124, 129-131, 134, 139-140, 145-146, 148, 152-154, 161-162, 164-167, 170
Deutsches Afrika Korps (DAK), 4–5, 31–33, 79, 82, 89, 117, 122–23, 125, 134, 137–38, 148–49

Corps
X Corps, 165
XIII Corps, 30, 32, 43, 47, 81, 90, 166
XXX Corps, 31, 48, 50, 64–65, 76, 122, 139, 160, 166
Deutsches Afrika Korps (DAK), 32–33, 68, 79, 82, 89, 116–117, 122–125, 134, 137, 142, 148–149, 170
XX Italian Corps, 82

Divisions
1st Armoured, 33, 37, 48, 51, 118, 126, 132, 138

1st South African, 38-39, 48, 111, 121, 138, 153, 156-157
2nd South African, 48, 136, 138, 155, 162
4th Indian, 38, 48
5th Indian, 33, 41, 49, 83, 91-92, 93, 103-104, 106, 141, 165, 17
7th Armoured, 42, 48, 66, 82, 92, 118, 147, 149-150, 160, 166, 169
10th Indian, 49, 103, 165
50th Division; 14, 30, 33, 37, 48, 57, 58, 61, 90, 111, 130, 135, 154-156, 171
Yeomanry Division, 122
15th Panzer Division, 14, 31, 79, 82, 89, 93, 99, 100, 102-104, 106-107, 111, 115-116, 118, 122, 124, 130, 136-137, 139, 142, 149
21st Panzer, 82, 89, 93, 111, 116, 122, 125, 134, 137, 139, 141-143, 149, 153, 156
90th Light, 31, 41, 82, 89-90, 106, 116, 122, 125, 132, 139-143, 146, 148-151
132nd Ariete, 33, 70, 93, 99, 118
27th Brescia, 92
17th Pavia, 93
60th Sabratha, 154
101st Trieste, 33, 89, 116

Brigades
1st Free French, 14, 38, 41, 44, 49, 110, 122-123, 144, 152, 165
1st Armoured, 49, 58, 117, 121, 123
1st Army Tank, (AT), 31-32, 58, 62, 86
1st South African, 153-154
2nd South African, 154
1st Support Group, 37-38
2nd Armoured, 21, 32-33, 34, 42, 52, 62, 77, 79-80, 102, 110, 112, 115-116, 118, 121, 125-127, 134, 160
2nd Demi-Brigade, 146
2nd Free French, 165
3rd Indian Motor, 49, 57, 65-66, 74, 146, 162, 165, 169
4th Armoured, 21, 31, 33, 41, 43, 49, 55, 62, 65-67, 73, 76, 78, 105, 108, 112, 114-121, 124-127, 134, 143, 151-152, 160-162, 166
5th New Zealand, 32, 43
5th Indian, 162, 165
7th Motor Brigade, 42, 44, 49, 56, 65, 67, 72, 119, 123, 140-141, 144, 150-151, 162
8th Armoured, 165
9th Indian, 92-95, 99, 109
10th Indian, 58, 92-96, 99, 101, 106, 116-117
11th Indian, 141
20th Indian, 142-143
21st Indian, 143, 165
22nd Armoured, 31, 33, 42, 50, 53, 60, 62, 76, 78, 80, 83, 86, 91-95, 98-101, 103, 112, 114-119, 121, 124-125, 127, 160, 170
25th Indian, 165
29th Indian, 43, 49, 58, 135, 165
32nd Army Tank (AT), 48, 58, 62, 90-92, 104, 127
50th Mobile Reserve, 86
69th Brigade, 57, 81, 87, 90, 155-157
150th Brigade, 14, 30, 37-38, 40, 44, 48, 57-58, 81-84, 87-88, 91, 106, 110-111, 114-116, 144, 148, 155-157, 165, 169
151st Brigade, 33, 57, 104, 130, 153, 156-157
161st Indian Motor Brigade, 165
201st Guards, 32-33, 38, 40-41, 48, 127
Polish Brigade, 38

Regiments/Battalions
1st RHA, 36, 55-56, 59, 79, 160
1st KRRC, 44, 74, 76, 78, 160
1st RTR, 118-121
1st Duke Cornwall Light Infantry (DCLI), 92, 103-104, 167
1st Worcesters, 126, 130, 134-136, 138, 140
1st Sherwood Foresters, 131, 136
1st South Wales Borderers, 142
1st Transvaal Scottish, 153-154
1st Regiment d'Artillerie, 146, 149-150
2nd KRRC, 65, 72
2nd RHA, 39-40, 132
2nd Scots Guards, 39-40, 126-127, 131-134, 136, 138
2nd Rifle Brigade, 43-44, 56, 72, 112, 161
2nd West Yorks, 92, 95, 99-100
2nd Highland Light Infantry (HLI), 92-93, 95, 97-98, 100, 102
2nd Royal Gloucester Hussars, 76-78, 92, 99, 101, 107-108, 112, 115, 119-120
2nd SA Armoured Car, 158
2nd Royal Lancers, 67, 70-72
2nd Field Regiment Indian Artillery, 69
3/2nd Punjab Regiment, 140-141
3rd Coldstreams, 39, 131, 135
3rd County London Yeomanry (CLY), 51, 54, 76-77, 80, 92, 102, 115-116, 119, 125, 127, 160, 170
3rd RTR, 55, 61, 65, 74, 112, 114-118, 120, 160-161

4th County London Yeomanry (CLY), 76-78, 92, 94, 102, 112, 115-116, 121, 127
4th East Yorks, 84-90
4th Green Howards, 85, 87-90
4th Royal Northumberland Fusiliers/ 50, Recce Bn, 50, 53-54, 94, 101, 109
4th South African Armoured Car Regt, 64, 67
2/4th Gurkhas, 92, 94-97, 105-107, 109, 165, 169-170
4th RTR, 32, 58, 62, 92, 94, 98-100, 115, 127
4th Hussars, 56, 120-121, 123, 125
4th RHA, 55, 73
4th Field Regiment RA, 95, 99, 107-108
5th RTR, 48, 55, 74-75, 114, 116-117, 120
5th Green Howards, 84, 87-90, 169
5th East Yorks, 156
1/5th Mahrattas, 139-141
6th RTR, 117-120, 126, 138, 160
6th Green Howards, 87, 155
6th Durham Light Infantry (DLI), 153, 157-158
6th South African Field Regiment SAA, 132
1/6th Rajputana Rifles, 142
7th RTR, 32, 104-105
7th Green Howards, 28, 58, 91-92, 105, 155-157
7th Medium Regiment RA, 169
8th RTR, 104-105
8th Hussars, 42, 51, 65, 73, 76, 78, 112, 120
8th Durham Light Infantry (DLI), 159
9th Royal Lancers, 52, 60, 77-78, 80, 111, 113-114, 119, 160-161
9th Rifle Brigade, 43, 118, 132, 161-162
9th KRRC, 33, 55, 72
9th Durham Light Infantry, (DLI), 130, 158-159
3/9th Jats, 92, 95-96, 100, 108, 169
4/10th Baluch Regiment, 92-93, 96-100, 102-103, 105-109
10th Hussars, 45, 52, 79, 110, 113-114, 116, 119
11th RHA, 52, 80, 112
11th Prince Albert Victors Own, (PAVO), 57, 67-70
12th Royal Lancers, 59, 83
3/12th Frontier Force Rifles Regiment (Piffers), 92, 100, 139
2/13th Demi-Brigade de Legion Étrangère, 146
18th King Edward's Own Cavalry, 67, 69-70
3/18th Garhwali Regiment, 143
28th Field Regiment RA, 101, 107
42nd RTR, 58, 86, 88, 104-105
44th RTR, 58, 79, 81, 86-87
74th Field Regiment RA, 159
95th Anti-Tank Regiment RA, 136
104th Field Regiment RA, 132
106th Anti-Tank Regt, 43
107th RHA, South Notts Hussars, 53-54, 92, 96, 101, 108-109
115th Rifle Regiment, 79, 125, 153
157th Field Regiment RA, 100
Battleaxe Medium Battery, 86-87
Kings Dragoon Guards, 33, 38
Queen's Bays, 52, 80, 114, 117, 120, 126